AF530980

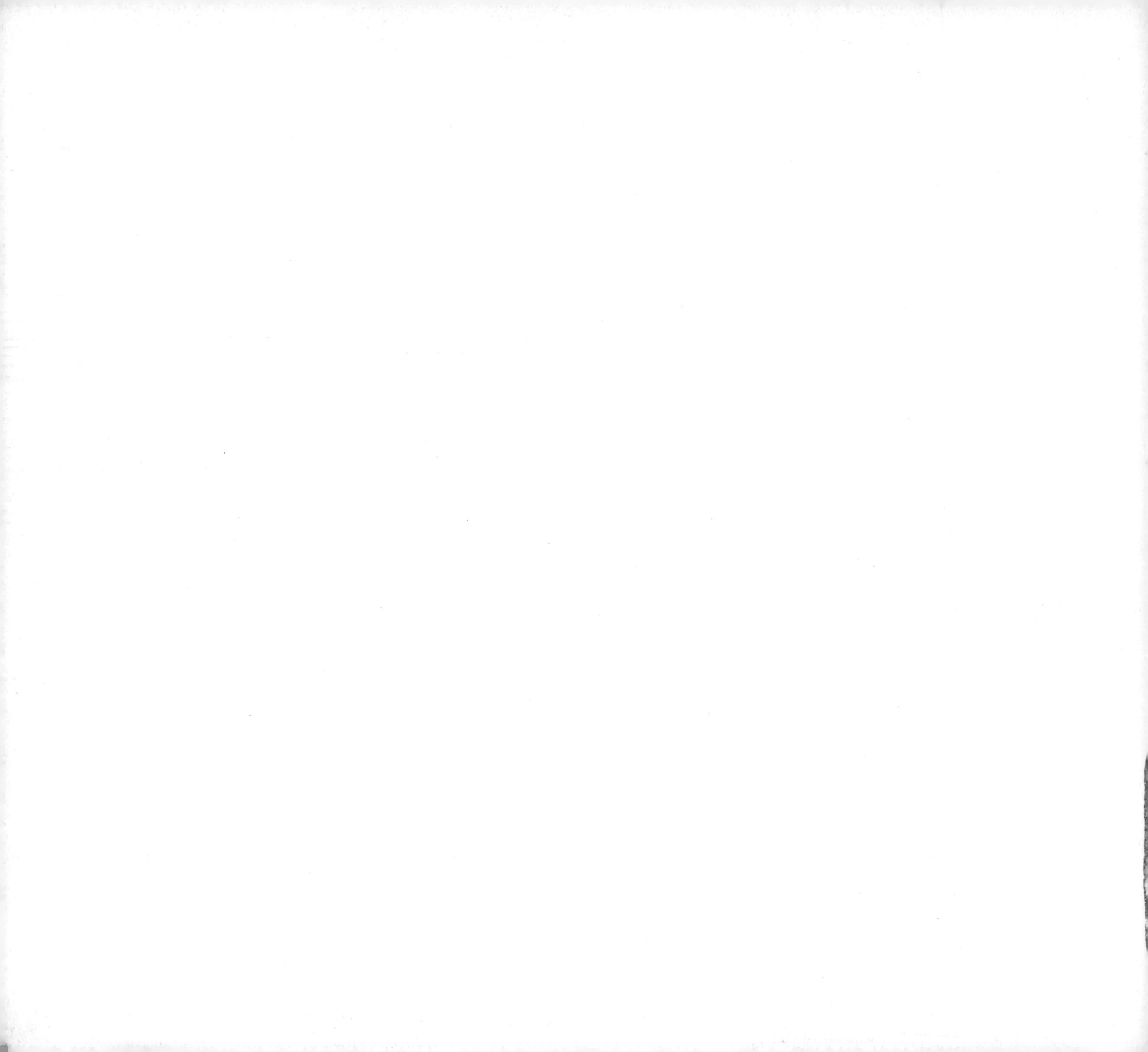

John Annerino

AMERICA'S OUTBACK

An Odyssey through the Great Southwest

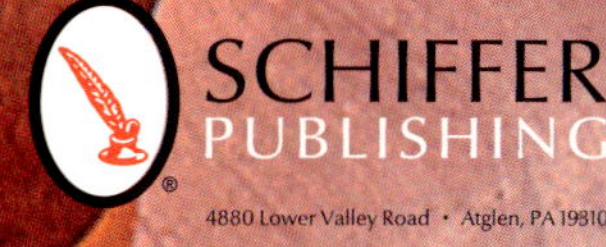

SCHIFFER PUBLISHING
4880 Lower Valley Road • Atglen, PA 19310

Other Schiffer Books by John Annerino:
In the Chasms of Water, Stone, and Light: Passages through the Grand Canyon, ISBN 978-0-7643-5760-2

Library of Congress Control Number: 2020943642

Designed by Ashley Millhouse
Cover design by Ashley Millhouse
Front and back cover photos: John Annerino; photo permissions: www.johnannerinophotography.com

Historical black-and-white and color photos courtesy of Library of Congress; Art Institute of Chicago / Wiki; Willa Cather Pioneer Memorial Foundation / Wiki; Heritage Auction Gallery / Wiki; Julio Reza Diaz, Mexican Association of Press Photographers (Julio Reza Diaz, Asociación Mexicana de Fotógrafos de Prensa); Missouri History Museum Archives; Easterly Daguerreotype Collection / Wiki; 20th Century Fox / Wiki; Aimé Dupont Studio; George Grantham Bain News Service; Harry Ransom Research Center, University of Texas at Austin; and the US Farm Security Administration.

Type set in Proxima Nova/Garamond

ISBN: 978-0-7643-6187-6
Printed in China

Published by Schiffer Publishing, Ltd.
4880 Lower Valley Road
Atglen, PA 19310
Phone: (610) 593-1777; Fax: (610) 593-2002
E-mail: Info@schifferbooks.com
Web: www.schifferbooks.com

FOR TOTO

for running down Cerro Colorado Crater as a child for as far as he could see into the wonder of El Pinacate.

AND FOR BILL

for crisscrossing the desolate sands of El Gran Desierto that engulfed the crater's lunar landscape.

With a magnificent Unknown looming thus suddenly above the horizon like an enchanted vision, [men and women have] not rested in their endeavor to explore the world, and leave no part unknown. Our own century has exhibited this spirit as powerfully as any gone before, but each year the field has grown narrower, and before long all *tierra incógnita* will have vanished.

—Frederick S. Dellenbaugh, explorer, 1897 American Geographical Society of New York

For many generations . . . the Hopi People have lived in the sacred place known to you as the Southwest and known to us to be the spiritual center of our continent.

—Thomas Banyacya, Hopi traditional elder, August 4, 1970,
in a letter to the president of the United States of America

My heart belongs to no one now, but the desert.

—Gertrude Bell, 1907 *Queen of the Desert*

No man can live this life and emerge unchanged.
He will carry, however faint, the imprint of the desert, the brand which marks the nomad; and he will have within him the yearning to return, weak or insistent according to his nature.
For this cruel land can cast a spell which no temperate clime can match.

—Sir Wilfred Thesiger, 1946, crossing the Rub' al Khali, "the Empty Quarter"

CONTENTS

FOREWORD

"If we don't spot the tinaja in the next five minutes, we should turn back or we'll run out of water." John Annerino is not being bossy, just factual. And he ought to know, because for decades he has led groups of novices and experts on hikes like this across harsh desert valleys, into boulder-choked canyons, and over precipitous ridges where a misstep afoot or a miscalculation about water could doom the trip. We had followed my memory instead of our map, up the wrong canyon to the spine of a bone-dry, scramble-rock range where only desert bighorn dare go. The month was July, and the sun had baked us from the moment we left the truck hours ago. I didn't argue since I knew he was right.

John himself is a lifetime veteran of such trips looking for hidden places, seeking unique photo points, or tracking ancient trails. For years he taught college students the rudiments and joys of hiking and camping skills, outdoor survival, and route finding in Arizona and on Tiburón Island in Sonora, Mexico. By blending his years as a Colorado River boatman, his own expeditions to *far*-out-of-the-way places such as Picacho del Diablo in Baja California Norte, stone towers in Arizona's Grand Canyon, and runs tracing ancient Native American trails, John has learned how to get back alive so he can share his story and impart the grandeur or mystery of the place. Not bad for a guy who took a long "screamer" fall early in his mountain-climbing career—it shattered his ankle so badly that surgeons wanted to amputate his foot and said he might never walk again.

He also photographs these places—"remote exposures," he calls them—so that when words fall short of describing the grand cliffs or delicate flowers, he can show them to us in brilliant color and fine detail. His second career has been writing and illustrating books, and doing contract photography for PBS, *Life Magazine*, *Newsweek*, *Time*, *National Geographic Adventure*, and *Arizona Highways*, as well as producing more than two dozen of his own wall calendars. His list of books now includes twenty-eight classics, with titles sweeping across a wide span of audiences. These include *Vanishing Borderlands*, *Adventuring Arizona*, *The Virgin of Guadalupe*, *Hiking the Grand Canyon*, *Running Wild*, *People of Legend*, *The Wild Country of Mexico*, and more. I've enjoyed them all, though *High Risk Photography* and *Dead in Their Tracks* may be the ones I most often revisit, as my well-thumbed copies show.

You may wonder why you seldom see John featured in your newspaper or rarely catch him promoting his book on TV or on a book festival panel. It is because he's camping on the ground 90 miles from town in the dead of winter to catch that perfect sunrise photo. He's out interviewing Navajos outside their hogans and cowboys at the rodeo arena, or he's plunging down slot canyons. And he's prowling a library or combing archives looking for hidden gems of history that quick-write authors didn't take time to find.

John finds and devours the firsthand reports and then maps his own hikes or camping trips through the heart of the maze in order to see, hear, and feel the pulse of the land. He lives to imagine what the first explorers or pioneers saw and did. He wants to know their fears and thrills. He has that adventurous spirit, and at times he must think he was born 200 years or more too late. John is attuned to Indigenous people, and he strives to present their accounts and perspectives of the world. He loves place names in O'odham, Navajo, or Paiute. And his photographs of Native Americans are some of the best modern portraits taken—take a look at his photography books *Apache, People of Legend* or *Indian Country*.

Annerino has a way of putting people at ease as he composes photos with his faithful Nikon. He has amassed a splendid collection of characters on film, ranging from border patrol agents to wranglers, from Apache princesses to field hands, and cave-dwelling Tarahumara to boatwomen rowing the Grand Canyon. His own days picking crops, working on forest fire crews, or exploring Indian reservations give him an edge, a patience, and instant camaraderie. He is a bit shy and unassuming, so foremost he offers them common-man respect and is instantly *simpático*.

Although his books are featured in bookstores and gift shops across the West, and his photographs appear everywhere, he himself is less known. If he were at a party for mountaineers and guides, you wouldn't spot him. Despite his international readership, he's not the one ordering the third round of beers or slapping the table while telling a string of boisterous stories. No, he'd be at a back-corner table quietly asking questions and taking notes, or hosting a string of professionals asking about roads to special canyons and routes up seldom climbed peaks. His *Hiking the Grand Canyon* guide is now in its fourth edition.

If I'm lucky, John phones me four or five times a year to suggest lunch, invariably at a favorite Mexican café with Sonoran or Oaxacan decor. He prefers frijoles and tortillas, chips and salsa. I order a beef taco or bowl of *albondigas*. Always he talks proudly about his family and his latest trips, and about half the time he has his latest publication under his arm to give me. We invariably swap the books we write, but he is so prolific that I'm embarrassed to say how many books I now owe him. In some years, he's published as many as four, a prodigious feat. This book, *America's*

Outback: An Odyssey through the Great Southwest, is one of his best and stands as a companion book to his award-winning *In the Chasms of Water, Stone, and Light*. John has dedicated his life's work to exploring mythic landscapes and secret places, with a focus on the people who lived or lingered there to map the geography, study its species, or run rivers and climb mountains.

On our trip to the tinaja, we rounded a knob a couple of minutes after John's warning and spotted our goal, the waterhole. We were safe, though not yet down from the heights and treacherous slopes. We sat beside the tank, ate scraps of lunch, and sipped some but not all of our remaining water. We were happy to find the spot and content to sit in a mountain hall known for bighorn sheep and golden eagles. But one more surprise awaited us. As we clambered down the last ridge to reach the bajada and mile hike to the truck, we were treated to a dust storm rolling across the sand dunes that mark this valley. It rolled like a breaking wave, engulfing everything along its path in a tawny cloud. We marveled at the raging wind and shifting colors—green plants took on a yellow hue, and black rocks turned to dull gray. Blown sand stung our legs, and we were forced to cover our faces with kerchiefs so we could breathe. But the maelstrom invigorated us with raw energy, the blast of a storm and power of wind. It was as if John had saved the best for last. Enjoy *America's Outback*—it's superb.

—Bill Broyles, author of *Among Unknown Tribes* and *Sunshot: Peril and Wonder in the Gran Desierto*

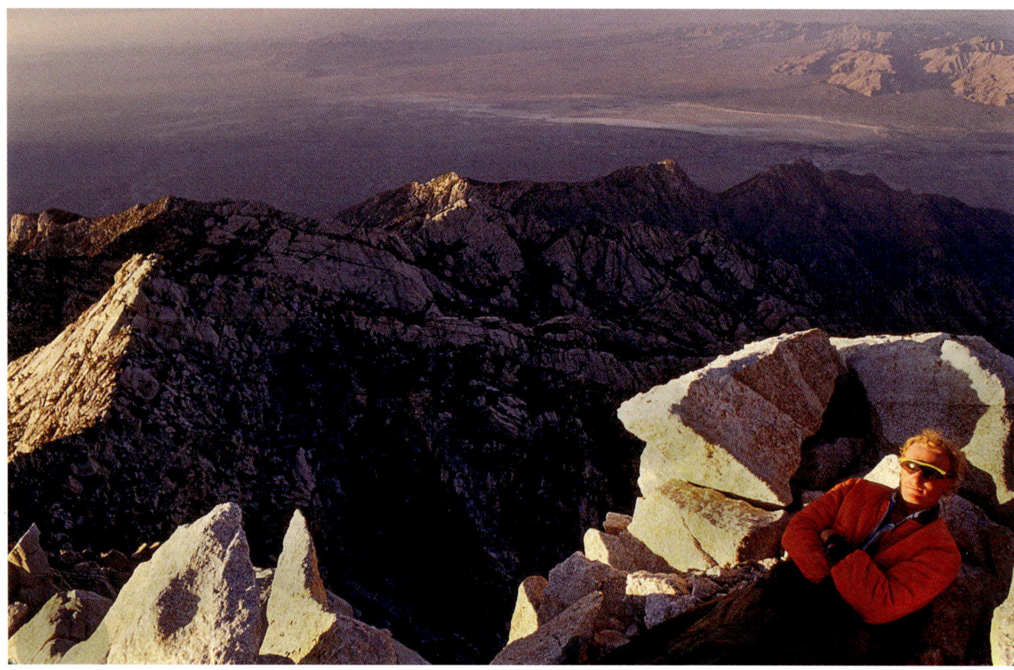

An American climber bivouacs atop 10,152-foot Picacho del Diablo (Peak of the Devil), the highest mountain on the 800-mile-long Baja Peninsula, Mexico.

ACKNOWLEDGMENTS

Inspiration for this odyssey came from many artists, adventurers, travelers, pilgrims, and Indigenous peoples. Their quests, discoveries, words, and images lit a fire and stirred my soul to venture beyond my horizon lines. Thanks to Carobeth Laird and George Laird for *The Chemehuevis*, Robyn Davidson for *Tracks*, Bruce Chatwin for *The Songlines*, Colin Fletcher for *The Thousand-Mile Summer*, Charles Bowden for *Blue Desert*, Donald McClain for his epic journey to Picacho del Diablo, Reinhold Messner for summiting *All 14 Eight-Thousanders* without oxygen, Georgia O'Keeffe for her artistic exploration of the Bisti Badlands, the late Robin Lange for climbing Baboquivari Peak, and Padre Eusebio Francisco Kino for his missionary journeys that traversed 7,500 miles of the *tierra incógnita* in Pimería Alta. Thanks also to photo editor and curator Donnamarie Barnes, author and ultra runner Kathleen "Kitty" Williams, Mexican photographer Julio Reza Díaz, and my editor Cheryl Weber for her talents. Thanks, especially, to *National Geographic Adventure*'s founding editor in chief John Rasmus—no one knows adventure and exploration better—who assigned me to map the early explorations of the Grand Canyon pioneers and later sent me twice into treacherous no man's land to photograph the US-Mexico border.

The remarkable black-and-white images that grace the pages of this book would not have been possible without the distinct vision of the pioneer photographers who created them. Thanks to Charles Milton Bell for his albumen print of Navajo headman Manuelito, Aimé Dupont for her platinum print of author Willa Cather, Ben Wittick for his ferrotype (tintype) of Billy the Kid, Alfred Stieglitz for his platinum print of artist Georgia O'Keeffe, A. Frank Randall for his studio portraits of Geronimo and Painted Boy, Michael Miley for his albumen print of Texas Ranger William A. A. "Bigfoot" Wallace, Thomas Martin Easterly for his daguerreotype of scalp hunter James "Santiago" Kirker, W. D. Smithers for his glass-plate negative print of the *curandero* (faith healer), Dorothea Lange for her nitrate negative print of horse whisperer Robert Lemmons, and Edward S. Curtis for his photomechanical print of the San Ildefonso offering, gelatin silver print of Yebichai war gods, photographic print of a Navajo woman, and photographic print of the Qahatika girl in the Sonoran Desert.

INTRODUCTION

DESIERTO / DESERT

[T]here is a nakedness about the Southwest, a bald truthfulness, and at the same time there is a sense of the hidden. The secret does not lie thinly veiled. It is deep down at the heart of things, only to be glimpsed after patient digging.

—Laura Adams Armer, "The Southwest," 1935

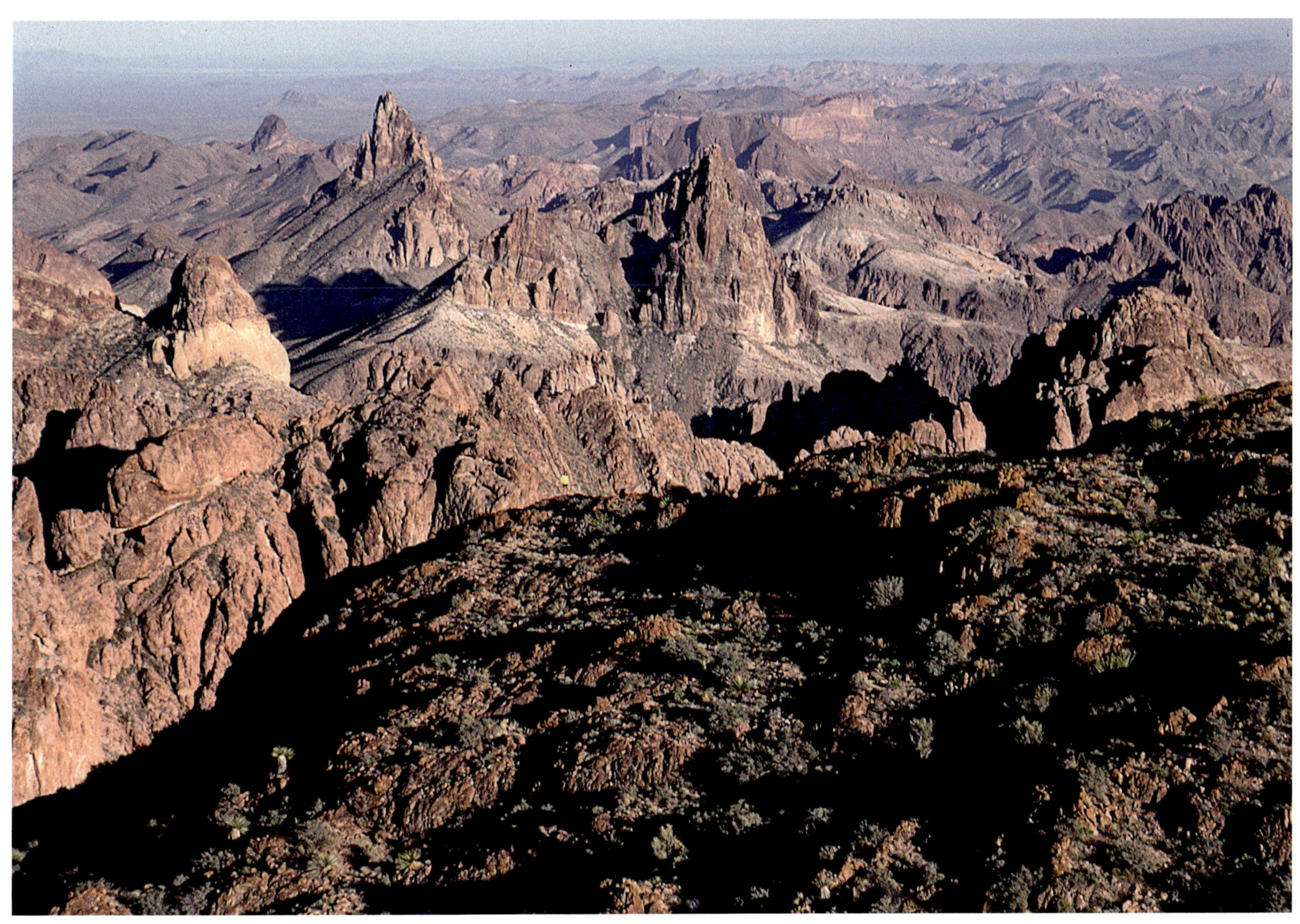

A lone hiker is dwarfed by the 4,877-foot Kofa Mountains, Kofa National Wildlife Refuge, Arizona.

The first time I glimpsed the Kofa Mountains, I was buffeted by a desert wind while balancing atop a shattered column of rock more than 2,000 feet above the desert floor. The striated pillar of lava and tuff was called the South Feather. It was one of three bronze plumes that were said to resemble "an eagle's tail sticking straight up into the air." The Feathers crowned the 3,640-foot summit of the Eagletail Mountains, a lonely range hidden in a secret wilderness of hardscrabble volcanic peaks, bajadas veiled with spiny wands of ocotillo, and bone-dry arroyos that thundered to life with flash floods during summer monsoons. This was the heart of what an early climber called the "outback." Teetering in the wind on the pedestal of rock, I crouched down before I was blown off my perch. I draped my legs over the top and yelled down to my climbing partner, "I'm up!" "On belay?" he yelled. "On belay," I yelled down to him. I pulled up my rope, belaying (safeguarding) him as he climbed the exposed fissure, mumbling about the crumbly rocks that tumbled beneath his feet.

I gazed into the western horizon, and a row of jagged pinnacles cast long shadows in the hypnotic mirage that shimmered across the back of beyond. Were they real—or were they *fata morgana*, seductive illusions of the Arthurian legend named after the Italian sorceress Morgana le Fey? They looked like snarling coyote fangs guarding a mystifying mountain range that floated in a sea of desert that remained, perhaps, the largest *despoblado*, uninhabited land, in the Great Southwest that included the United States and Mexico. Cut by a half-dozen ribbons of asphalt carrying drivers and passengers numb from the "monotonous" scenery drifting by their windows, this 10,000-square-mile Empty Quarter stretched southwest to the blue waters of the Gulf of California, Mexico, west to the meandering currents of the lower Colorado River, north to the sere streambeds of the Bill Williams River, and southeast to the Great Bend of the Gila River.

One range stood out among others that erupted from the sweep of bald desert that ran to the horizon in every direction: the Kofa Mountains. It was named after the King of Arizona Mine, a deep underground treasure shaft that by 1910 had yielded $3.5 million in fine-grain gold and silver from a burning "wasteland" that many had nonetheless forsaken. The Kofa Mountains were sacred to the Yavapai. They called it Wi:kasayeo, and it was home to their mountain spirit Akaka, who "could be heard calling in summer." It offered refuge to magnificent desert bighorn sheep, rarely seen desert tortoise, timid beaded-lizards called Gila monsters, coyotes and cactus wrens, and an Ice Age oasis of California fan palm trees that took root 150 miles distant from its nearest offshoots in the Mojave Desert.

No one lived out there, where names like Charlie Died Tank marked a dry waterhole that stuck to the landscape. It was rarely visited. Every Spanish and American explorer who headed West, and every Jesuit and Franciscan missionary; mountain man and trapper; boundary surveyor and forty-niner; pioneer and settler; artist, writer, and photographer; and horse, wagon, Pony Express, and stagecoach trail gave the Kofas a wide berth. Today, it remains No Man's Land, what early explorers called *tierra incógnita*, unknown country. I had to go there.

Not long after my climbing partner and I rappelled off the South Feather, fearing it would topple over, I made the long drive down the interstate across the Sonoran Desert toward California. I turned north along the Colorado River on an empty two-lane highway and drove past the largest military gunnery range in the West. I turned east and rattled down the rutted washboard road to the foot of mountain ramparts of the Kofas. I parked on the streambed placer-gravel road at the junction of Indian and Ten Ewe Canyons. That was my route description to climb the mountain. There were no trails or signposts—this was off the grid. Native peoples had climbed up the hanging canyons to hunt mountain sheep, *amuukyat*, or *muu*, their sacred prey, so I should be able to find my way, I'd reasoned. The next morning I led two friends up the steep canyons until they braided, then picked our way cross-country through jumbled igneous boulders, Spanish dagger-tipped century plants, and scarlet-stemmed chuparosa to the summit. We planned to bivouac there for the night. Except for the 1949 US Coast and Geodetic Survey benchmark atop the 4,877-foot peak, we saw no evidence that anyone had climbed it recently.

From the breathtaking vista, we took in a view bathed in luminescent amber that was almost palpable in the setting sun. The colorful shroud stretched east across the Kofa Pinnacles. *Remolinos* (dust devils) danced over the Palomas Plain and the craggy bluffs of the Little Horn Mountains. The distant Eagletail Mountains waited silently beyond. The air was still. The Feathers were dabbled with a hint of red and gold that lit up like flickering candle lanterns in the desert sea.

Caressed by the warm spring breeze, it was not difficult to imagine that the only people who ventured into this haunting but beautifully empty *despoblado*—apart from inquisitive miners wandering about from the King of Arizona Mine—were Native peoples and archeologists who sleuthed their deceptive and desolate wanderings. Indigenous to this seldom-visited ecosphere were nomadic Western Yavapai (Đo:lkabaya) bands, including the Mađqwadabaya, or Desert People. They roamed, hunted, and gathered in what pioneer archeologist Malcolm Rogers called the Great Malpaís area. The name referred to the discovery of ancient artifacts that predated Paleo-Indians who wrested a meager living 6,000 to 7,000 BCE from what eighteenth-century Spanish explorers later called *malpaís*, bad country. Those who followed their ancient trails included fleet-footed Yuma, Mojave, Pima, and Maricopa peoples who traced faint paths grooved into the living patina of desert varnish to hunt bighorn sheep, mule deer, and rabbits in their unending quest for food and water.

Living water was nearly nonexistent in their ancestral homelands, forcing them to rely on seasonal rock tanks of rainfall called tinajas. They slept in nomadic fire-lit camps in lofty Kofa Mountain caves and under the stars on the desert floor, where they protected themselves from cold winds by huddling together in sleeping circles of stone. They painted pictographs with crystals and ceremonial red paint and used hammerstones to etch petroglyphs of anthropomorphic shamans, figurative art of hunters and bighorn sheep, and abstract patterns of trails and grids. Their rock art puzzled occasional hikers, scientists, and prospectors hundreds and thousands of years later.

More mystifying, perhaps, than the bedrock mortars, manos and metates, ceremonial dance circles, and fragile patterns of arrowheads, broken pots, and lithic scatters that ancient peoples left behind were intaglios and geoglyphs of giant snakes, stick-figured men, vision quest rings, creation myths, and earth figures they'd outlined and scraped into the desert varnish. The intaglios had been likened to the zoomorphic geoglyphs of Peru's Nazca Desert. Seen from peaks and mountaintops, the mysterious earth carvings still glimmered across the outback in the warm glow of daybreak, hot midday sun, and cool fuchsia wisps of twilight.

Archeologists believe that one intriguing intaglio symbolized, perhaps, the Mađqwadabaya's "spirit living in the Kofa Mountains." The ancient hunters of this far western desert traveled up to 50 miles from their river settlements along the Colorado and the Gila Rivers into the breach of the Kofa Mountains. They used a maze of incipient trails, marked by trail shrines, that "were said to be links of spiritual power in a sacred network" that guided them during their desert quests as far east as the Eagletail Mountains. Then they disappeared from their hallowed grounds as silently as they had come. Archeologists concluded that the Mađqwadabaya as a people had ceased to exist. But their spirits lived on and touched those who still entered their forgotten realm.

Strangers later called such country Untrodden Lands, No-Man's Land, the Outback, Back of Beyond, Off the Grid, Land's End, Big Empty, End of the Trail, Whole Lot of Nothing, Middle of Nowhere, Out West, 30 Miles from Water—2 feet from Hell!, Tierra Incógnita, Despoblado, Malpaís, El Gran Desierto, and a Hell of a Place to Lose a Cow. The first time I'd considered the phrase "unknown land," a companion and I had made an end-to-end traverse along the crest of the Sierra de la Estrella (Mountain of the Stars). It was located on the western horizon of metropolitan Phoenix, and it towered over a dangerous pioneer route called the Jornada de las Estrellas (Day's Journey from the Stars). We were surprised to discover that the Sierra Estrella was still home to nimble-footed desert bighorn sheep. They bounded across the ridgeline in front of us. Geologist and Harvard professor Kirk Bryan described the daunting 25-mile-long range in 1925: "Climbing this range is arduous work, and many of the slopes can be ascended by a pedestrian only with the greatest difficulty. Much of the topography and scenery is as rugged, wild, and grand as any found in the Rocky Mountains of the United States or Alaska."

Staggering out of the Sierra Estrella without water after three and half days of traversing the humbling *cuchillo* (knife-edge ridge), we stopped at the first home we came to and asked a Pima elder if we could drink out of his garden hose. Sizing up our ragged appearance, he asked us where we'd come from. I pointed at the wall of mountains behind the little mission church nearby and said, "across the mountain from the other end." He shook his head, turned on the garden hose, and said, "Nobody's ever been up there before. Those mountains [*komadk*] are a mystery to everybody."

As sundown faded into twilight, the light dimmed on the tips of the Feathers, and the dreamscape that captivated us far below had vanished. The beguiling Kofas and Eagletails, lost in this vast corner of the Great Southwest, was just one region among others that drew me deeper and deeper into the far corners of the primal earthscapes featured between the covers of this book. On its surface it was indeed an uninhabited land, and it remains so today. At times I called it America's Outback. It formed the heart of 515,149 square miles of mysterious, beautiful, and brutal deserts, canyons, mountains, rivers, and inland seas that encompassed the American Southwest, northwestern Mexico, Baja California Peninsula, and La Frontera (the Frontier) of the US-Mexico border.

Further defining the scope of the region were the conceptual boundaries of the Great Southwest. They were composed by archeologist Erik K. Reed when he wrote: "The Greater Southwest . . . extends approximately from Durango, Colorado, to Durango, Mexico, and from Las Vegas, New Mexico, to Las Vegas, Nevada." Reed's conception of the Great Southwest was illuminated on a National Geographic Society map of the Southwest that hangs above my desk. Over the years it's been my dreamscape of trails—what Australian outback Aboriginals called "songlines" and "dream tracks," and what the Chemehuevi of California's Mojave Desert sang as territorial hunting songs that pinpointed sacred routes and destinations—that I followed across the marvelous quarter where my spirit had touched down.

I'd discovered I had not been the only one who dreamed through maps. In author Charles Bowden's thought-provoking book *Desierto*, he wrote of his own affinity for the maps he used for long walks across the empty ground of the Southwest: "For years I'd pored over the maps . . . [and] the forbidden zone," Bowden wrote. "I would rehearse long walks through the map, my legs tightening on the rises, my ears alert for the sound of a rattlesnake in the summer's darkness."

Depending on one's own perceptions of the mythic region that author and adventuress Mary Hunter Austin describes in her book *Land of Little Rain*, the fluid boundaries of the Great Southwest reached far beyond and were limited only by one's imagination and by putting one foot in front of the other: "Not the law, but the land sets the limit," Austin wrote, "as far into the heart of it as a man dare go." By any name, America's Outback encompasses the "least inhabited, last explored region" in the contiguous United States" and northwestern Mexico.

Austin had also penned a graphic warning about venturing into such country: "First and last, accept no man's statement that he knows this Country of Lost Borders well. A great number having lost their lives in the process of proving where it is not safe to go," Austin wrote, and added "which began with the finding of a dead man, clothless as the desert dead mostly are, with a bag of nuggets clutched in his mummied hands."

After years of exploring far beyond Austin's own land of "lost borders . . . little rain . . . and lost rivers," it was plain to me that the Great Southwest's extraordinary geography was sculpted by forces of nature that touched my soul. Volcanic mountain islands erupted high above desert seas, sometimes creating elliptical craters that resembled the surface of the moon. Thundering cataracts tumbled into flood-swollen rivers that carved deep chasms through cliffs, canyons, and sierras. Towering monuments and mysterious hoodoos, honed by wind, water, and stone-splitting freeze-thaw erosion, resembled ancient deities like the Navajo's Haashch'eeh diné (Holy People who turned to stone). Cryptic stone murals and otherworldly figures, etched and painted by Native hands, remain hidden among wind-scoured terra-cotta mesas that stretched across the Four Corners and Painted Desert region from one glorious sunrise to the next. Once home to ancient people such as the Hohokam (Those Who Are Gone), Mukwic (People We Never Saw), Anaasází (Enemy Ancestors), and Hisat. sinom (People Who Lived Long Ago), they survived in a perilous landscape they revered. Spanish missionaries, explorers, surveyors, settlers, writers, artists, and photographers also forged routes across their magnificent, rugged, and sacred lands. Their journeys defined their character as much as their handwritten journals, prose, poems, and albumen silver print photographs later defined our modern perceptions of the Great Southwest.

Territorial army wife Martha Summerhayes, for one, captured her impressions of the region in her journal in 1875, or thereabouts: "The scenery was wild and grand; in fact, beyond all that I had ever dreamed of; more than that, it seemed so untrod, so fresh, somehow, and I do not suppose that even now, in the day of railroads and tourists, many people have had the view."

Crossing empty ground on foot from dawn to dusk, I bore witness to nature's palette, brushstrokes, and ever-changing hues of color and came to realize this landscape was like no place on earth. The hallowed mesas, spires, buttes, and red sands of Monument Valley in Navajoland compelled Hollywood icon John Wayne to conclude, "So this is where God put the West." West of the Pecos, American scalp hunters and banditos—armed to the teeth—and Lone Star Texas Rangers, horse whisperers, and *curanderos* (faith healers) prowled West Texas and the wild river canyons of Big Bend. The canyons were carved by the ageless corrosion of the storm-fed Rio Grande / Río Bravo del Norte. The river's Big Bend was called El Columpio del Diablo (the Devils Swing) by neighbors living across the river. Towering 10,000 feet, the cloud-piercing granite horns of Picacho del Diablo (Peak of the Devil) soared over Jesuit missions built in the devil's playground. White sands, charcoal stone hoodoos, and the Tierras Encantadas (Enchanted Lands) of New Mexico inspired American modernist Georgia O'Keeffe to paint her celebrated oil-on-canvas Black Place series. It was the same high desert that Pulitzer Prize–winning novelist Willa Cather wrote of in her evocative novel *Death Comes for the Archbishop*.

One line in the book, among others, convinced me that Cather had lived and breathed in the crisp, clean air of her enchanted lands: "The whole western sky was the colour of golden ashes, with here and there a flush of red on the lip of a little cloud. High above the horizon the evening-star flickered like a lamp just lit, and close beside it was another star of constant light."

Across the Four Corners of Utah, sandstone-terraced mountains called the Bears Ears were the birthplace of Navajo headman

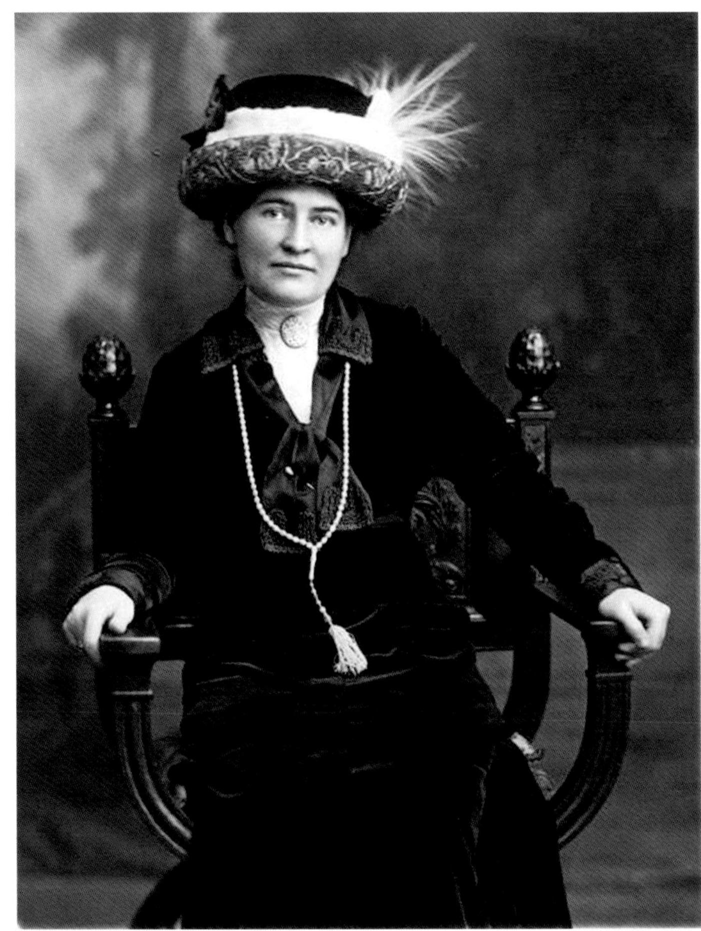

Willa Cather, platinum print by Aimé Dupont Studio, 1911, New York. *Courtesy of Willa Cather Pioneer Memorial Foundation / Wiki*

Manuelito (Nabááh Jiłt'áá: Warrior Grabbed Enemy), who brokered peace for his people after their traumatic Hwéeldi (Long Walk). The peaks, cockscombs, and canyon lands near Bears Ears offered the elusive hideout of Robbers Roost for dynamite-wielding train robbers Butch Cassidy, the Sundance Kid, the Wild Bunch, and their mysterious and alluring companion, Etta Place. They stayed hell-bent on the outriding Pinkerton Detectives dogging their dusty trails. Roaming the slickrock country a century later, the wilderness of stone inspired environmentalist Edward Abbey to write his masterpiece, *Desert Solitaire*. In his seminal book, the high priest of slick rock offered his legions his *benedicto*: "May your trails be crooked, winding, lonesome, dangerous, leading to the most amazing view."

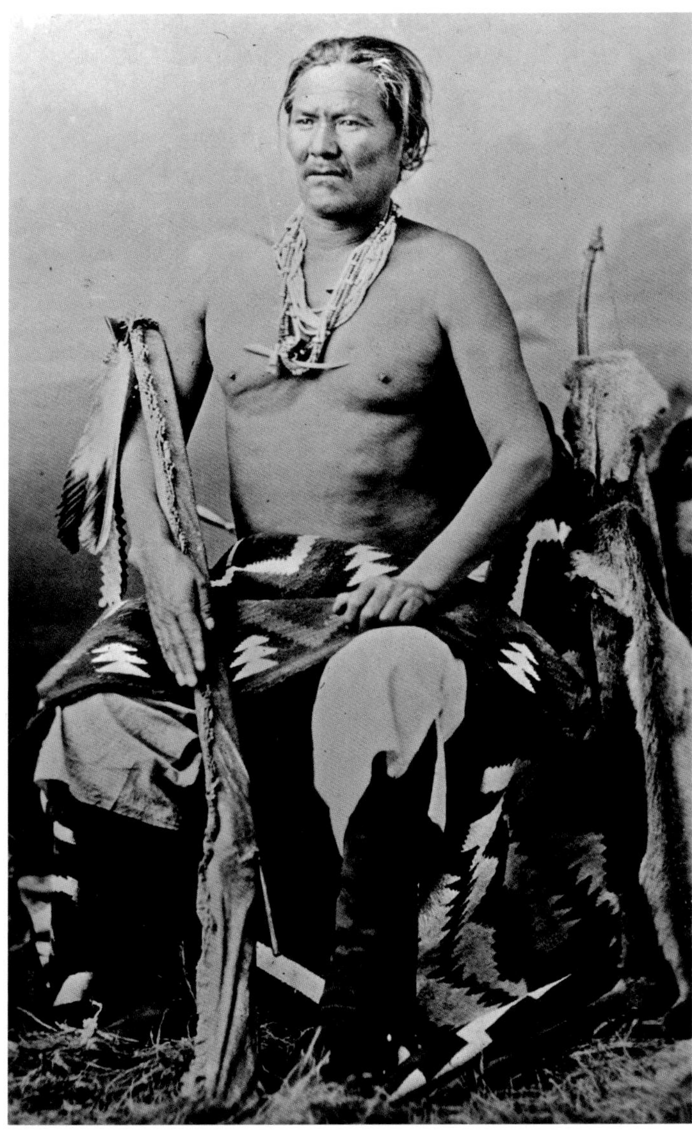

Navajo headman Manuelito, Nabááh Jiłt'aa (Warrior Grabbed Enemy). Albumen photographic print by Charles Milton Bell, 1873. *Courtesy of Library of Congress / Wiki*

The Grand Canyon of the flood-swollen Colorado River challenged all comers. But far to the south, where the deadly tidal bore of the Colorado River delta emptied into the Gulf of California, Nobel laureate John Steinbeck navigated the sometimes "quiet and strange" Sea of Cortés with biologist Ed Ricketts. Their 2,000-mile, coastal-hugging voyage aboard the 76-foot sardine boat the *Western Flyer* from Cannery Row in Monterey, California, around Lands End of the Baja Peninsula inspired Steinbeck to pen his environmental siren call, *The Log from the Sea of Cortez*. In the distant barrancas and *quebradas* (broken country) of mainland Mexico's Sierra Madre—still home to tales of lost gold and "lost tribes"—producer John Huston directed Humphrey Bogart in his Academy Award–winning cinema *The Treasure of the Sierra Madre*. The film classic was adapted from the novel by B. Traven, a mysterious German author who lived quietly in Mexico as an American. In their quest for gold, the treasure hunters, Traven wrote, "had to march nearly fourteen hundred miles from the mine to the capital, through deserts, across rivers and ravines, and up ten thousand feet across the high passes of the Sierra Madre."

In these regions and other once-blank spots on the maps, medieval cartographers might have inscribed with their quill pens "Here be the dragons," or cannibals, scorpions, lions, dog-headed creatures, sea serpents, and other mythic beasts and beings. The unknown lands of America's Outback include the sublime, forgotten, and eternal landscapes of the Great Southwest. For years I'd made it my mission to go off the grid into its unknown lands in search of affable locals, enduring traditions, and rarely seen earthscapes that I explored by foot, raft, rope, canoe, sea kayak, seagoing panga, and, ill-advisedly, from the back of an ornery mule. I wanted to disappear into the landscape to photograph my journeys with the colors of the earth, note my perceptions, and compose evocative essays. Often those explorations necessitated climbing and bivouacking alone atop remote mountain peaks to photograph the glory of sunrise and the spellbinding magic of sunset. There was no better reward for my efforts.

Before artist, poet, and "vagabond for beauty" Everett Ruess mysteriously vanished in 1934 in what later became Grand Staircase–Escalante National Monument, Utah, he wrote of one such aerie: "I found a trail and have just left it to make [a] dry camp on what seems like the rim of the world. My camp is on the very point of the divide, with the country falling away to the blue horizon on east and west. The last rays of the sun at evening and the first at dawn reach me."

Many of the wild landscapes, serpentine trails, and faded wagon routes that often remained beyond the horizon line for early travelers have since been designated United Nations Man and the Biosphere programs, UNESCO World Heritage Sites and UNESCO Biosphere Reserves, national parks, national monuments, national wildlife refuges, national wilderness areas, national historic trails, national scenic byways, national wild and scenic rivers, and Native American Sacred Lands. Moreover, the Wilderness Act of 1964 officially defined many modern *despoblados*: "A wilderness . . . is hereby recognized as an area where the earth and its community of life are untrammeled by man, where man himself is a visitor who does not remain."

This book is about my explorations of vanishing *despoblados* and *malpaís*. I've organized the book into four far-flung explorations, interwoven with discoveries, adventures, historical vignettes, and galleries of earthscapes. Many of the color photographs are paired with literary quotes from the Great Southwest's early travelers, authors, characters, and Native peoples to illuminate the landscapes they traveled through and exemplify how their raw earth wanderings changed, inspired, and often repelled them. Their words and images continue to shape our modern perceptions of the living landscapes and the hardy people who still inhabit them. Where they're known and verified, I've included Indigenous names of public sacred lands, and Spanish names and toponyms, because their cultural legacies and names had often been lost, erased, or anglicized by early cartographers. The bibliography includes the primary sources I used for my research. The literature cited includes the quotes and literary sources I selected. And the captions include each landscape's celebrated designation.

Sit back, relax, and enjoy the journey—or head out the door, breathe in the fresh air, and discover the wonders that await you in your own back of beyond.

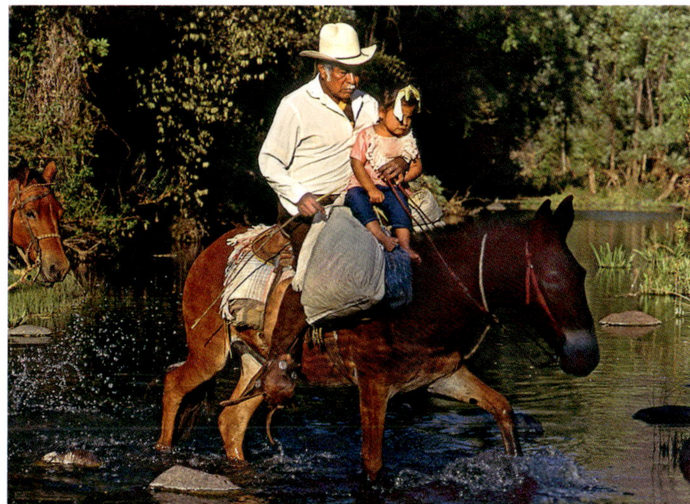

ABOVE: In the roadless depths of the Sierra Madre's Río Guajaray, an *arriero* (muleskinner) travels to a remote village, carrying his granddaughter, food, supplies, and mail to the Guarijío, the last tribe of Indigenous people discovered in Mexico, which some called the lost tribe. Elders told researchers they were never lost: "We've always been here."

RIGHT: Cascada de Basaseachi (Basaseachic Falls) plummets 805 feet into Candameña Canyon and forms the headwaters of the Río Mayo, which flows through the heart of the Sierra Madre into the Sea of Cortés. Basaseachic Falls National Park, Chihuahua, Mexico. *Parque Nacional Cascada de Basaseachi.*

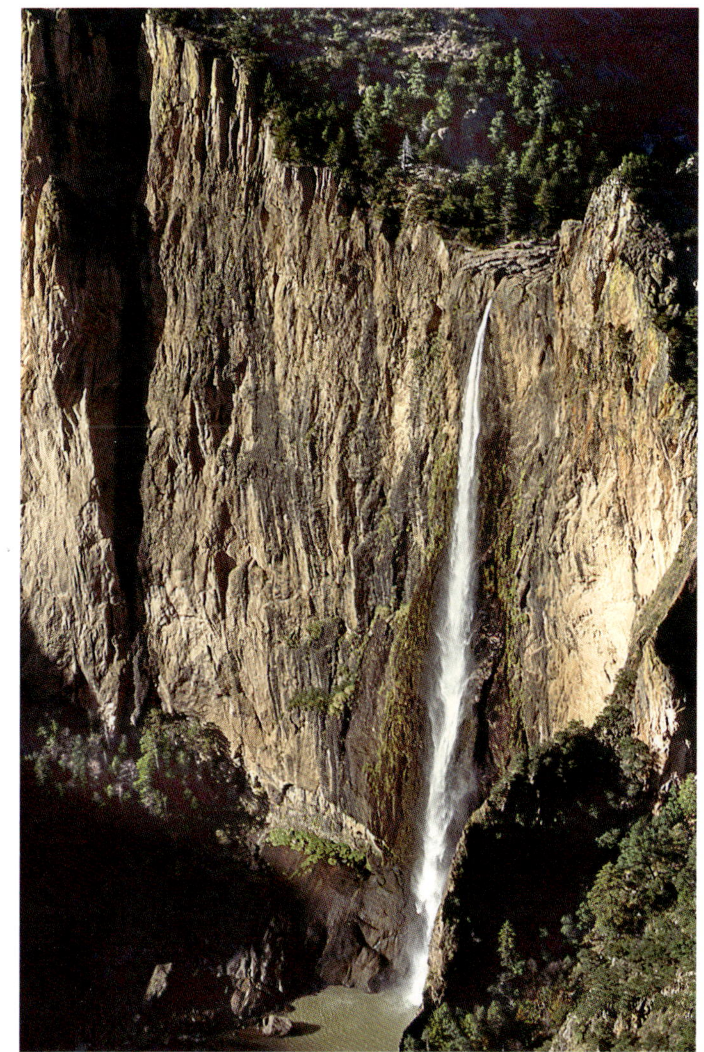

A traveler scarcely knows just where he is hidden or from which direction the tortuous trail has brought him.

—Howard Scott Gentry, *The Warihio Indians*, 1963

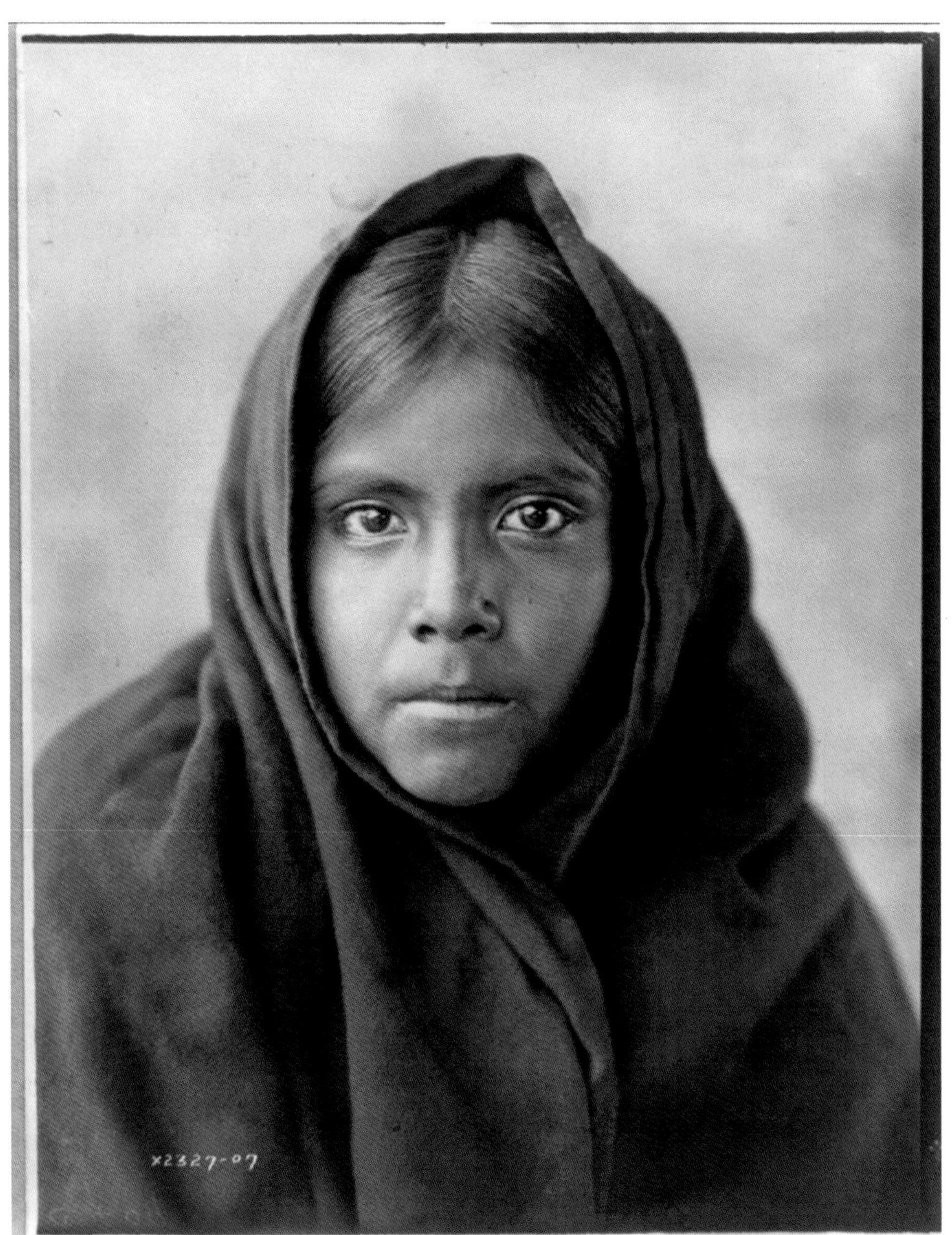

A Qahatika girl wearing a shawl in the Sonoran Desert, Arizona. Photographic print by Edward S. Curtis, September 14, 1907. *Courtesy of Library of Congress*

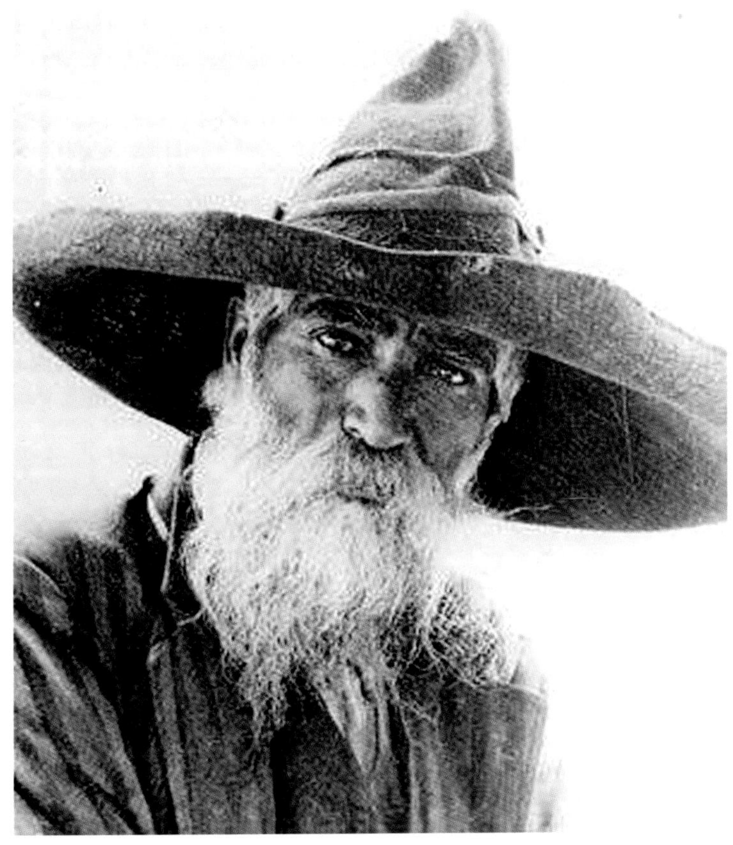

Curandero (faith healer), Big Bend, Texas. Glass-plate negative print by W. D. Smithers, ca. 1920s. *Courtesy of Harry Ransom Research Center, University of Texas at Austin*

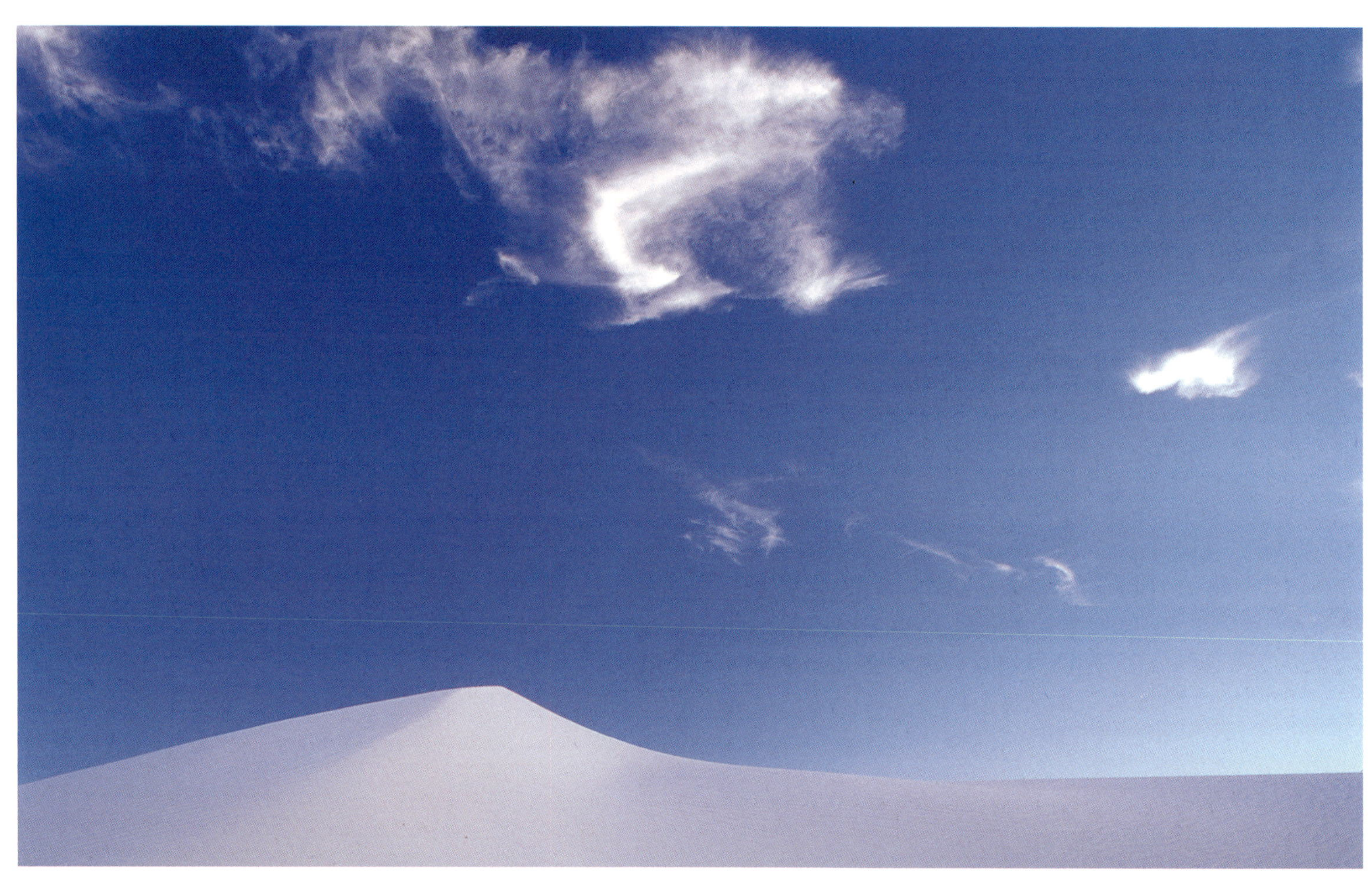

Cloud wisps hint at the mysterious winds of Pavla Blanca, White Sands National Park, New Mexico. UNESCO World Heritage Site Nomination.

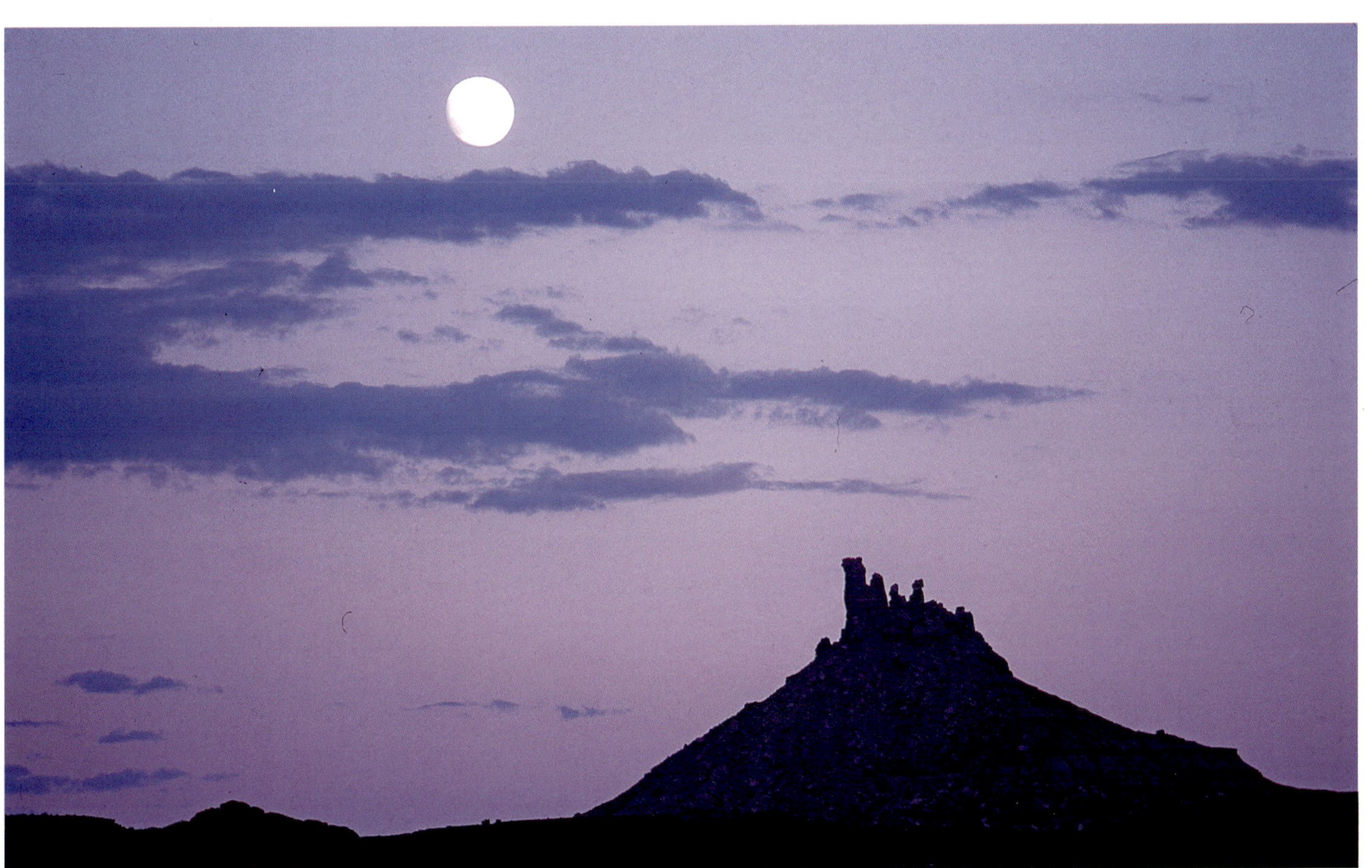

Moonrise, 6,379-foot North Six-Shooter Peak, Bears Ears National Monument, Utah. Navajo headman and warrior Manuelito was born in Bears Ears ca. 1818.

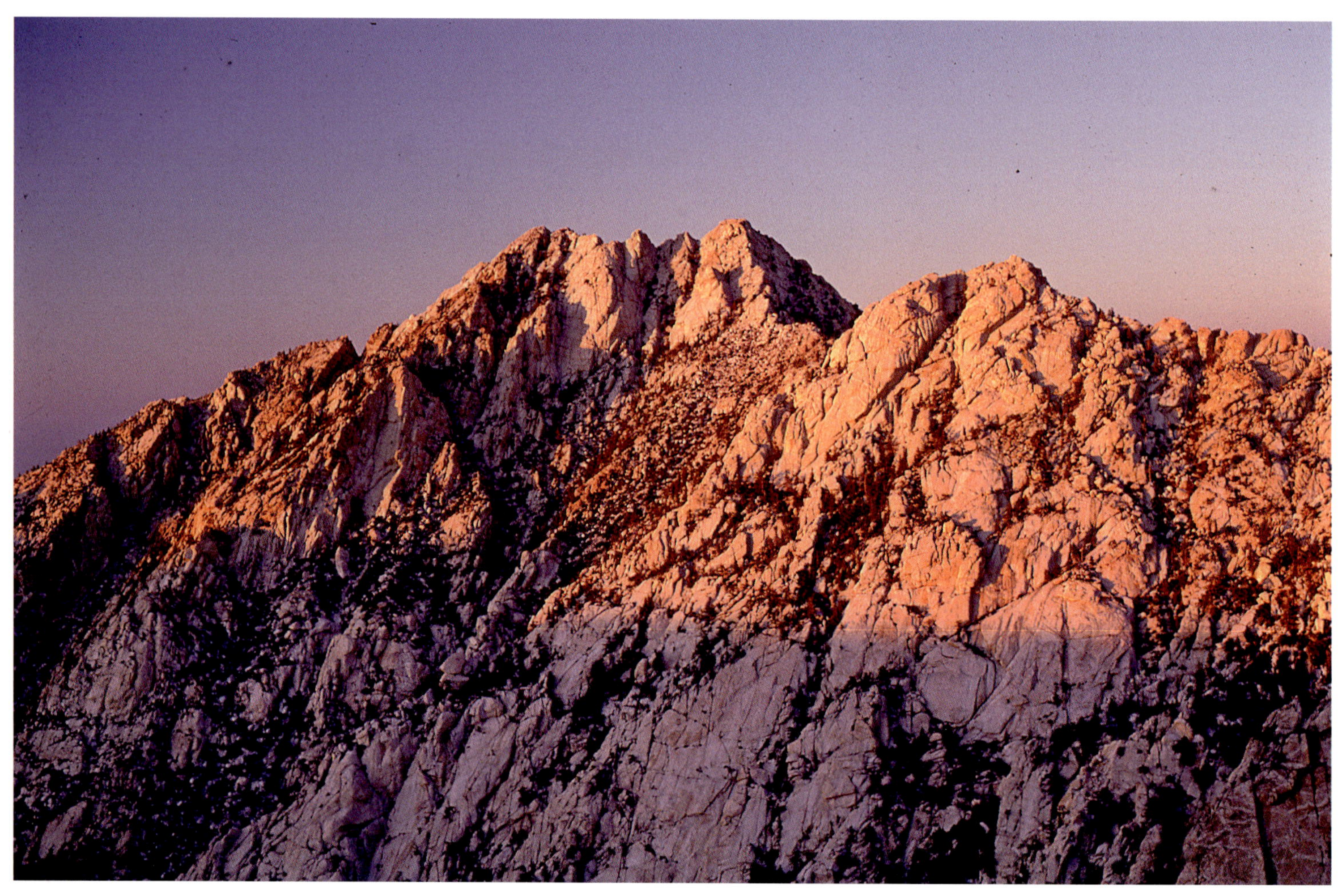

The serrated summit of 10,154-foot Picacho del Diablo (Peak of the Devil) challenges climbers, who face the daunting ascent of the most remote and rugged mountain in the Great Southwest. The summit towers two vertical miles above the San Felipe Desert, Baja California Norte. Sierra San Pedro de Mártir National Park (Parque Nacional Sierra de San Pedro Mártir).

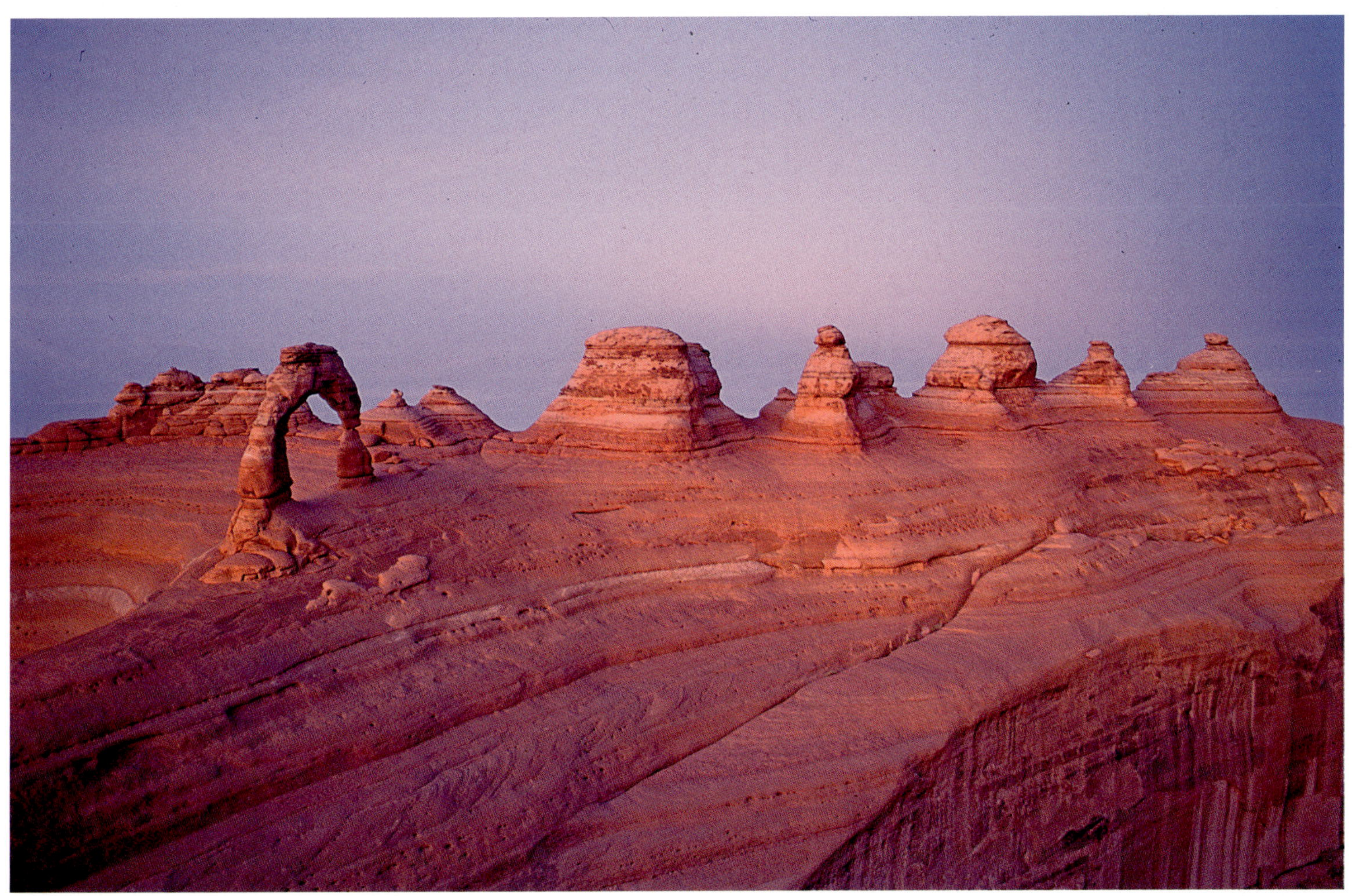

Earth glow illuminates the slickrock ridge of Delicate Arch, Arches National Park, Utah.

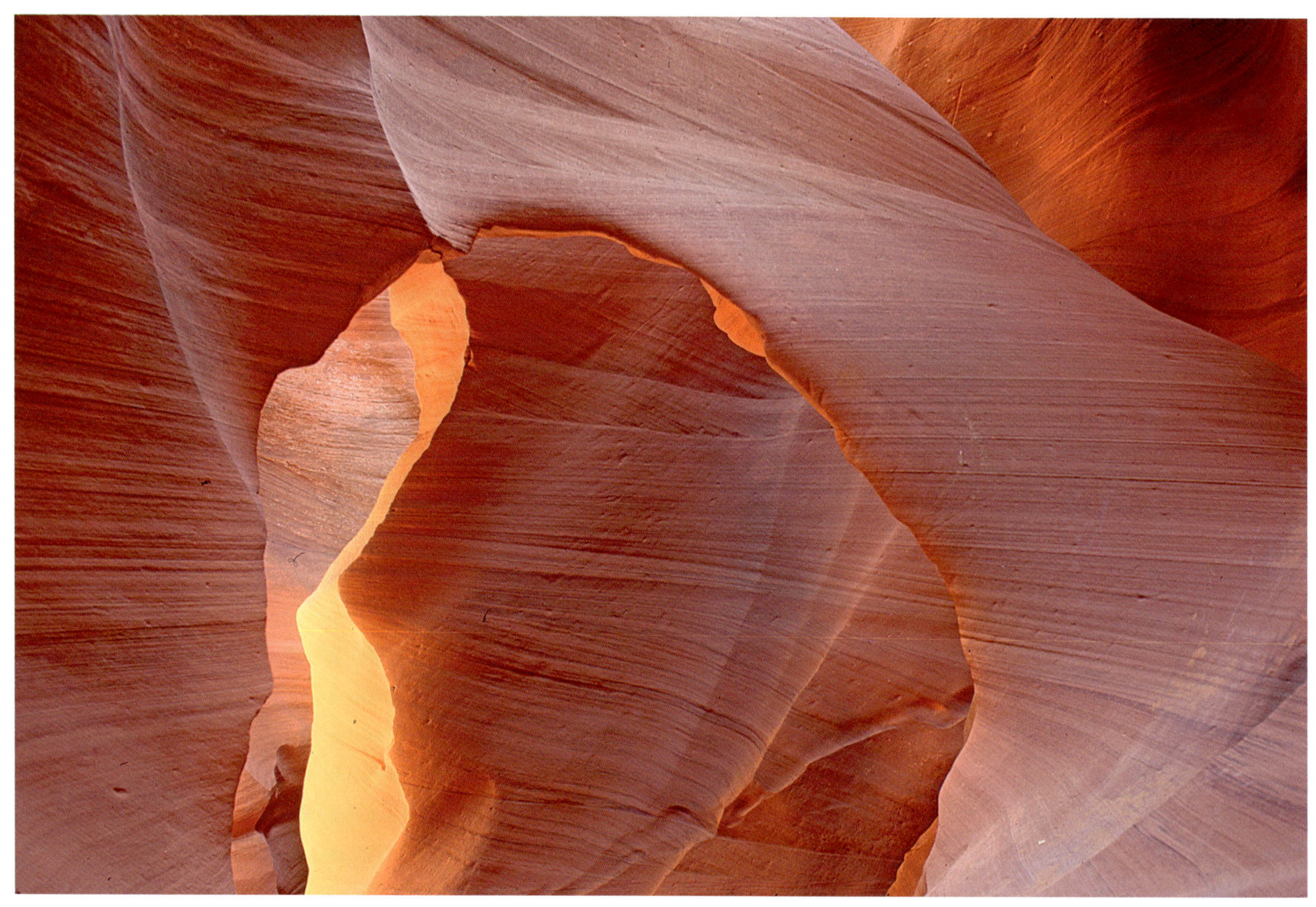

Hidden passage, Lower Antelope Canyon, Glen Canyon National Monument tributary, Arizona. The Navajo named this subterranean window of stone Hazdistazí (Spiral Rock Arch).

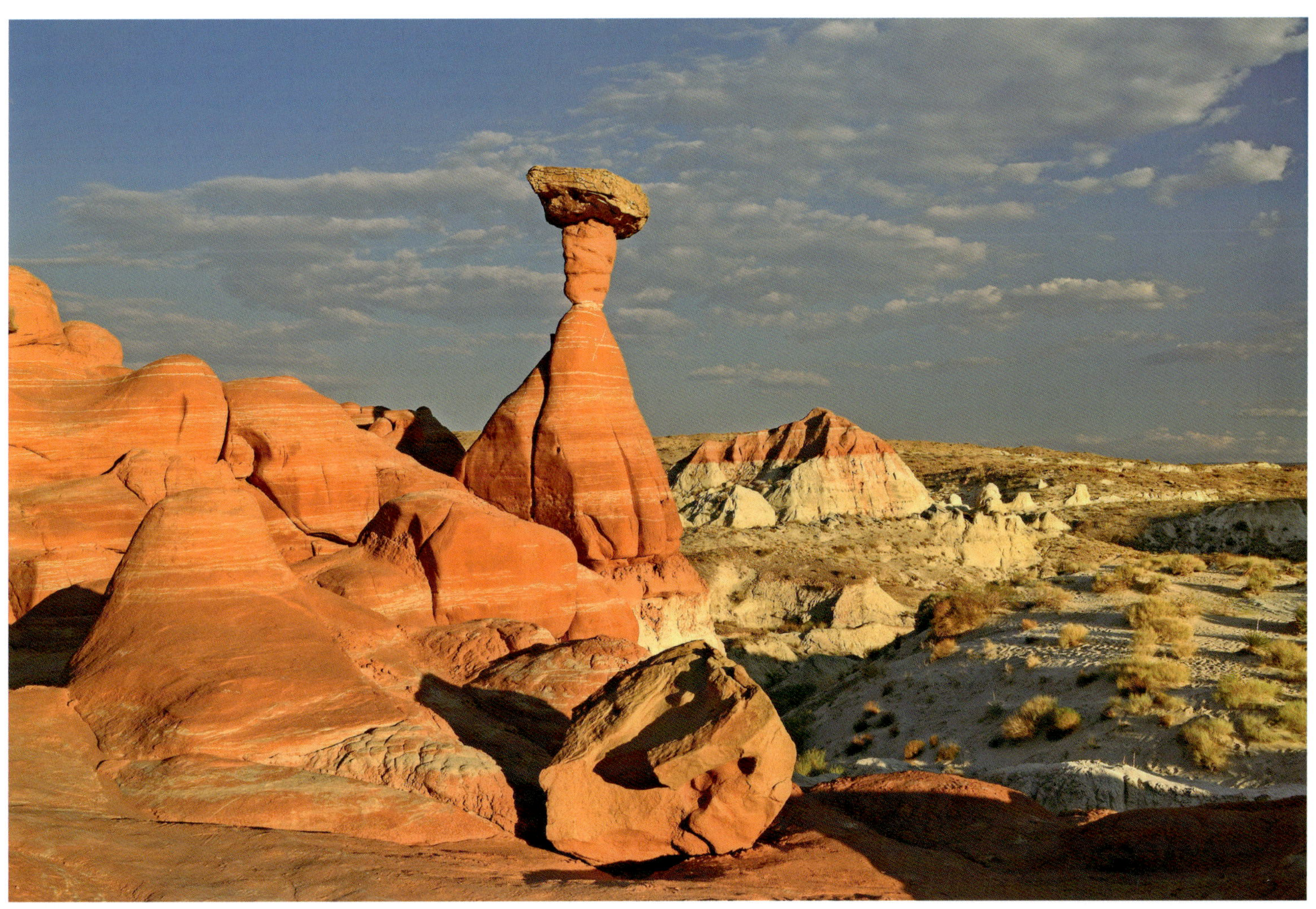

A caprock hoodoo stands sentinel beneath the southern escarpment of the Vermilion Cliffs, Grand Staircase–Escalante National Monument, Utah.

I. *TIERRA INCÓGNITA* / UNKNOWN LAND

LOST HORIZONS, MOUNTAIN ISLANDS, AND DESERT SEAS

The long, hot days, the stark, wind-beaten nights;
No human presence, human sight or sound;
Grim, silent land of wasted hopes, where they
Who came for gold ofttimes have madness found.

—Sharlot M. Hall, "Sheep-Herding," 1901

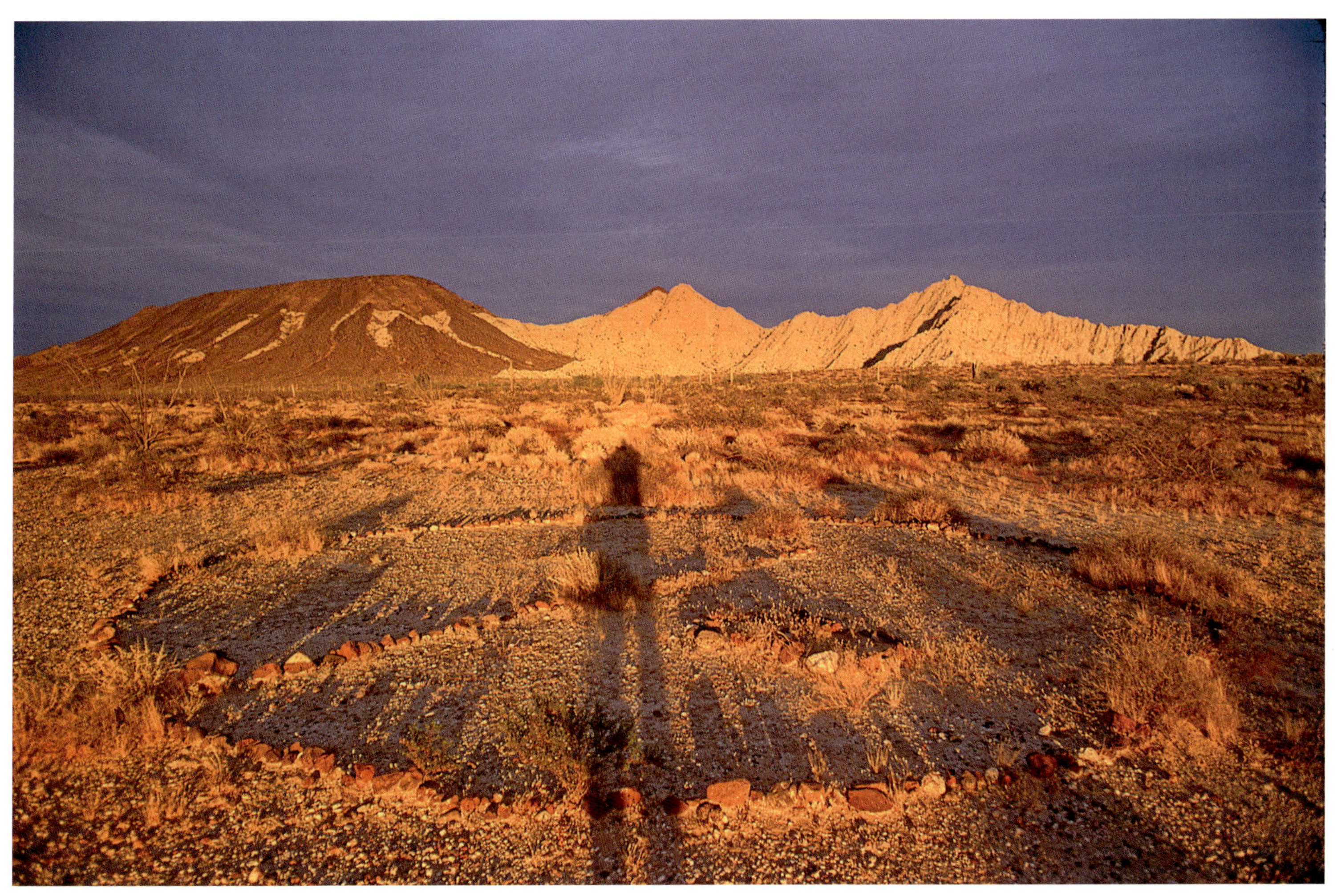

Sundial, circle of eight stone grave markers, El Camino del Diablo (Road of the Devil), Cabeza Prieta National Wildlife Refuge, Arizona. National Register of Historic Places.

South by southwest from El Desierto was a chimera of myths and legends that cast a spell or a curse on most all who entered. Dreams were sought, hopes were often dashed, and life nearly always hung in the balance. At times, that included my own. Among the sinuous paths that crisscrossed the heart of the southwestern United States and northwestern Mexico were those of missionary cartographers who first discovered the land passage to California from the summit of an ancient volcano. There were lost explorers who vanished with little trace after their hands were staked to wooden planks in a hallucination called El Desierto Purgatorio (the Purgatory of the Desert). And there were gold seekers, scientists, adventurers, and moonwalkers who crossed what looked like the last place on earth.

This tract of *tierra incógnita* in what became the Spanish Southwest was defined by mountain islands that floated over desert seas, including Gulf of California waters that lapped against sun-scorched shores. A wild and lonely country of primeval beauty, it stretched from La Palma de la Mano de Dios (the Hollow of God's Hand) in California's Mojave Desert to El Camino del Diablo (the Road of the Devil) in Arizona's Sonoran Desert, and from Picacho del Diablo, which soared 2 vertical miles above Laguna Diablo (Devils Lake) in northern Baja California to the haunted isle of Isla Tiburón (Shark Island) in the Sea of Cortés and beyond.

It was not cheery country to travel through, whatever notions or dreams tugged at their souls and lured them deeper into a trance until they dropped in their own shadows, carrying the promise of God, Glory, and Gold sealed between their cracked lips. When Irish-born American author, artist, and world traveler J. Ross Browne first ventured into the American West in 1863, he wrote: "It is not a jolly country. The graves of murdered men, and boundless sand deserts, and parched mountains, and dried-up rivers, and scenes of ruin and desolation are profoundly interesting; but they are not subjects for the indulgence of rollicking humor."

My travels throughout these lost horizons of mountain islands and desert seas forged my will and honed my vision like no other corner of the Great Southwest.

Tiburón Island floated in the Sea of Cortés like a mythic leatherback sea turtle. The Seri named it *moosnípol* (sea turtle—its blackness). It was the largest reptile that swam the Seven Seas, including the Sea of Cortés. The Seri, or Comcáac (the People), lived between the blistering desert and the cimarron sea. Their ancestral home of Tahéöjc (Tiburón Island) was the center of their creation story of "Hant Caai, he who made the land." It was their refuge from Spaniards, who decimated the Comcáac from 3,000 people until fewer than 175 survivors remained. It was their hunting grounds, where they stalked mule deer with poison-tipped arrows, and gathered magical plants such as hapis, which was said to have supernatural power. And it was a sanctuary where they meditated in secret caves during *heecot coom* (vision quests) until they were touched by spirits. "With three other medicine men, I went to the Sacred Cave," Santo Blanco, one of the "last of the Seri," had said, "and for the four days we were there, we ate no food and drank no water. . . . After which the Spirit which lives there came to see us."

The 450-square-mile Tiburón Island is the largest in the Sea of Cortés. Together with the Midriff Islands, it formed an archipelago of fabled stepping stones that the "superhuman . . . *xica coosyatoj* Giants" used to journey from the Baja Peninsula to Tiburón Island. It became a crossroads for Spanish conquistadors who raided the island, American gold seekers who found madness and death on its shores, and world travelers who went in quest of discovery. *Kon Tiki* adventurer Thor Heyerdahl ventured onto Tiburón Island to study the Seri's use of *hascam* (balsa rafts) for his seagoing RA Expeditions. "There was no path," Heyerdahl wrote. "No trace of anything, but deer, hare, lizards, snakes, and rodents. Shark Island had been uninhabited by human beings." It was known to the Seri as Tahéöjc Imozit (heart of Tiburón), and I had traveled across a forgotten corner of the Great Southwest to climb the island's unknown mountain, the 2,871-foot Sierra Kunkaak. It was uninhabited. The Seri named the peak Cójocam Iti Yaii (where the flee-ers were). I'd fled there too. I found solace to contemplate nature alone and photograph the lay of the land from the summit to the sea. Over time, the summit became a friend, a doorway, and a stepping-stone to my own quests that awaited me beyond.

When the "Father of Denali National Park," Charles Sheldon, hunted deer on Tiburón Island for the Seri, he made a telling note in his journal on December 30, 1921: "The Seris assert that mule deer, rabbits, lions, coyotes, jaguars, and rattlesnakes swim back and forth from the mainland to Tiburón. I have asked all of them and have been very careful that they understood, and they still assert this." As a result of Tiburón Island's textured cultural history and rich biodiversity, the Comcáac's homeland was inscribed along with other gulf isles as a UNESCO World Biosphere Reserve, the Islas de Golfo California (Islands of the Gulf of California). It merged with a neighboring UNESCO Biosphere Reserve, the Alto Golfo de California (Upper Gulf of California). Together, they formed the northern half of what undersea explorer and oceanographer Jacques Cousteau called "the world's aquarium" during his epochal Farewell Voyage of Rediscovery.

The hard rock spine of the Sierra de San Pedro Mártir is the highest, most rugged, and spectacular range of granite peaks on the 800 mile-long Baja Peninsula. At 10,154 feet, Picacho del Diablo was seen from the Pacific Ocean during the sixteenth century by Spanish mariners and from the Gulf of California by Indigenous peoples. It was a nearly impregnable massif for Jesuit missionary explorer Padre Weceslaus Linck, who traversed the sierra from coast to coast by mule and on foot, and it was the lost world of the canyon—and mountain-dwelling Kiliwa (Koléew Ñaja') peoples until their clock tragically ran out in 1829. A beacon for *gambusinos* (miners) who searched for gold in wild canyons cursed with the names Cañón del Diablo (Devil's Canyon) and Cañón del Diablito (Little Devil's Canyon).

One of the first explorers to be lured by the mountain's stark beauty was Donald McLain. In 1911 the California topographer boated down the lower Colorado River from Yuma, Arizona, sailed a small skiff down the Sea of Cortés, walked across the San Felipe Desert, and climbed for the heavens where no one had stood before, Picacho del Diablo. Before McClain returned home to Altadina, California, by the same way he first ventured, he'd noted: "I finally reached the north peak. There was no evidence of any previous visit. I found it hard to believe no one had been there before." McLain's first recorded ascent of Picacho del Diablo "via an old Indian trail in San Pedro Canyon [Cañón el Cajon]" remained a remarkable quest in the annals of adventure.

It would take more than two decades before anyone else took up the challenge of climbing the most difficult mountain in Baja. Among them was legendary Sierra Nevada climber Norman Clyde. He led a small group of Sierra Club climbers during a second attempt on the peak in 1932. In an epic plagued by fatigue and thirst, Clyde led his party on a perilous, rarely repeated traverse of Pinnacle Ridge. From the summit of the mountain, Clyde wrote: "On every side the peak dropped away precipitously to deep gorges leading to the desert some 10,000 feet below."

On rare occasions, climbers continued to thread the brutal maze of boulders and cataracts from the San Felipe Desert through Cañón del Diablo. I was among them. No other terrain had brought me to my knees the way the great sierra had. On the second day of a retreat off the peak with a friend who'd reached her limit, I'd skip-jumped onto a large boulder; it rolled over my left leg and wedged it against another rock. I spent the next ten hours limping, resting, peg-legging, and coaxing my partner all the way back down to my truck. It was parked near the mouth of Cañón del Diablo, not far from the smugglers' airstrip on Playa del Diablo.

But the mountain had a hold on me. I came back two weeks later and finally climbed and bivouacked atop the roof of Baja to photograph sunset and sunrise from what McCain had called "the solemn, majestic La Provdencia Peak." In Spanish it was called Cerro de la Encantada (Mountain of the Enchanted One). The twin summits of the daunting peak I'd viewed through my camera lens formed the southern terminus of a great transpeninsular mountain range that ran 200 miles north to 10,834-foot San Jacinto Peak (Saint Hyacinthe) near Palm Springs, California. Today, the Sierra de San Pedro Mártir is celebrated as a national park, and the summit still beckons climbers where eagles dare.

Few places on earth resembled the 770-square-mile lunarscape of El Pinacate and Gran Desierto. And no missionary explorer was more tenacious than Padre Eusebio Francisco Kino. In 1706, the Jesuit cartographer crossed the alien terrain of *maar* (steam blast) craters, cinder cones, and volcanic peaks, shields, and lava flows that would have proven hell on earth for tender-footed novitiates. Traversing 7,500 miles on foot in leather sandals, by horse, and mule, Kino founded a string of Spanish colonial missions throughout Pimería Alta (Upper Pima Lands) between 1694 and 1701. In the process, Kino forged trails across a foreboding desert inhabited by the hardiest desert people next to the Seri, the Hia Ced O'odham (People of the Sand). They roamed the Pinacate and Gran Desierto—the largest sand sea in North America—in a never-ending quest for food and water that included *hía tatk* (sand root) tubers that grew in barren but beautiful star dunes. On November 5, the tireless Padre Kino wrote of climbing 3,957-foot Volcán de Santa Clara, which reigned over the Pinacate. From the summit he'd discovered that California was not an island, as early explorers professed: "Selecting the best mules, we ascended this very high peak . . . and we saw very plainly the connection of this our land with that of the west."

Inspired by Kino, I ventured alone into what, without my trusty pickup truck, would have remained a hidden realm on the far side of civilization. I parked at a remote camp called Cono Rojo (Red Cone), and I had the Pinacates to myself. Coyotes howled and the moon lit up the dark landscape. The next morning, I crawled, often upended like a *pinacatl* (pinacate beetle), to negotiate tortured blocks of lava before I began a climb of Sisyphus. For every step I took forward, I slid a half foot down, regained my footstep, and slid another half foot down, until I finally reached the summit. I sat down and gazed at the mysterious terrain beneath my feet.

Few dared enter the forgotten domain for many years after Padre Kino stood atop the Volcán de Santa Clara. Norwegian explorer Carl Lumholtz sought out Juan Caravales, the last "Indian hermit," or Hia Ced O'odham, whom he called Sand Papago. Caravales unimaginably lived alone in the 2,200-square-mile sand sea until 1910. Then came salt-of-the-earth wood cutters, miners, and ranchers—all trying to eke out a living from what geographer Ronald L. Ives called the "land of lava, ash, and sand." In a 1934 letter to his parents, Ives wrote of his passion for wandering such deserts: "If at any time I get an invitation to accompany any bona-fide expedition anywhere, even to hell to bring back the devil, I will take it."

During the 1950s, archeologist Julian Hayden turned academia on its ear after he began examining the Pinacate's ancient trails, stone tools, and mystifying bighorn sheep cremation shrines, evidence that early people inhabited the great desert long before 11,000 BCE. Two of the three Apollo 14 astronauts, Commander Alan Shepard and Lunar Module Pilot Edgar Mitchell, landed in the lunarscape in 1970 to train for the third lunar landing and moonwalk. There were terrestrial walkers and writers Charles Bowden and Bill Broyles, who crisscrossed the "Empty Quarter of the Sonoran Desert" on foot from sunrise to the Sea of Cortés.

Then there was the contemporary sage of the desert, Edward Abbey, who proffered wisdom from the desert sea to the slickrock canyons. Few characterized the Pinacate more colorfully than Abbey when he wrote:

"The ultimate among the various provinces of The Great American Desert is Sonora's Pinacate region. . . . This region is the bleakest, flattest, hottest, grittiest, grimmest, dreariest, ugliest, most useless, most senseless desert of them all. It is the villain among badlands, most wasted of wastelands, most foreboding of forbidden realms."

> Show a hiker a map with blank space and some innate impulse roars, "Go there." A feature, a mood, a line beckons. So with the Gran Desierto. If one outlines the Gran Desierto and then X's the heart, we have a mythical center of power, a heartland, a geographical center, a median of some improbable significance.
>
> —**Bill Broyles**, *Sunshot: Peril and Wonder in the Gran Desierto*, **2006**

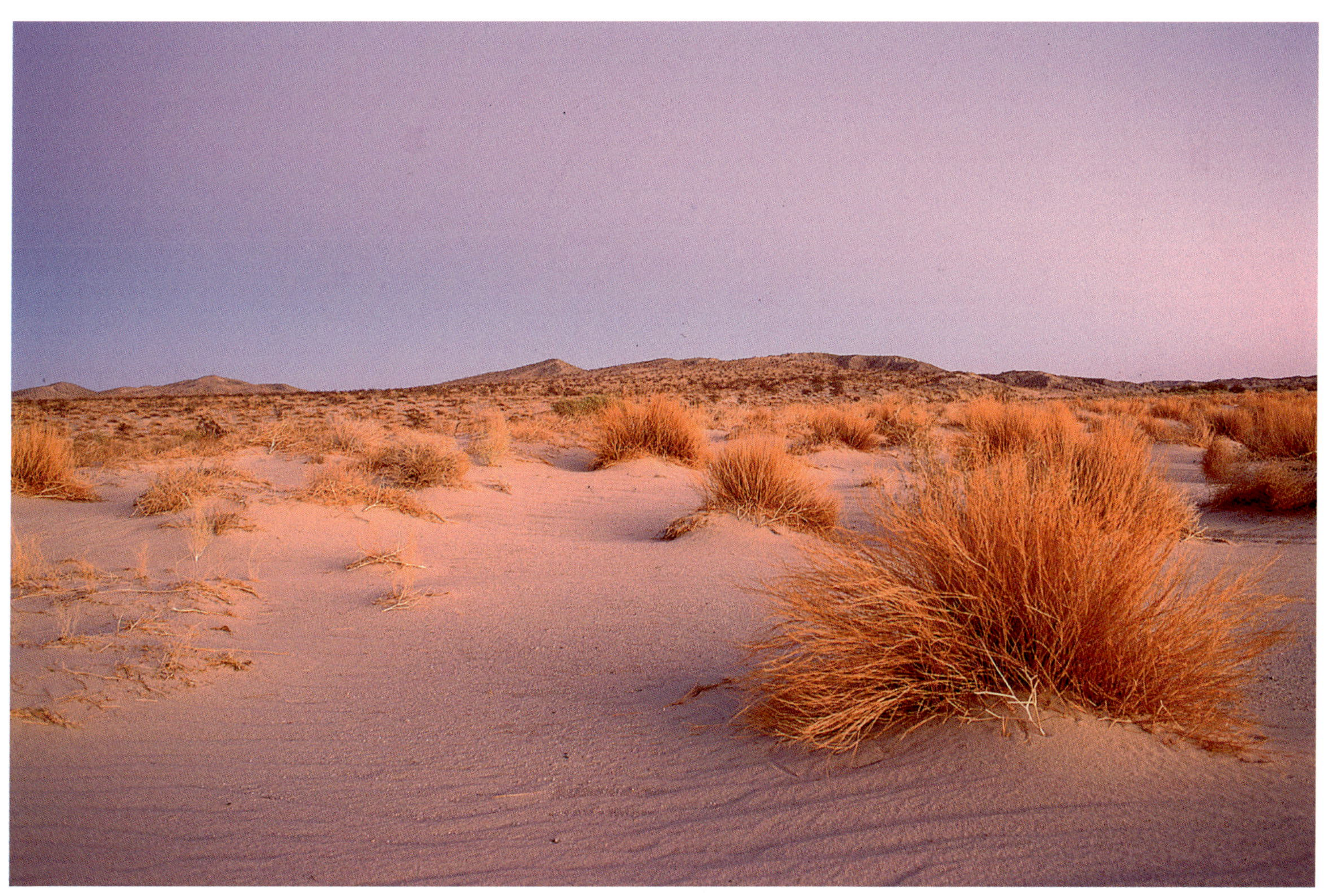

The barren Colorado Desert typifies the harsh region that pioneers struggled across and called La Palma de la Mano de Dios (the Palm of God's Hand), in Anza Borrego Desert State Park, California. UNESCO Mojave and Colorado Deserts Biosphere Reserve.

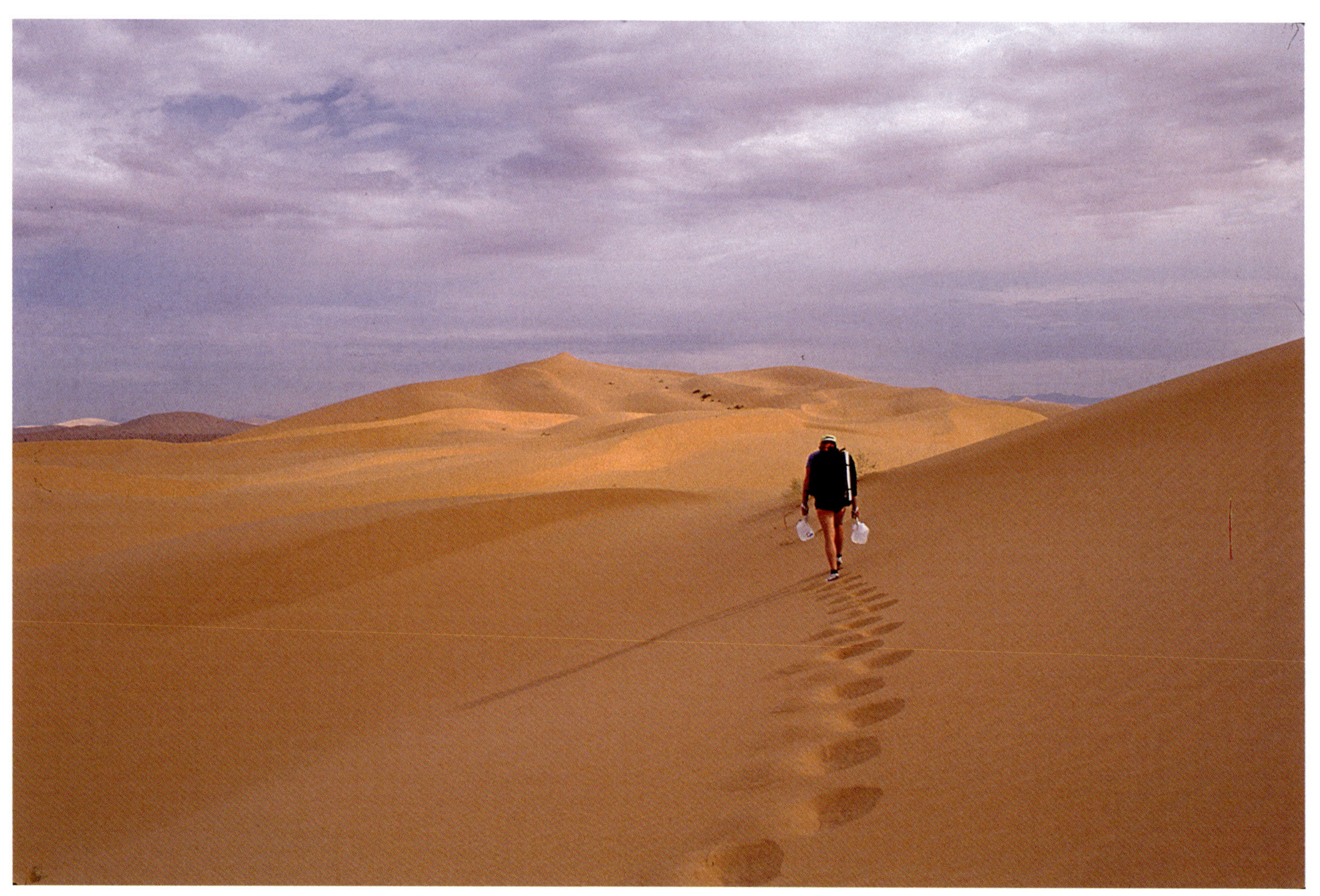

Crossing the lost horizon of El Gran Desierto sand sea, UNESCO El Pinacate and Gran Desierto de Altar Biosphere Reserve, Sonora, Mexico

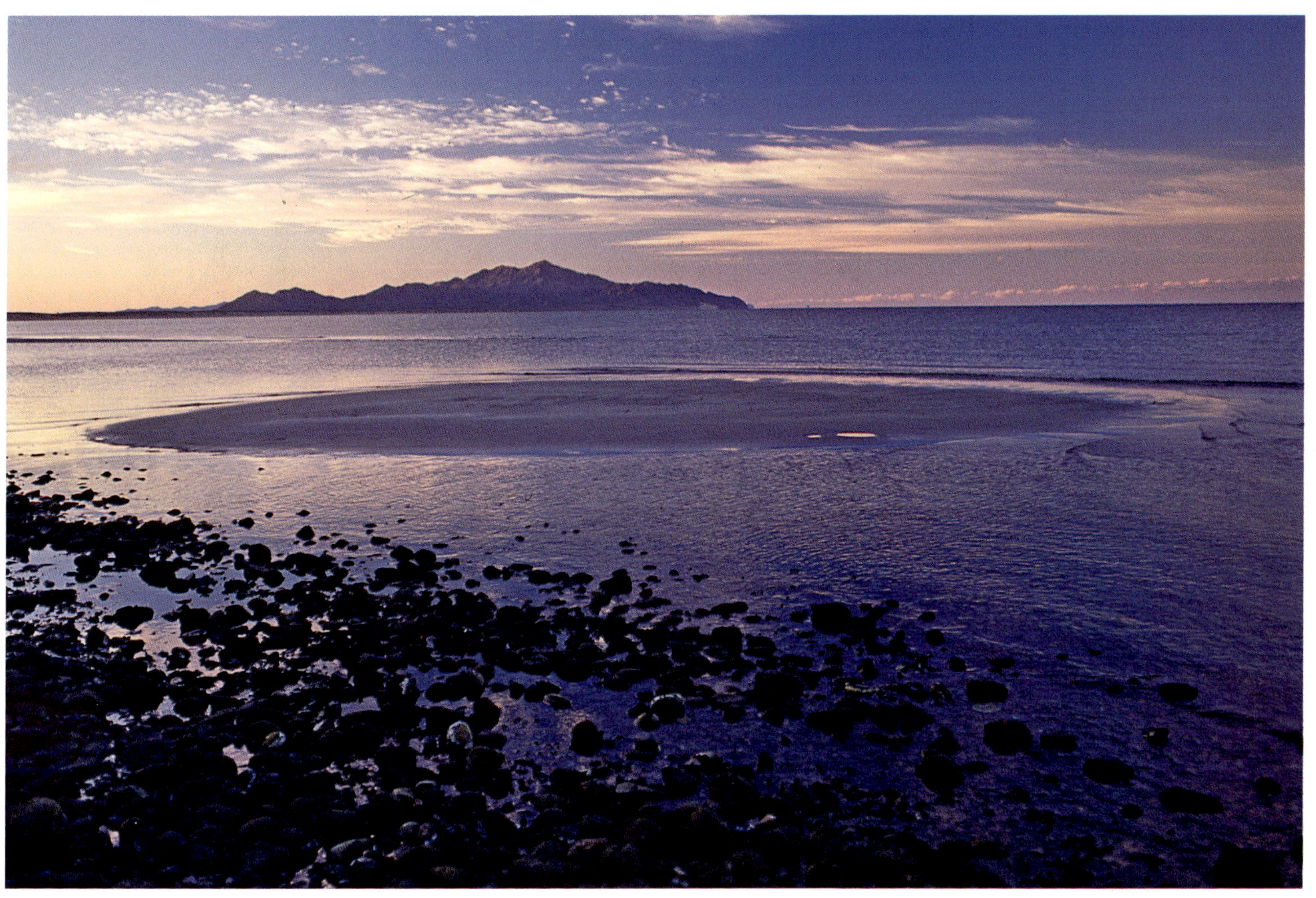

Sunrise, Punta Tepoca (Tepoca Point), Sea of Cortés, Sonora, Mexico. UNESCO Islands and Protected Areas of the Gulf of California (UNESCO Islas y Áreas Protegidas del Golfo de California).

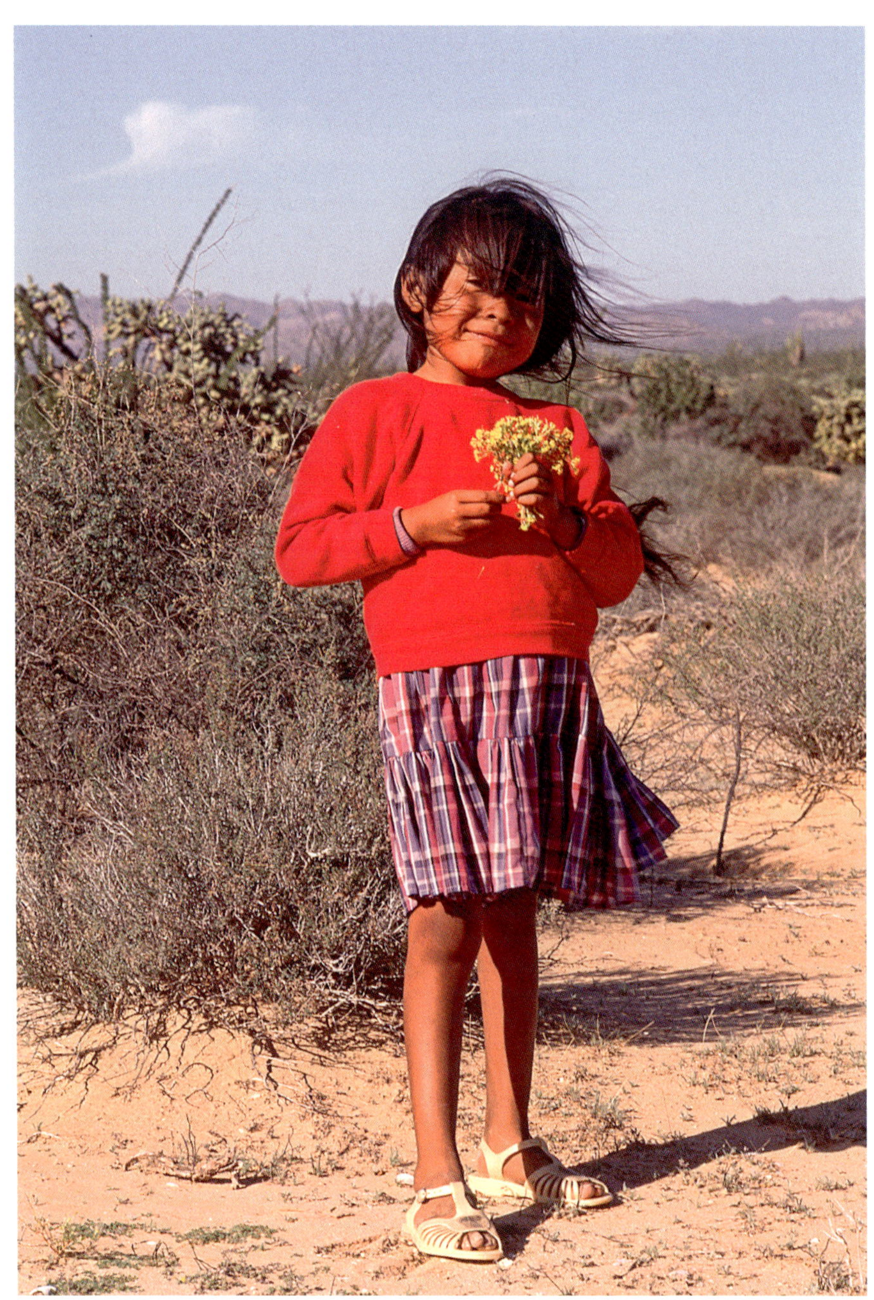

A Seri girl holds a bouquet of yellow flowers she gathered in the coastal desert near her village of El Desemboque de los Seris (Haxöl Iihom), Sonora, Mexico.

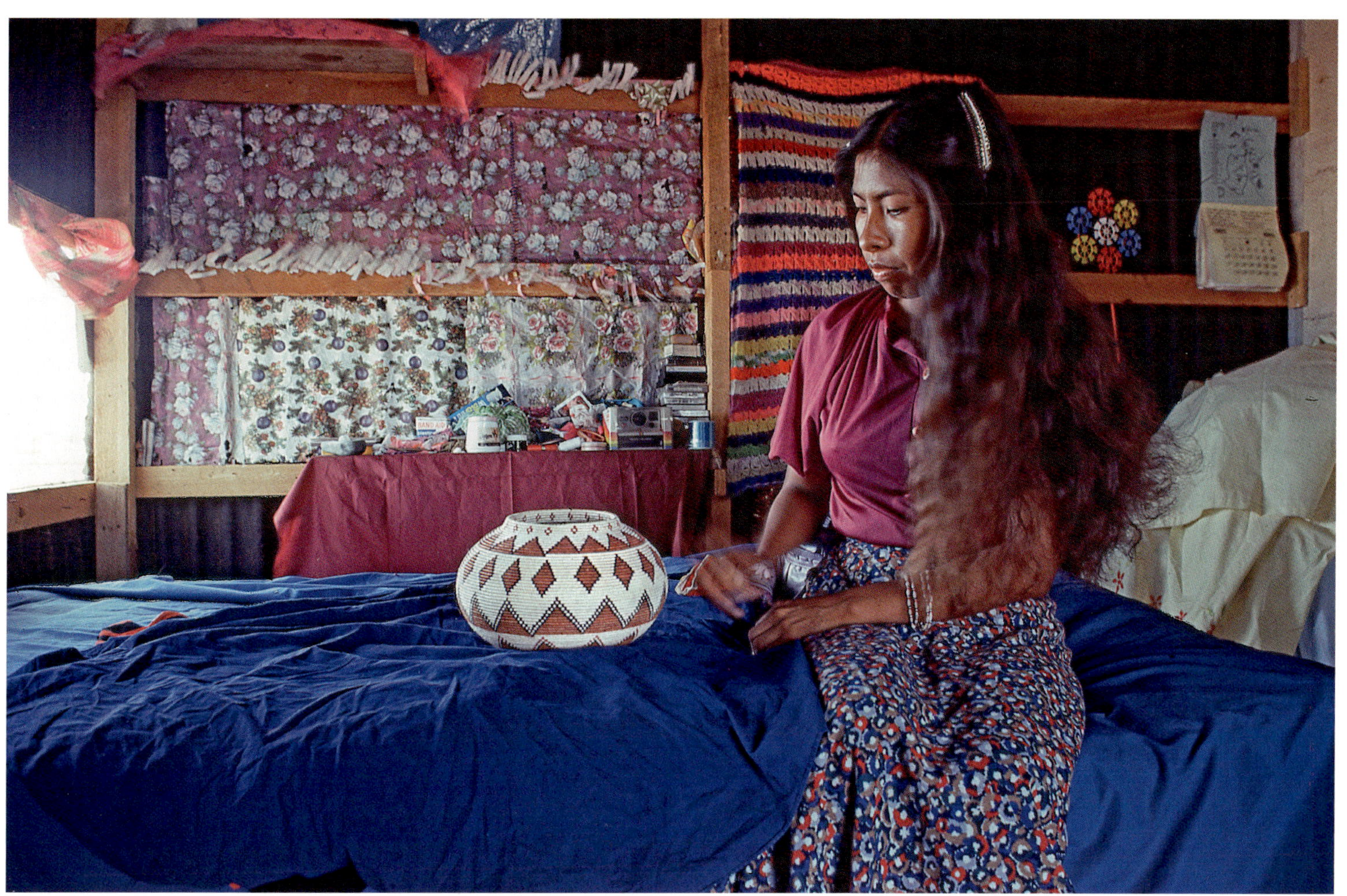

Aurelia Molina holds one of her prized pot-styled (*haat hanoohcö*) baskets that was handwoven from limber bush (*haat*), colored with natural dyes, and bought by an American collector.

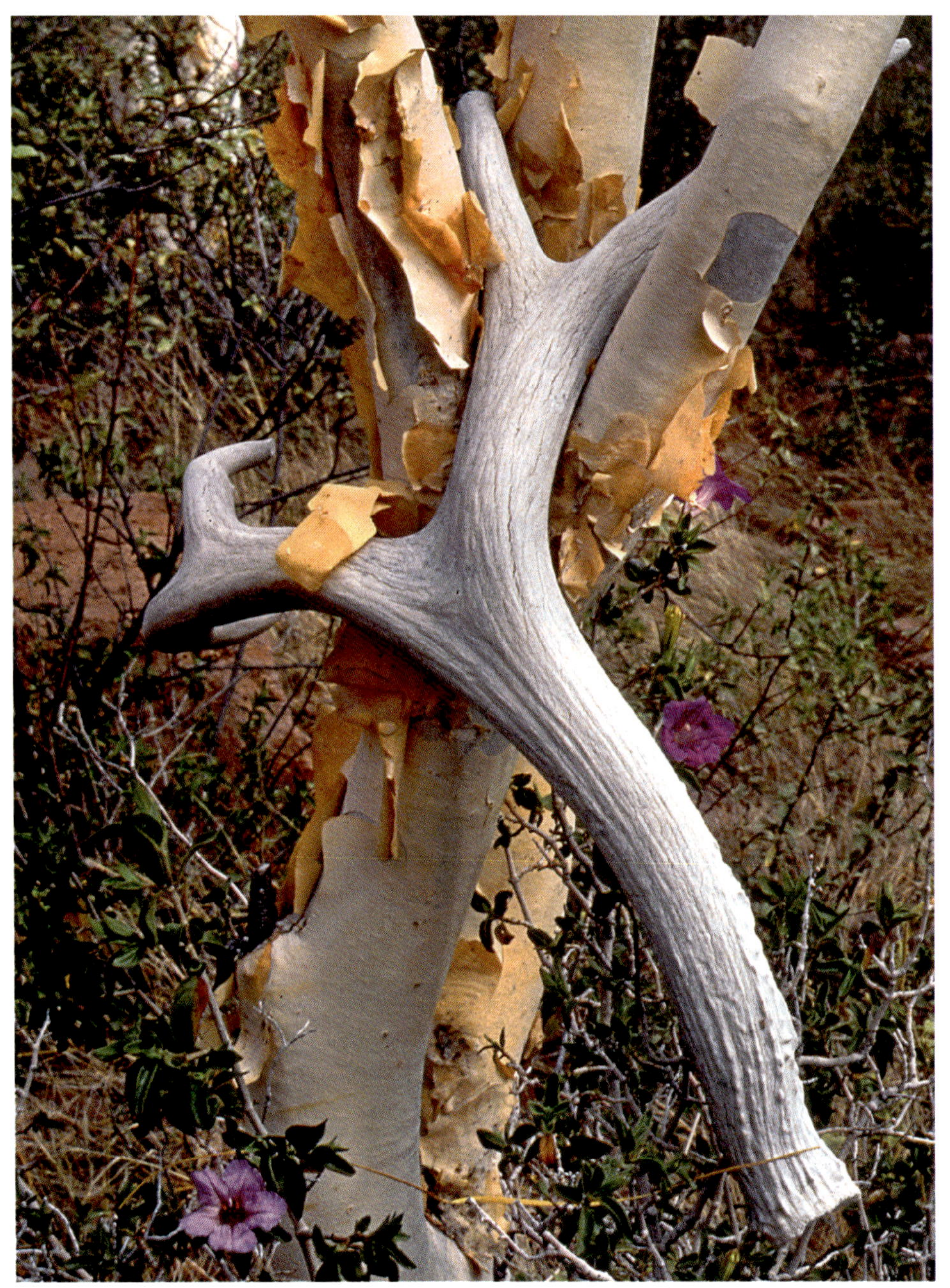

It was puzzling to see the antler of a Tiburón Island buro (mule deer) caught in this palo blanco tree on the way to the summit of the Sierra Kunkaak, Sonora.

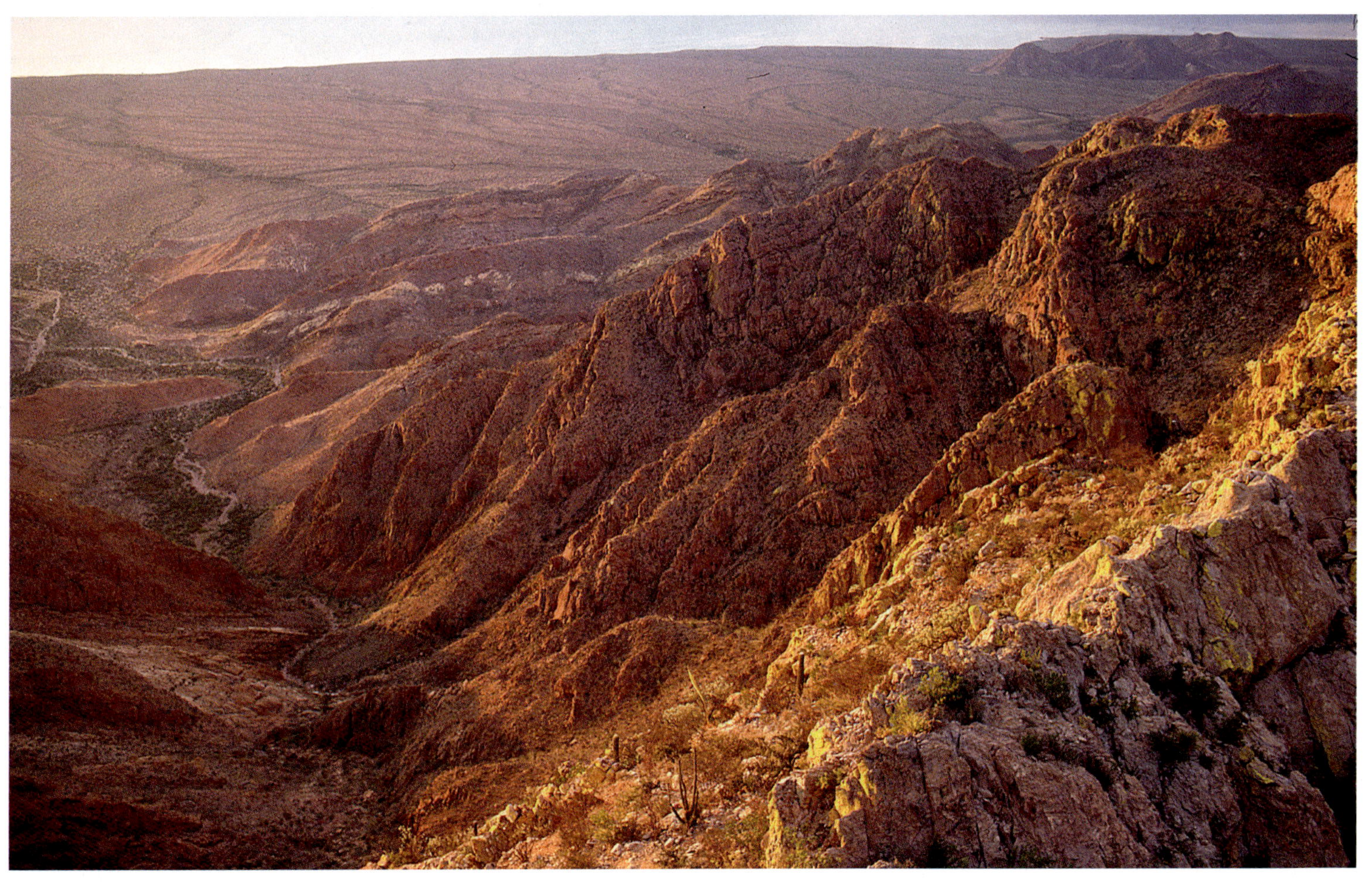

Sunrise, looking east on the summit ridge of the Sierra Kunkaak, Cójocam Iti Yaii (Where the Flee-ers Were), Tiburón Island, Sea of Cortés, Sonora, Mexico.

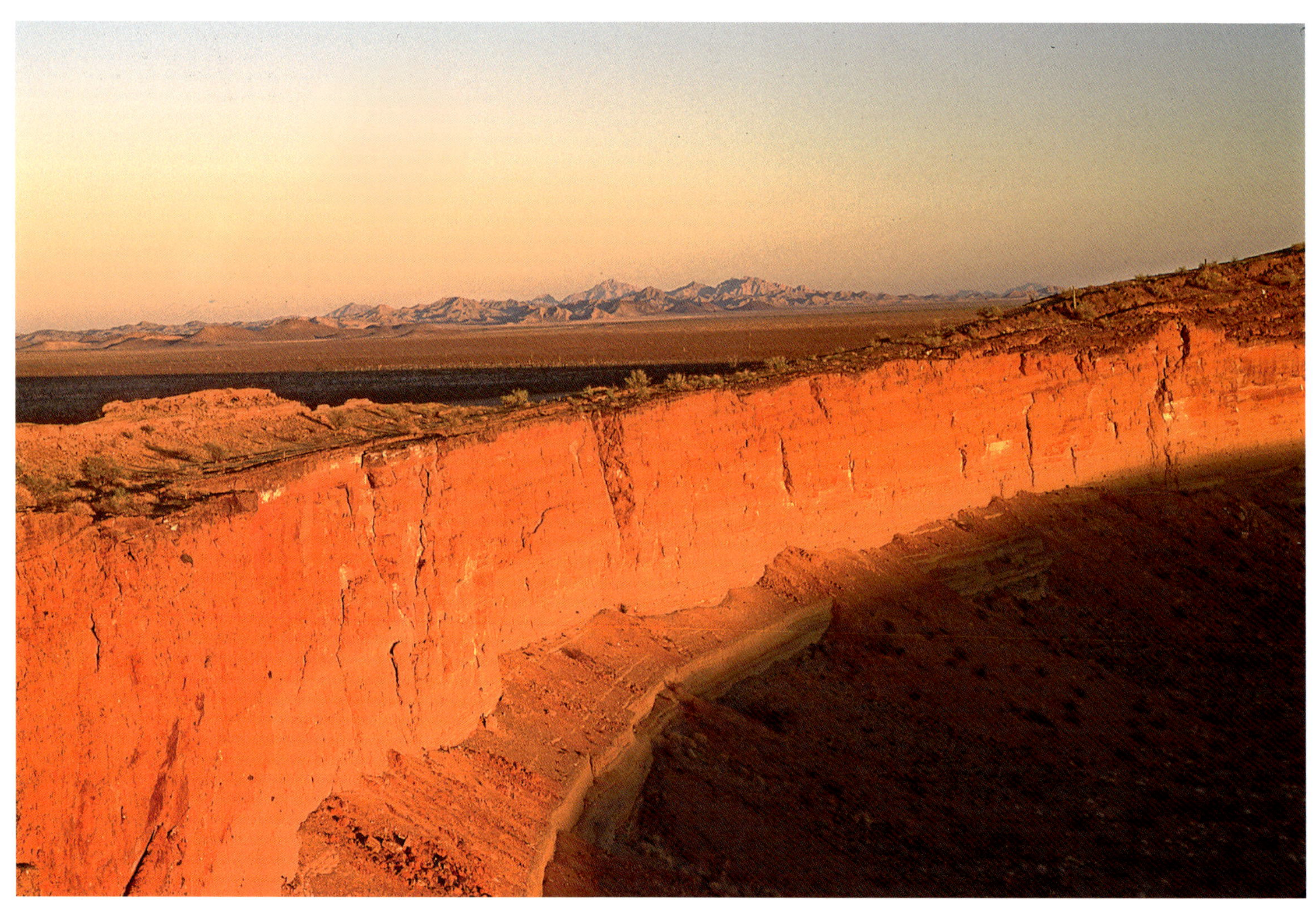

Cerro Colorado Crater, Sonora, Mexico. UNESCO El Pinacate and Gran Desierto de Altar Biosphere Reserve.

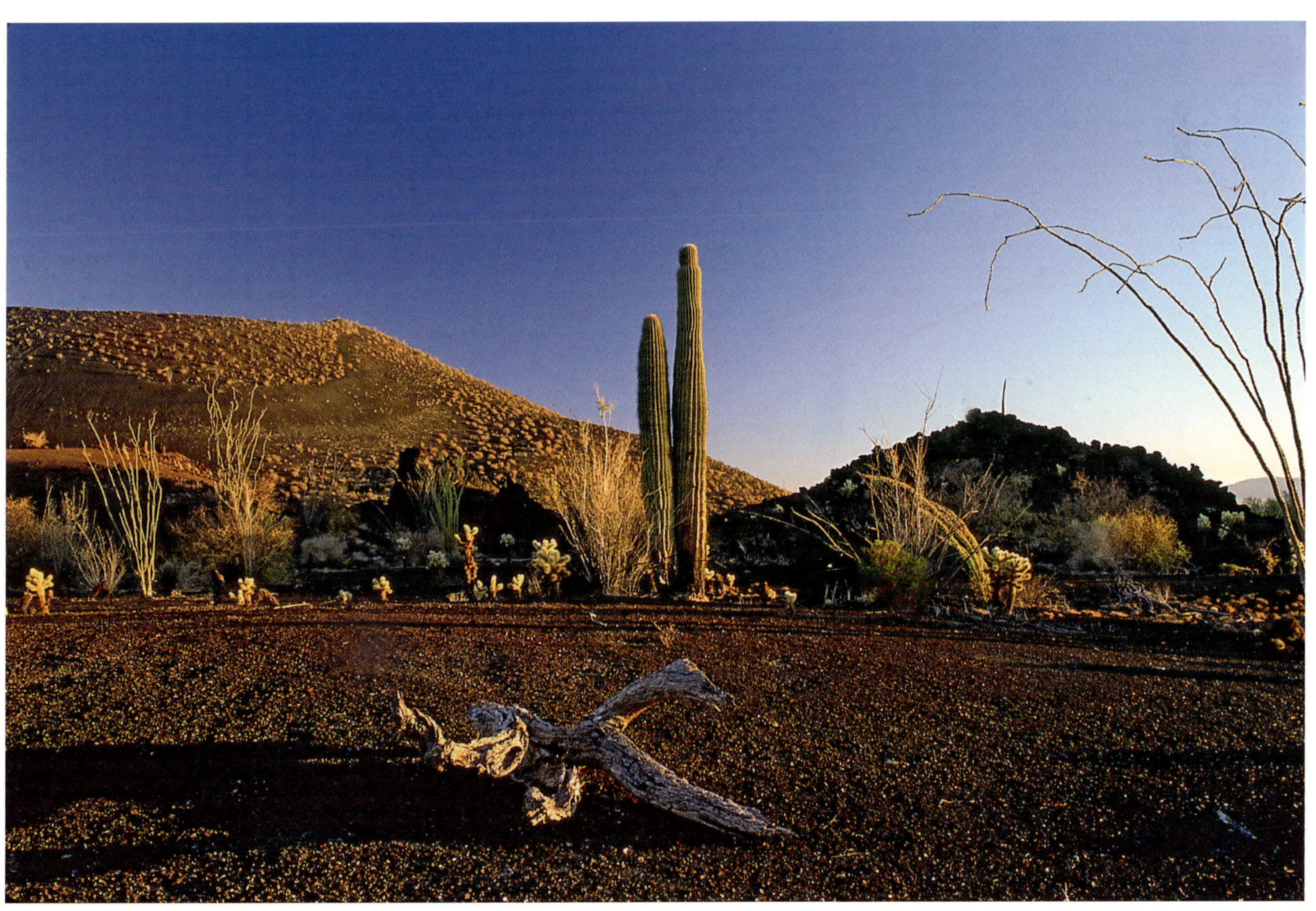

First light, Altar Desert, Sonora, Mexico. UNESCO El Pinacate and Gran Desierto de Altar Biosphere Reserve.

II. *TIERRAS ENCANTADAS* / ENCHANTED LANDS

STANDING ROCKS, WHITE SANDS, BADLANDS, AND ANCIENT CITIES

Pretty soon he [my brother] would be hundreds and hundreds of miles away on the great plains and deserts, and among the mountains of the Far West, and . . . have all kinds of adventures, and maybe get hanged or scalped, and have ever such a fine time, and write home and tell us all about it, and be a hero.

—Mark Twain, *Roughing It*, 1913

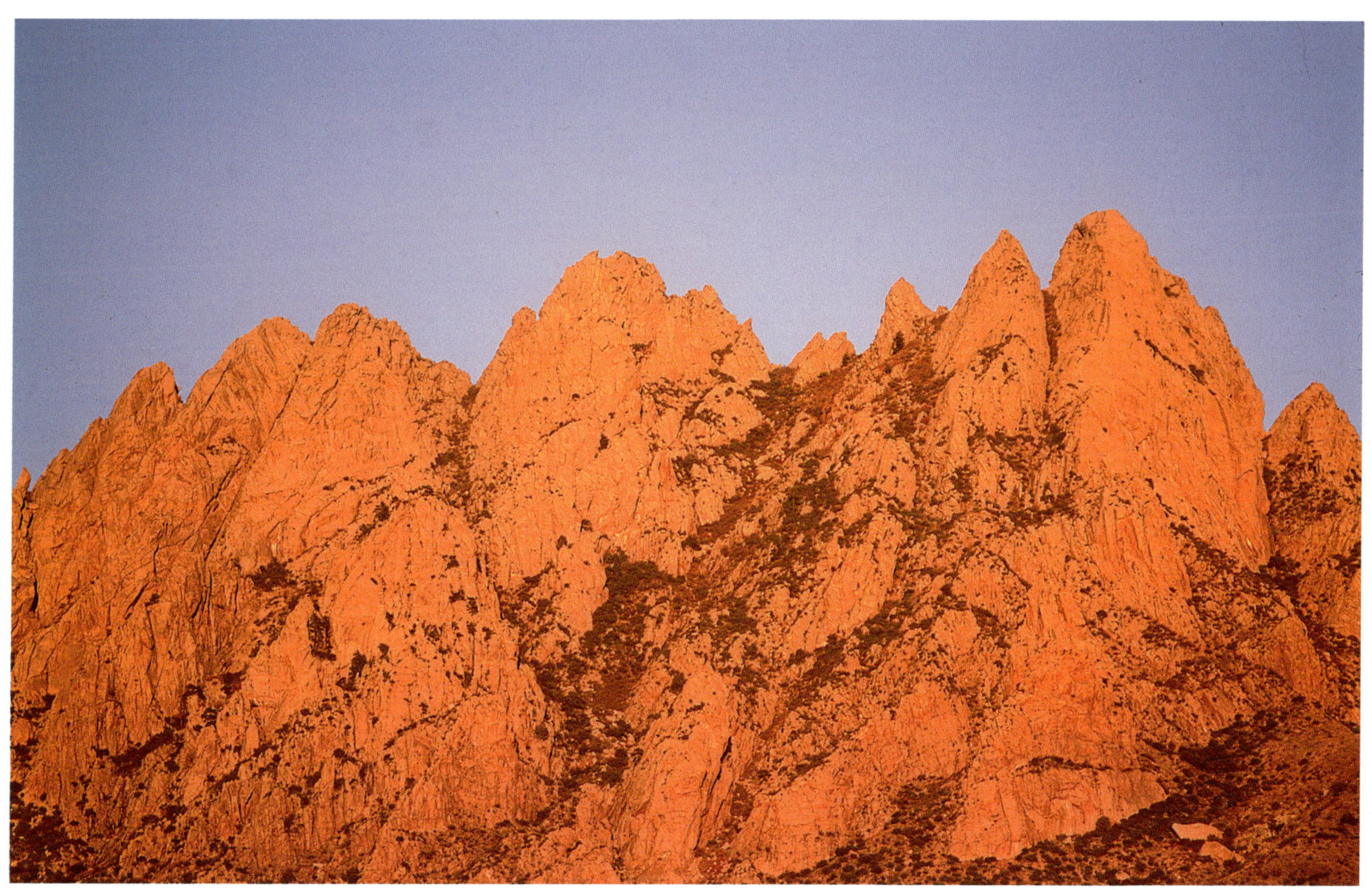

Organ Mountains, Desert Peaks National Monument, New Mexico. The biological "sky island" was a landmark along the Jornada del Muerto for Spanish conquistador Don Juan de Onate y Salazar's 1598 expedition. As J. B. Priestly wrote in *Midnight on the Desert*: "At sunset, the land throws up pink summits and saw-toothed ridges of amethyst, and there are miracles of fire in the sky."

Between here and there, the ancient craters of the Sierra Pinacate disappeared at twilight and shape-shifted at daybreak among the mountains of the Far West. The granite strongholds and sky islands of the Chiricahua Apache glowed hundreds of miles east as sunrise winked over holy ground. The sylvan heights were the dwelling places of benevolent *ga'an* (mountain spirits) that blessed the Ndé (the People) during times of ceremony and siege. Soldiers dogged Geronimo wherever he rode and ran like the wind, deep into the forgotten sierras of Mexico and across the Bootheel of New Mexico. Still, there was beauty to behold standing atop lofty lookouts and tracing the roseate streams of the Rio Grande. Spaniards called the country Tierra Encantada (Enchanted Land), and you could see it wherever you found peace and light after darkness.

Turn north along the Continental Divide, as 400 Spanish, Indian, and mestizo settlers had done following Spanish conquistador Don Juan de Oñate y Salazar in 1598. They faced privation and death, buoyed by prayers and penitence as they struggled across the Jornada del Muerto (Journey of the Deadman). At times, enchantment was seen at nearly every turn, from the gypsum dunes of White Sands to the pink minarets of what Oñate called the Sierra del Olvido (Mountains of Forgetfulness). The trail Oñate followed along the Río del Norte, from mission pueblo to pueblo, veered west from the Spanish capital of Santa Fé de Nuevo México to the Zuni pueblo of Acoma. Death followed in his wake. Eight and a half months after Oñate's colonizing expedition crossed the Rio Grande at El Paseo del Norte (the Pass of the North), his troops massacred 800 Acoma men, women, and children in a dispute over the pueblo's precious stores of food.

Beyond the dark and bloody ground across the high, wide sagebrush desert and hoodoo-staked badlands, fertile canyons and terra-cotta mesas were home to ancient civilizations. Over the horizon, "Out Where the West Begins," poet Arthur Chapman hinted in 1917 that there was a place like no other on the planet. Above all others, it epitomized the American West: "Out where the skies are a trifle bluer, Out where the friendship's a little truer, That's where the West begins."

My journeys across the enchanted lands of what once was New Mexico and Arizona Territory were redefined by songs, myths, and images of sacred lands, Western landscapes, and scenes that defied belief.

STANDING-UP ROCKS, NIGHT OF THE JAGUAR, AND SKY ISLANDS

On the run from General George Crook, Geronimo and his fleet-footed, fast-riding band of thirty-eight Chiricahua Apache found refuge in the sky islands that poked out of a sea of grass stretching south across the border into the Sierra Madre, Mexico, west into Cochise Stronghold, and deep into the heart of the Chiricahua Mountains. The Apache were said to call their refuge the Land of Standing-Up Rocks. Cataclysmic eruptions millions of years earlier created a fantasy of volcanic totems that stood like effigies huddled together. By day, the garden of stones and canopies of pine and oak trees were home to brilliantly plumed *guacamaya* (macaw), red-tailed hawks, banded-rock rattlesnakes, spotted lynx, whitetail deer, and black bear. In the dark of the moon, the rhyolite tuff megaliths looked eerily like the shadows of ghosts that still haunted the mysterious landscape. Among them were puma (mountain lion) and *pantera* (Mexican jaguar) stealthily prowling the sierras and barrancas of fifty-seven biological sky islands towering over the grasslands and borderlands that remained home to Mountain Spirits.

Starker Leopold wrote in 1959:

> Around the camp fires of Mexico there is no animal more talked about, more romanticized and glamorized, than *el tigre*.
>
> The chesty roar of a jaguar in the night causes men to edge toward the blaze and draw serapes tighter. . . . From time to time, it is rumored that a jaguar has become a man-eater.

The Land of Standing-Up Rocks was small and accessible at 17 square miles, compared to Tiburón Island, Picacho del Diablo, and Gran Desierto. But if you wanted to walk in to photograph a sunset vista, you had to hike out in the dark. Camping was off-limits.

It was a pleasant afternoon when I hiked down from the rim at Massai Point into Heart of the Rocks. "On the way," Angie Debo wrote, "Geronimo looked out towards the familiar Chiricahua Mountains and remarked . . . "Once I moved about like the wind." There were a hundred places where guerrilla fighters such as Geronimo and the Chiricahua could have hidden in the maze of pinnacles. I stopped and waited for the sun to dip into the horizon. It crowned Balanced Rock with gold and then fuchsia at twilight. I packed up my camera and tripod and headed out the trail. It was almost pitch black, but I used the last hint of ambient light before turning on my flashlight. I shined the beam down the trail, then turned it off until I was enveloped by darkness. I flicked on the light again and began to see a shadow slinking back and forth on the dark path ahead of me. *Not again*, I whispered to myself.

Years earlier, I'd climbed the Dos Cabeza Mountains during a sky island traverse of the Chiricahua Apache homelands, from Mexico across the Chiricahua, Winchester, and Galiuro Mountains to Aravapai Canyon. I was a week into the 250-mile crossing, and exhausted. I started a small fire of twigs and bivouacked beneath the rocky bluffs of Dos Cabezas (Two Heads). I'd drifted to sleep when a big cat growled at me. I stumbled out of my sleeping bag and fumbled with my stove fuel. I splashed it on my stack of firewood and threw the bundle into the fire pit. I jumped back as the fire exploded into a roaring blaze. Overhead, I glimpsed the terrifying eyes of the snarling cat. I couldn't go anywhere, so I screamed back at the growling silhouette, dancing back and forth in front of the flames, trying to cast my shadow larger than life. I pulled out my bowie knife, but in the blink of an eye the cat disappeared. I didn't see clearly if it was jaguar—the Dos Cabezas was its home range—but I stood there shaking and wondering what I would have done with the knife. . . . I ran down the dark trail through the Chiricahuas, expecting to be pounced on at any moment. *El tigre* or *león*? I couldn't tell for certain. For some reason it didn't follow me over the rim. I'd been blessed. The Apache might have said I'd been guarded by the Mountain Spirits.

Few places on the continent are thought to be as mystical as the barren sweep of gypsum dunes of White Sands. A mirage of sand within reach of the Jornada del Muerto, it's been called Like No Place Else on Earth. It was home to ancient peoples who roamed the Tularosa Valley 7,000 to 10,000 years BCE, when the 275-square-mile dune field first formed. It was the place of dreams, visions, and apparitions, where cottonwood trees still grew half-buried in the sand. It was the haunt of Manuela, a mythical spirit that sometimes appeared near dusk as a dervish of wind. She whispered across the cloudscape of sand, trailing her flowing white dress in an unending search for her lover, sixteenth-century Spanish conquistador Hernando de Luna. There was no beginning to their trail of unrequited love—some said it began in Mexico City—and there was no end to it, either. Others professed that Luna was swallowed up in the heart of the great white dunes. Believers insisted that Manuela, or La Pavla Blanca (the White Dread), is still out there.

"[I]n the desert of dead men, the sun beat in smothering waves upon the white sands, the stark rocks, the black wastes of volcanic obsidian," Cleve Hallenbeck and Juanita H. Williams wrote in *The Journey of Death*. "Moving slowly through the heat-shimmer was the emaciated form of a man, clad in rags, his head bowed upon his chest. In his right hand he held a sword, the point of which had been broken off, and he was using his blade as a cane to steady his footsteps. Occasionally he stopped and stared with bloodshot eyes."

Many had ventured into the dunes since the time of legends. The Mescalero Apache, or Mashgalénde (People Close to the

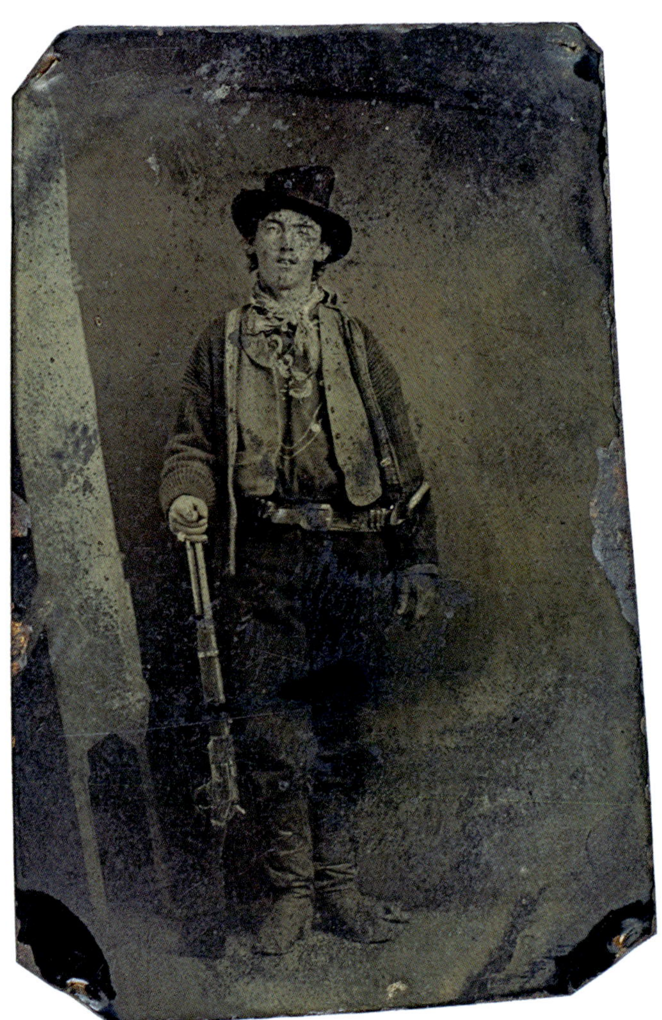

Twenty-year-old cattle rustler and outlaw Billy the Kid, Fort Sumner, New Mexico Territory. Ferrotype (tintype) by Ben Wittick, 1879–80. *Courtesy of Wikimedia*

Mountains), had used the old trails to cross the hallowed dunes to pay homage at their sacred mountains: Sierra Blanca, Guadalupe Mountains, Three Sisters Mountain, and Oscura Mountain Peak. "These mountains," the late Mescalero Apache elder Wendell Chino had written, "represent the four directions of the universe." In what became the White Sands Missile Range, Chief Victorio and the Warm Springs Apache fought African American buffalo soldiers in 1880 rather than give up their land. A year later, during the Lincoln County War, Sheriff Pat Garrett tracked down gunslinger Billy the Kid (a.k.a. William H. Bonney) and shot and killed him at Fort Sumner on April 28. Locals suspected that Garrett staged the shooting out of friendship to the Kid so he could escape. Some speculated that Billy the Kid may have fled into the dunes, but no one was sure. But over the years, others had stepped out of the legend and claimed *they* were William H. Bonney. For a time, White Sands was nearly as quiet as fallen snow. Then at 5:29 a.m. on July 16, 1945, the stillness was broken by the earth-shattering nuclear detonation of "the Gadget" in the Jornada del Muerto Desert.

White Sands was still a place where you could walk off the face of the earth, get buried in the sand, or simply disappear like Billy the Kid. Imagine walking through a mirage with no beginning, no end, and no directions. I'd picked the dreariest of cloudy days, not by choice, but to search out the best vantage to photograph the pure white dunes. Taking a bead on the heart of the dunes, I walked fifteen minutes. I checked my bearings and walked thirty minutes. I checked my bearings again and walked sixty minutes. I stopped and turned around. I felt like I'd fallen through the soul of nowhere, where only the wind and spirits sang. I watched the breeze whisk away my footprints. They were my lifeline. I'd kept my eye on the horizon line. But once I started taking photographs, I started to lose my bearings. It was dizzying. I reoriented a distant peak over my left shoulder and trudged north through the dunes until I reached the park road two hours later. I missed my truck by a quarter mile, but I'd made it out at last light. I could have gone in another direction, and then where would I have ended up? Lost in a cloudscape searching for a trail without beginning or end.

The otherworldly terrain of Bisti Badlands is perhaps the most surreal haunt in the United States. I'd witnessed it firsthand as I crossed open ground that had unimaginably yielded the sixty-five-million-year-old bones of a genus of tyrannosaur named *Bistahieversor* in 1998. It was nicknamed the Bisti Beast. There were no trails, there were no conveniences, and there were no destinations. There was simply wandering through what the Navajo (Diné) called Bistahí (among the adobe formations). But there was color, texture, and form, which is what lured free spirits, archeologists, geologists, and artists into the stark high desert on the edge of Navajoland. Georgia O'Keeffe had discovered the forlorn sanctuary in 1936. She called it the "Black Place." For the next fourteen years, O'Keeffe walked, camped, and found inspiration among batwing totems, caprock hoodoos, and charcoal hills cut by deep arroyos that formed a 62-square-mile landscape that looked like it was the beginning—or the end—of time. O'Keeffe interpreted the dark, whimsical landscapes with oil on canvas and became the Mother of American Modernism in part for her celebrated Black Place series. In time the area became known as Bisti/De-Na-Zin Wilderness. It took its name from the Navajo, Bistahí, and Déél Náázíní (Standing Crane), and it drew rare visitors such as myself who were coming from or going to ancient cities such as Chaco Canyon.

Dark skies shrouded the *malpaís* when I'd started hurrying across the sand, silt, and mudstone, haunted by a lone wailing I heard in the distance. It may have been wind blowing through the hoodoos. But I suspected it might be something else. On the way into the badlands I'd seen a bone lying on the side of a gray hill. O'Keeffe had collected them and wrote: "The bones seem to cut sharply to the center of something that is keenly alive on the desert even tho' it is vast and empty and untouchable." The bone I'd seen was out in the open, but it was not one that I would have picked up. It was a leg bone, and its power spooked me. D. H. Lawrence wrote in *New Mexico* that "It had a splendid silent terror." I started running. I felt like I was being chased. The wailing continued. I wondered if the bone had been dug up. Was it the work of a were-person howling at me like a wolf after digging into a secret crypt? It was taboo to think about it. But the hair on my neck stood on end. I ran faster over the charcoal-colored ground, and faster, as darkness smothered the landscape. When I reached my truck, I looked behind me. I didn't see anyone, but I still heard the wailing. I was struck with fear. I got in the truck, locked the doors, and thought they would be pulled off. I headed down the road, drove out of sight, and took a deep breath. Had I been chased by a Navajo *ch'įįdii* (ghost)?

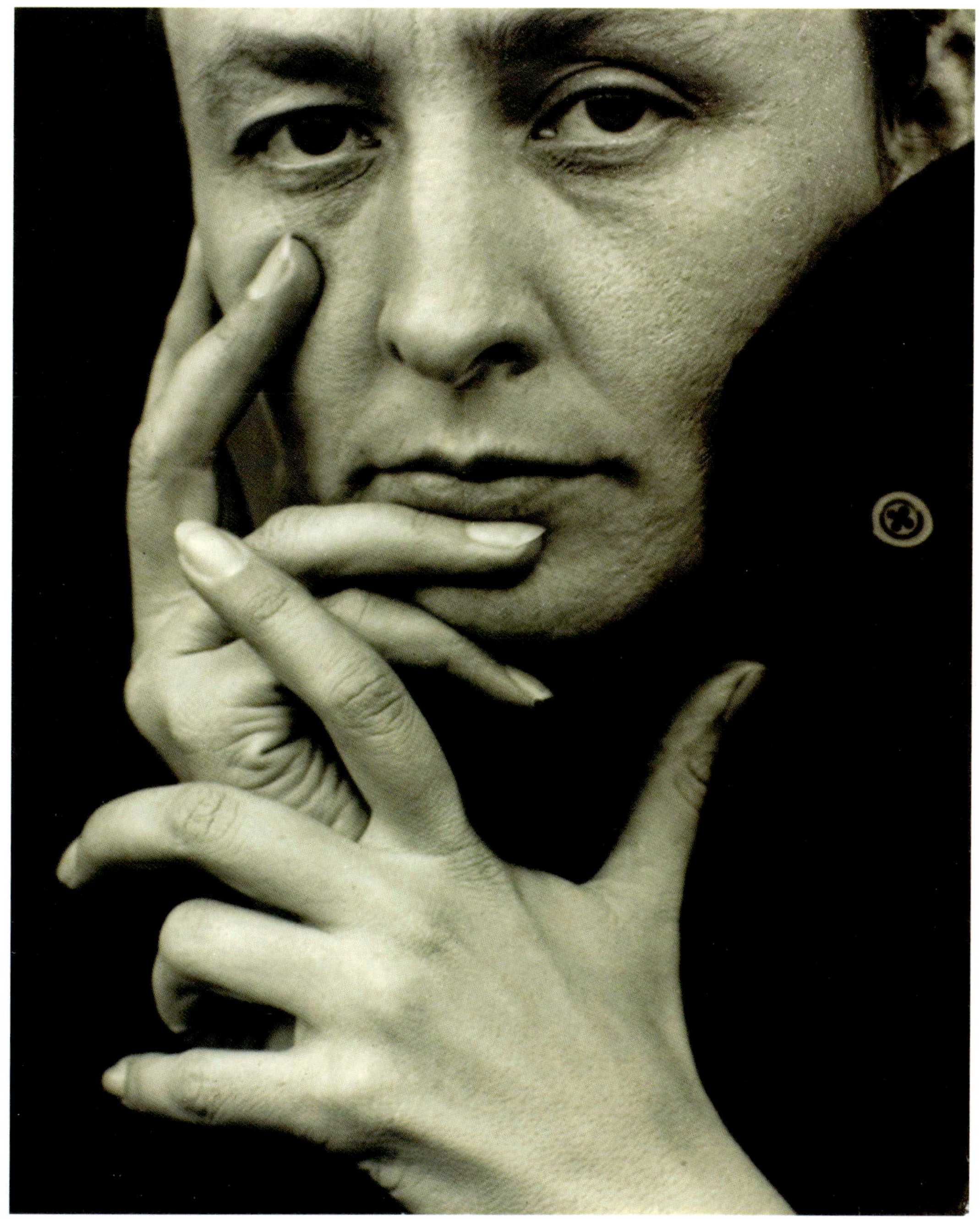

Georgia O'Keeffe, Hands. Platinum print by Alfred Stieglitz, 1918. *Courtesy of Art Institute of Chicago / Wiki*

I drove north from Gallup, New Mexico, and followed a maze of roads across a beautiful but lonely sweep of the 4,770-square-mile San Juan Basin. Bisti Badlands, I'd thought, was as deep into nowhere as I could get. But Chaco Canyon was deeper in the high desert by way of its isolation within the four cardinal directions. Prowling trails of the ancients, I'd discovered they'd led to spirit roads, stone shrines, ceremonial kivas, great houses, and astronomical observatories. Late that winter afternoon, I pulled into Chaco's empty campground and was surprised that the park was deserted. A lone elk stood on the rim above camp, holding its rack of horns like a crown. In the distance the banded cliffs of Fajada Butte were painted gold in the setting sun. A temple to the cosmos, it held the mysterious secret of "sun daggers," arrows of solar light that pierced spiral petroglyphs during times of equinox and solstice. That night Chaco's dark skies lit up with meteor showers before an icy cloud floated over the rim. The elk vanished and snow flurries hissed in my campfire. I nodded off.

Standing in the dark early the next morning, I saw the faint silhouette of Fajada Butte, and Venus, Mercury, Jupiter, and the moon glowing over the horizon. When the ranger pulled up and unlocked the gate, he said, "You've got Chaco to yourself." I drove down the empty park road to Pueblo Bonito (beautiful town). The Navajo named it Tsebiyaanii' aha (Leaning Rock Gap). It was Chaco's finest great house, one among a dozen that still stood a millennium later. I traced my fingers across Pueblo Bonito's main wall of hand-cut stones, which aligned with true north and south. Two hundred forty thousand timbers had also been cut by hand, hauled 60 miles across the desert from the San Mateo and Chuska Mountains, and used as beams to support the roofs, floors, and walls of the 100-to-700-room pueblos and kivas. An advanced civilization of more than 13,000 Ancestral Puebloans flourished in Chaco Canyon, a cultural and ceremonial center and trade crossroads between 950 and 1150 CE.

Leading 60 miles from Chaco along the Great North Road to the settlement of Aztec, Chaco's South Road led due south along the 108th meridian some 390 miles to the Mesoamerican trade center of Paquimé in Casas Grandes, Chihuahua, Mexico. Who traveled the mystical Chaco Meridian in either direction on roads that in places were 30 feet wide and aligned within 2 degrees of true north? The Chacoans on pilgrimage from Pueblo Bonito to Pueblo Alto and beyond? Mayans who journeyed 1,200 miles north from Central America to Pueblo Bonito, where they introduced the ritual drink of cacao—and the 114 cylindrical jars that had been excavated from Pueblo Bonito? Toltec warriors, whom some professed journeyed from the interior of Mexico and unleashed a reign of terror against the peaceful Chacoans? No one knew for sure. But it was a bit strange to wander alone on foot through a city of the dead that had been ravaged by drought and violence and finally abandoned.

Over the next two days, I explored the same ancient settlement Mary Hunter Austin had visited when she observed, "Everywhere there is the evidence of Chaco as a center of intertribal trade, trade in salt, trade in sea-shells, and turquoise from the south."

At the end of each day I went back to study 6,623-foot Fajada Butte from afar—it was off-limits to visitors.

"I had to adopt the Indian's method of studying unlimited spaces in the desert," Zane Great wrote in *Tales of Lonely Trails*, "to look with slow contracted eyes from near to far." Sacred to Native peoples including the Hopi, Navajo, and Pueblo peoples, the sanctuary was called Tsé Diyil (Sky Reaching Rock) by the Navajo. For many years, shamans, sun priests, and astronomers made pilgrimages across the sagebrush desert to the lofty observatory, where offerings of turquoise and prayer feathers were made. Ancient astronomers stationed atop Fajada Butte observed each day that with the cycle of sun and moon came death and rebirth. Chaco Culture National Historical Park has since been reborn as a UNESCO World Heritage Site.

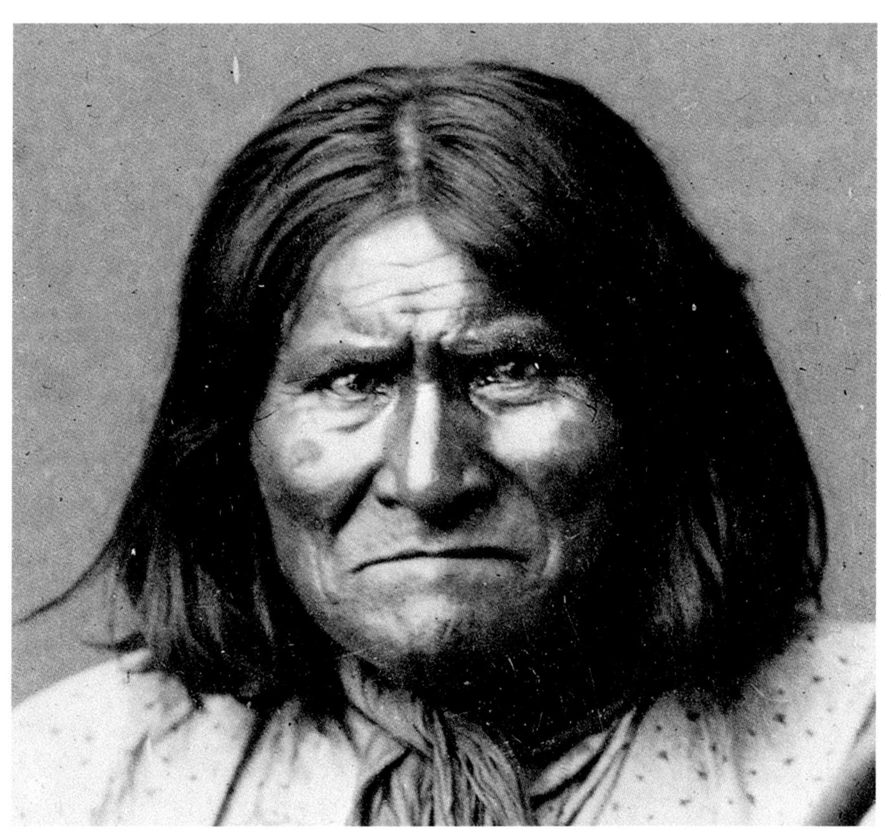

Geronimo portrait, *Goyahkla* (The One Who Yawns), Wilcox, Arizona Territory. Photographic print by A. Frank Randall, 1886. *Courtesy of Library of Congress*

> The eddy took shape as it neared the summit of the dune; it filled out—it was a woman. Right at the crest she stood erect and bent forward, as if peering into the shadows beyond the hill upon which she stood. Pavlo Blanco, the White Wraith, dressed in her flowing wedding gown. She poised for an instant, still looking, then she ran along the rippled edge of the dune. She disappeared with a sound that was halfway between a sigh and a sob.
>
> —Mrs. Tom "Bula" Charles, after visiting White Sands National Park for the first time, 1910

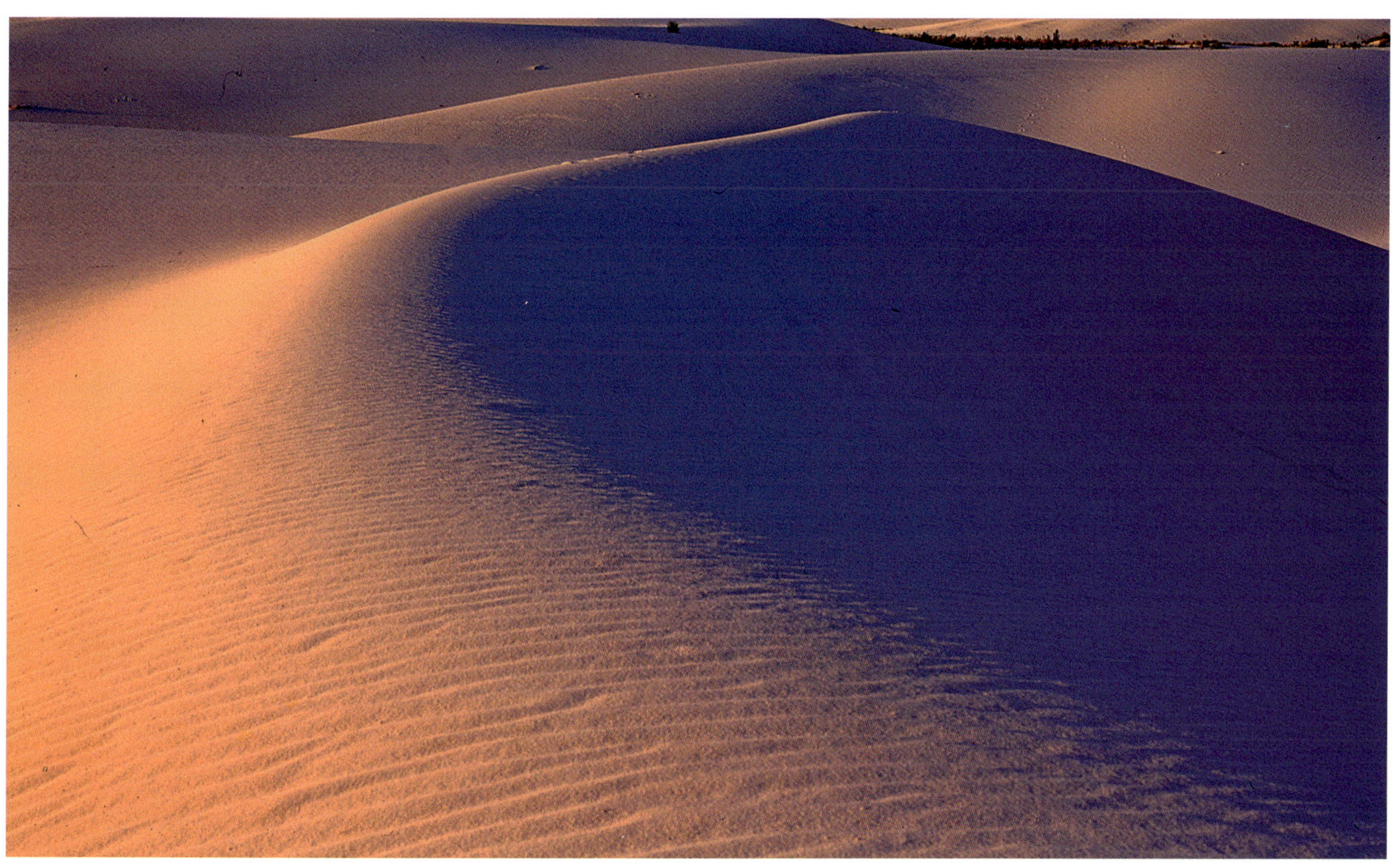

The spirit of Pavla Blanca is still said to roam the gypsum dunes of White Sands National Park, New Mexico. UNESCO Biosphere Reserve Nomination.

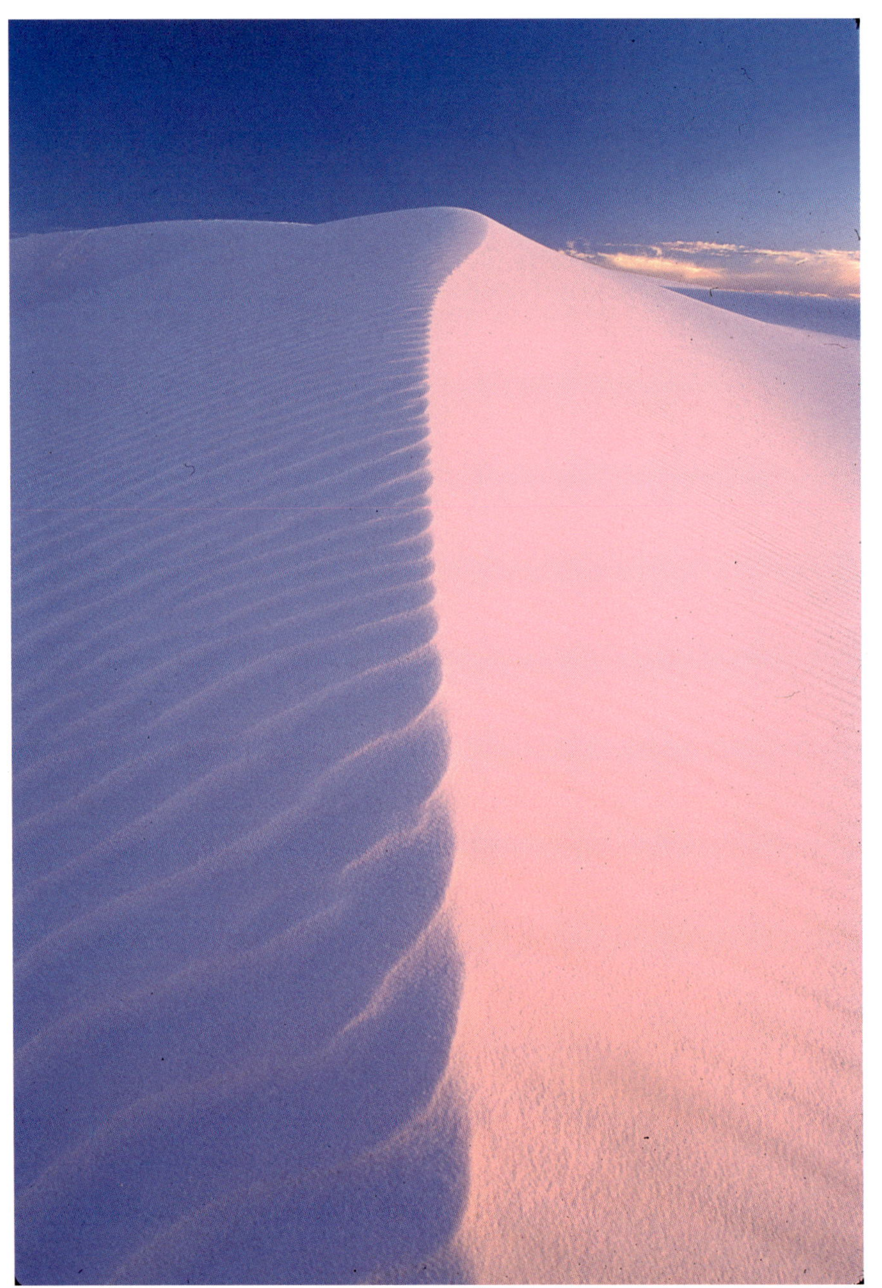

Shadow line, White Sands National Park, New Mexico

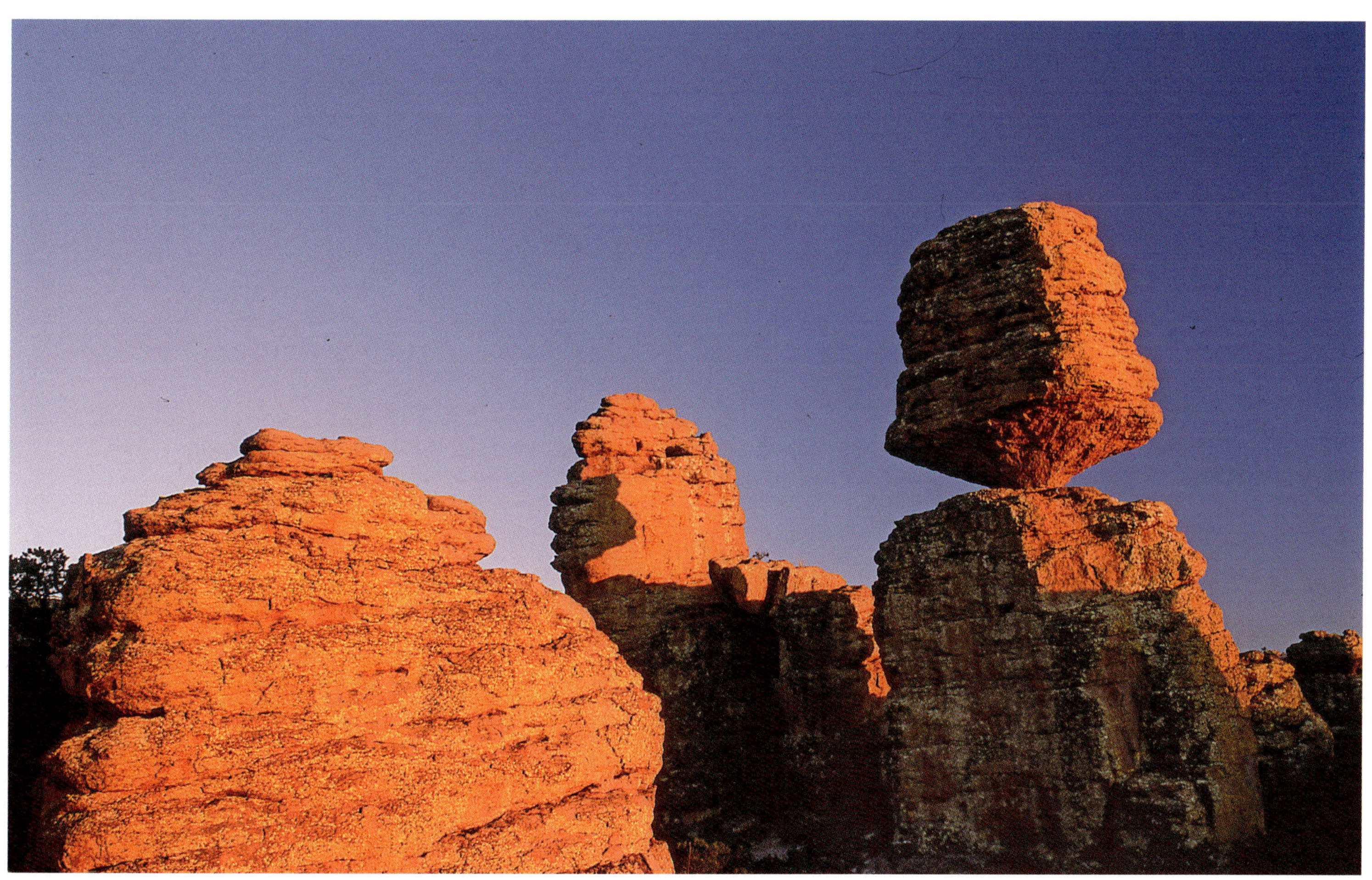

Balanced Rock in the Land of Standing-Up Rocks was the heart of stone for Geronimo and the Chiricahua Indian Reservation. *Chiricahua National Monument, Arizona.*

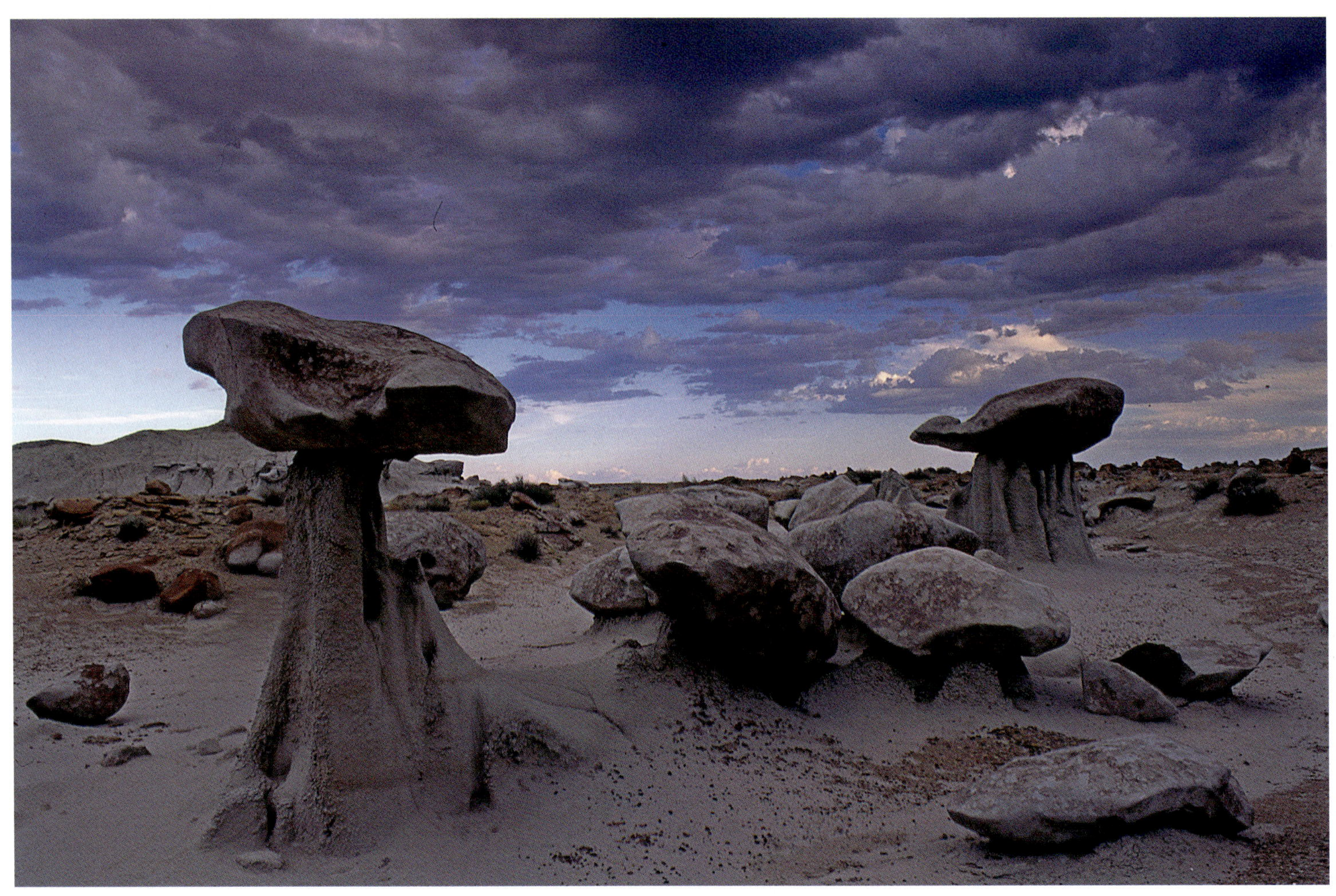

Georgia O'Keeffe drew inspiration from Navajo country's badlands and hoodoos to paint her celebrated oil on canvas *Black Place* in 1944. It later became known as the Bisti/De-Na-Zin Wilderness, New Mexico.

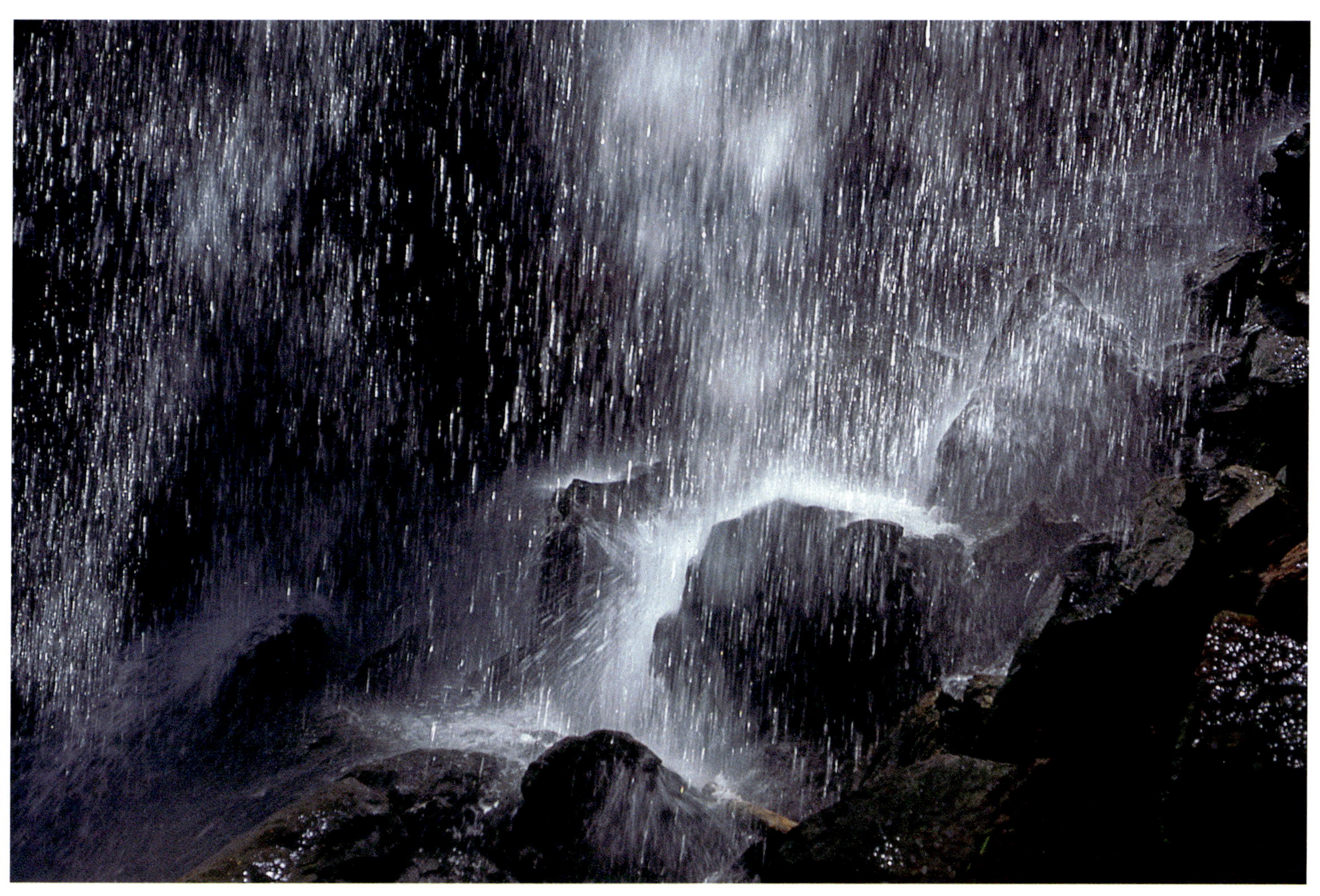

Haunted waters? The apparition of a skull appears in the dark waters of Frijole Falls, Bandelier National Monument, New Mexico.

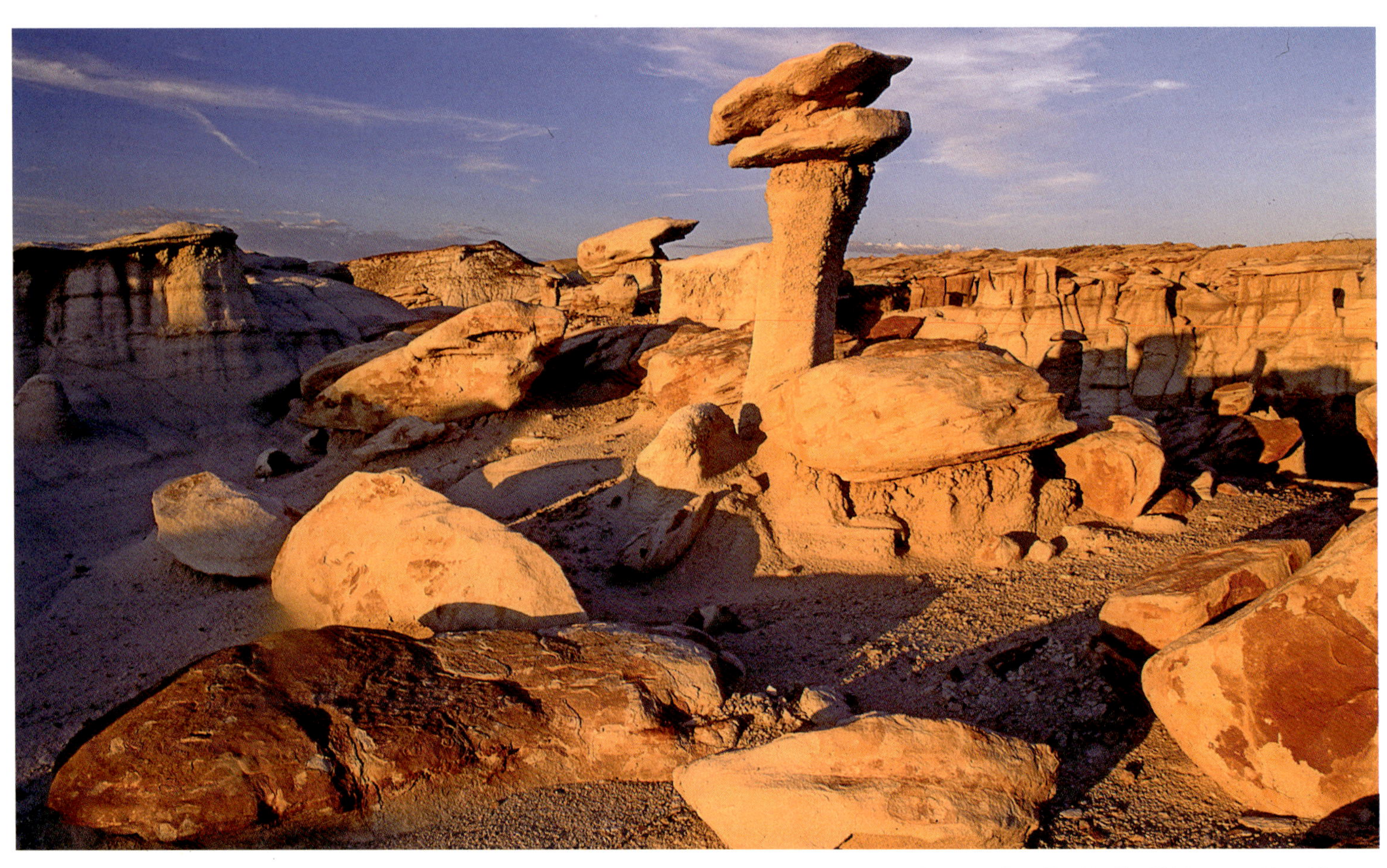

Hoodoo garden of stones, Bisti/De-Na-Zin Wilderness, New Mexico.
The name comes from the 1878 Tiz Nat Zin Trading Post, derived from the Navajo description of three *déłí nįįzķnķ* (standing sandhill cranes) in a hidden petroglyph.

An adobe food storage granary dates back to the Mogollon people who inhabited the region in 1275 CE. Gila Cliffs Dwellings National Monument, New Mexico.

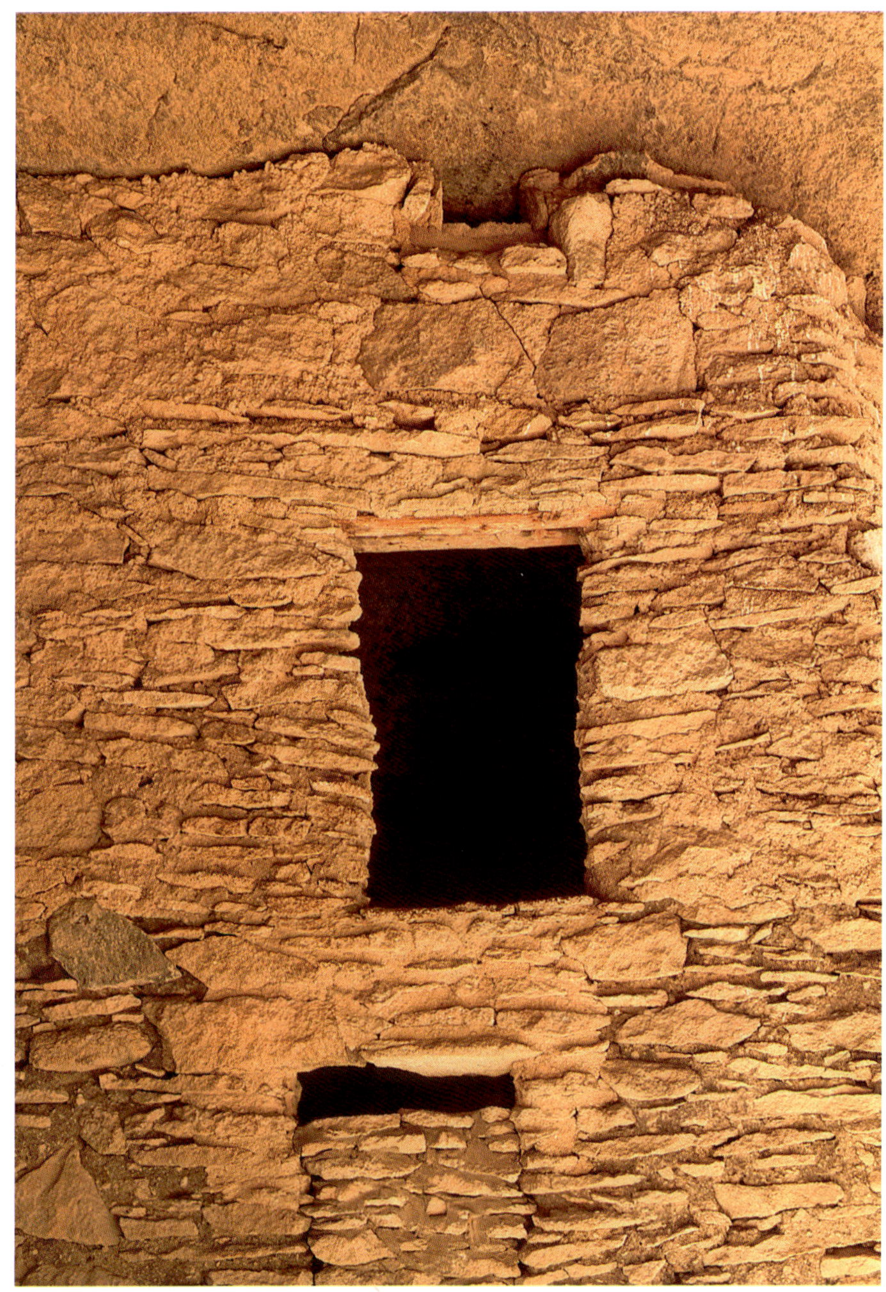

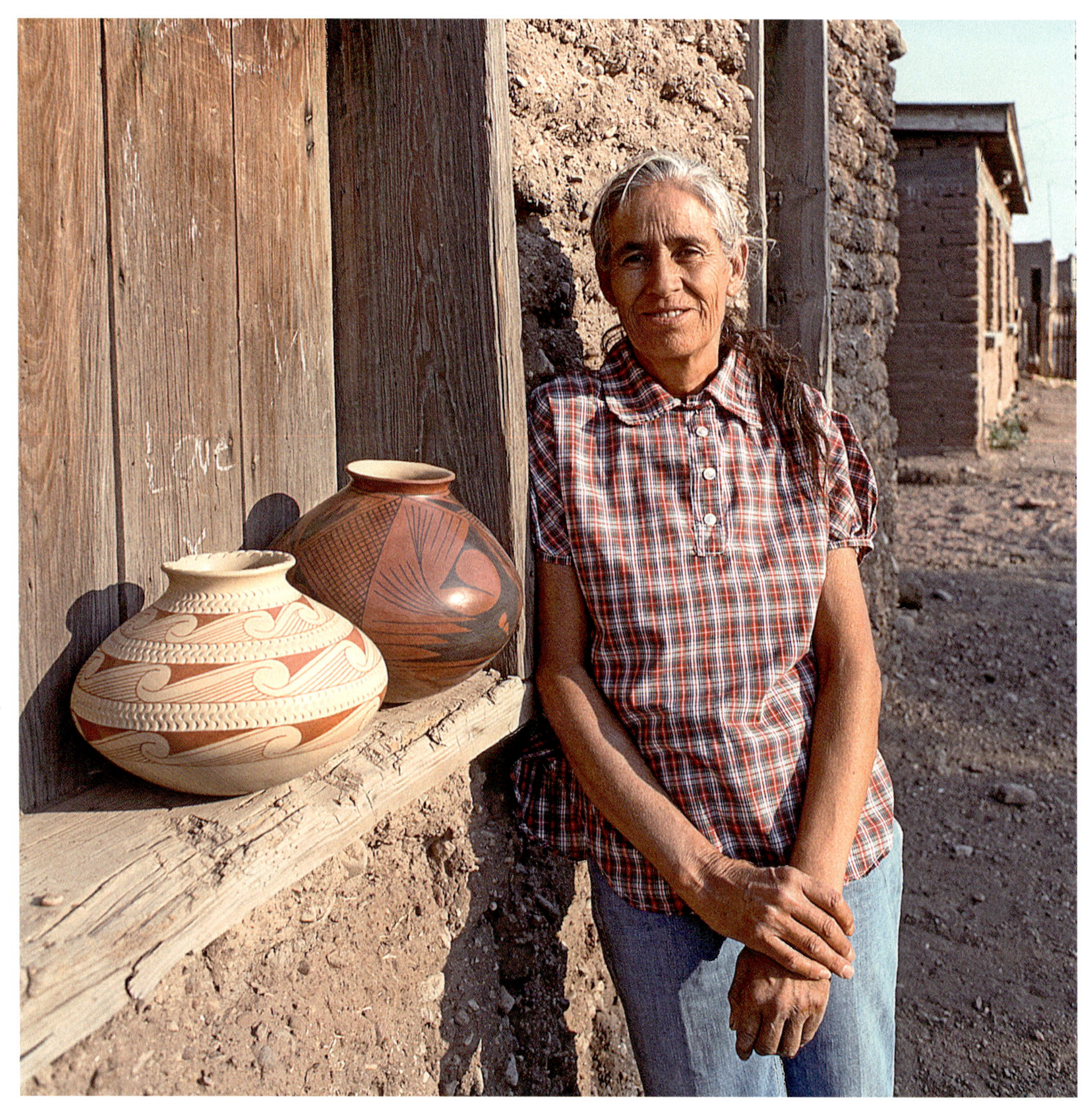

One of the original Mata Ortiz potters, artisan Consolación Quezada Celado poses with her signature pots in the dusty streets of Mata Ortiz, Chihuahua, Mexico.

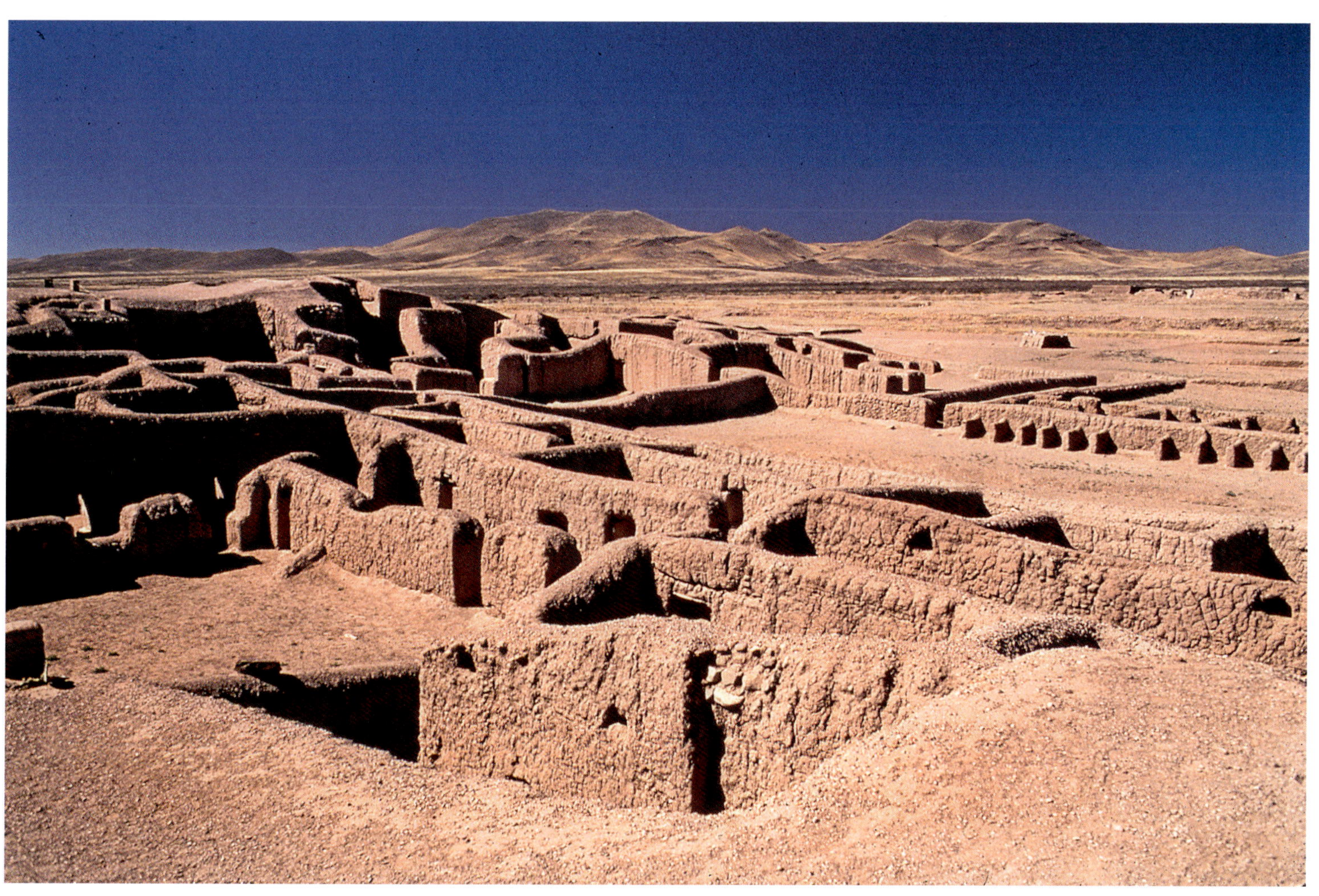

The fifteenth-century Mesoamerican settlement of Paquimé once traded with the Anaasází, or Ancestral Puebloans, of Chaco Canyon. The Mogollon-era pottery excavated here inspired the potters of Mata Ortiz (opposite), a tradition revived by Juan Quezada Celado. UNESCO World Heritage Site Archaeological Zone of Paquimé, Casas Grandes, Chihuahua (UNESCO Zona Arqueológica de Paquimé, Casas Grande).

III. *LA FRONTERA* / THE FRONTIER

BIG BEND, DEVILS SWING, AND RÍO BRAVO

Down in the gorge . . . The scream of the panther was heard there, the squall of the wildcat, the cough of the jaguar. Like other parts of the great Lone Star State, this section of Texas was a world in itself . . . winding trails led down into that free and never-disturbed paradise of outlaws—the Big Bend.

—Zane Grey, *The Lone Star Ranger*, 1915

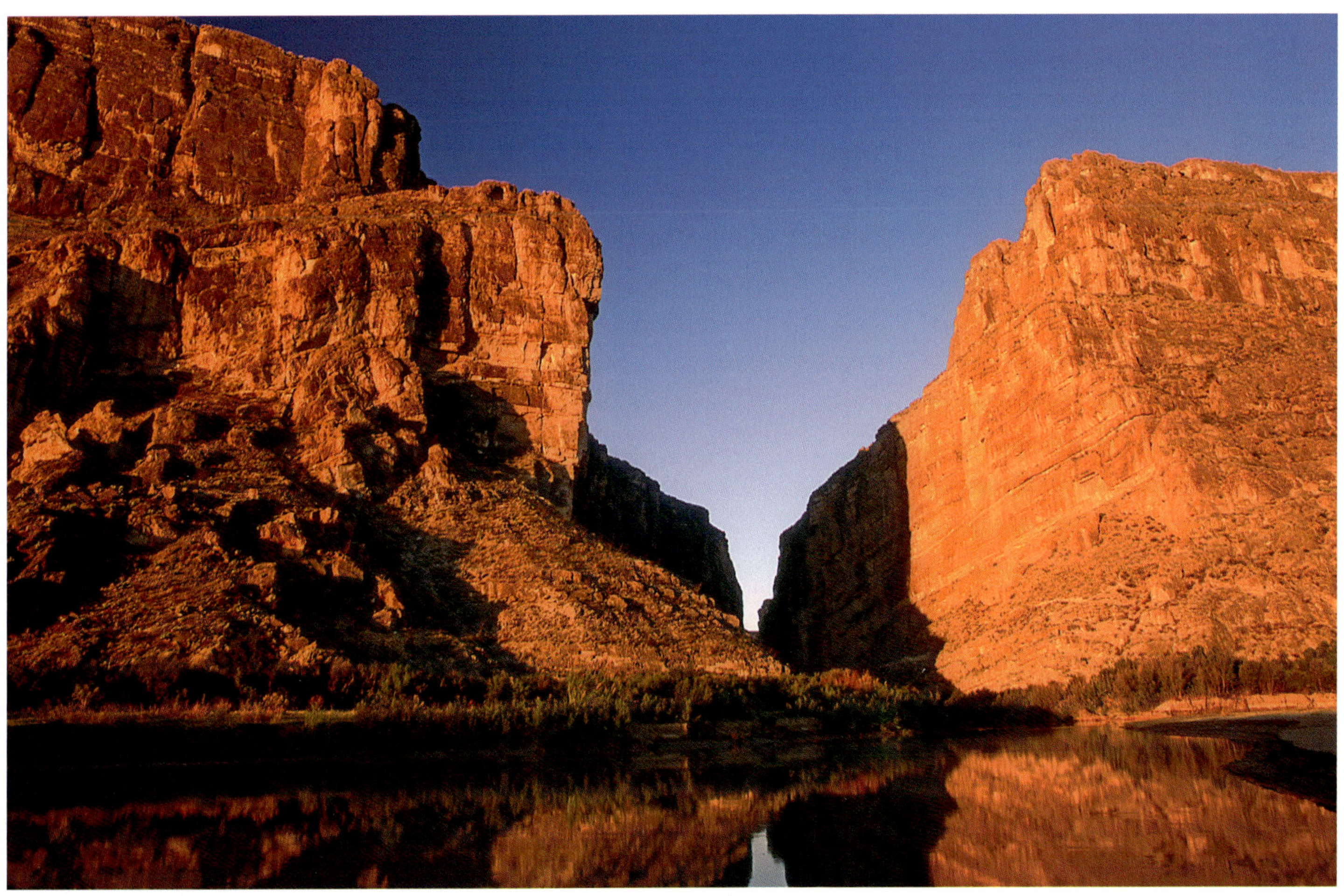

Two striking landforms come together on the US-Mexico border at Santa Elena Canyon. *Left*: Big Bend National Park, UNESCO Biosphere Reserve, Texas. *Right*: El Área de Protección de Flora y Fauna Cañón de Santa Elena, Chihuahua, México (Protected Area of Flora and Fauna, Santa Elena Canyon).

West Texas. It was neither here nor there. It was west of the Pecos River, south of the Llano Estacado (Staked Plains), and north of the Rio Grande. Comprising 2,500 square miles of burning Chihuahuan Desert, it encompassed the crimson heights of the Chisos Mountains and Sierra del Carmen, Mexico, as well as tortuous gorges of the Colorado, Santa Elena, Mariscal, and Boquillas Canyons, which carried the river to the sea. It was the most remote and beautiful wedge of land in the Great Southwest, flanked by La Frontera (the Frontier) of Mexico. Neighbors who lived north of the Rio Grande called the river's dogleg turn the Big Bend, and those who lived south of the river (known as Río Bravo del Norte) called the river's turn El Columpio del Diablo (the Devils Swing). Since the sixteenth century, nomads, explorers, and settlers have been drawn to this crossroads of paradise and hell for the same reason: the river that divided two countries also joined multilingual peoples—Mexicans, Indians, Texans, and Texicans (residents of Mexican Texas). "They spent their lives crossing frontiers, theirs and those that belonged to others," Carlos Fuentes wrote in *Gringo Viejo* (Old Gringo), "and now the old man [Ambrose Bierce] had crossed to the south because he didn't have any frontiers left to cross."

Many strangers came into the frontier; some would test the reader's credulity. Spanish explorer-turned-healer Álvar Núñez Cabeza de Vaca was the first European to cross into West Texas near La Junta de los Ríos (the Union of Rivers) of the Río Conchos and Rio Grande. After surviving a shipwreck on Texas's Galveston Island in 1528, Cabeza de Vaca was enslaved by Indigenous Karankawa when he performed the first open-heart surgery in North America. "Here they brought a man to me and said . . . the arrowhead was lodged over the heart," Cabeza de Vaca wrote in *La relación*. "With a knife I had I opened his chest . . . I continued to cut, inserted the point of the knife, and with great difficulty I finally extracted it. When I had removed the arrowhead they asked me for it and I gave it to them. The entire village came to see it . . . [and] they had many dances and festivities."

Cabeza de Vaca spent eight extraordinary years leading Indigenous peoples from Texas across the Southwest into northern Mexico. Yet, this did not eclipse the purported travels of a desert mystic known as the Lady in Blue who arrived in West Texas a century later. A Franciscan abbess, Sor María de Jesús de Ágreda claimed she had been teleported from the hallowed Monastery of the Immaculate Conception in Ágreda, Spain, to the deserts of West Texas and New Mexico. She reportedly told Fray Alonso de Benavides, who traveled from New Mexico to Spain to interview her, that she had made 500 mystical bilocations between 1620 and 1623 to convert the Indigenous Jumano peoples. The Jumano later reported to the Franciscan friary of San Antonio, Isleta, New Mexico, that they'd been visited by a mysterious "Woman in Blue." The Venerable María had prepared them for the missionaries' arrival. Fray Juan de Salas launched an expedition to West Texas where 2,000 Jumanos had gathered to be baptized.

"And so I say that this is what befell me in the provinces of New Mexico, Quivira, the Jumanos, and other nations," the Venerable María wrote from her convent on May 15, 1631. "I was taken by the will of God. By the hand and aid of His Angels I was carried wherever they took me, and I saw and did all that I have told the father [Alonso de Benavides]." To this day, no one knows where the Venerable María once stood on this continent.

It was dark when I followed the winding trail into the river bottom. I felt my way across the sun-cracked river mud, one crunching footstep after another until first light winked out of the empty horizon over the river's black surface. The breath of light crept higher and higher up the canyon walls until it became clear. Jaws of limestone stood 1,500 feet high and plunged miles deep though a narrow canyon passage that carried Southern Plains Comanche, Mescalero Apache, *curanderos* (faith healers), Texas Rangers, scalp hunters, *contrabandistas* (smugglers), and Villistas (followers of Francisco "Pancho" Villa). Few river chasms in the Great Southwest presented such a dramatic profile as Santa Elena Canyon, named for the Saint Helena. I stood near the edge of the Rio Grande, set up my tripod, and photographed a golden mirror of river light that reflected the canyon walls. Birds sang, the river flowed quietly, and beauty reigned. It was not always as sublime.

Displaced by wagon caravans of American settlers headed west, the Comanche rode south across West Texas during what frightened pioneers warned was September's "Comanche Moon." Mounted raiders called the Lords of the Plains, the Comanche rode deep into Mexico as far south as Durango, Zacatecas, and Jalisco, where 100,000 livestock were stolen and thousands of Mexicans were killed or kidnapped. Desperate to stop the scourge, the Cuban-born Mexican governor of Chihuahua, General José Joaquín del Calvo López, hired American scalp hunters to hunt down the Comanche and Mescalero Apache to "harvest" their scalps. Bounties paid were 200 pesos for warriors, 100 pesos for women, and 50 pesos for children, the equivalent of one American

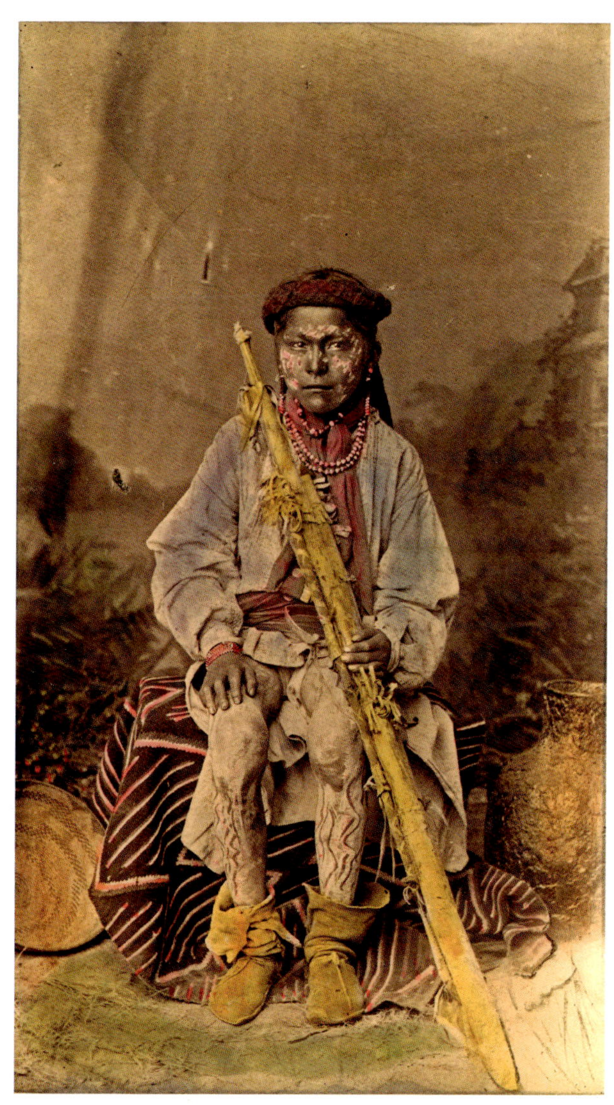

Mescalero Apache, *Painted Boy*. Hand-colored photo print by A. Frank Randall, 1883–1888. *Courtesy of Wikipedia*

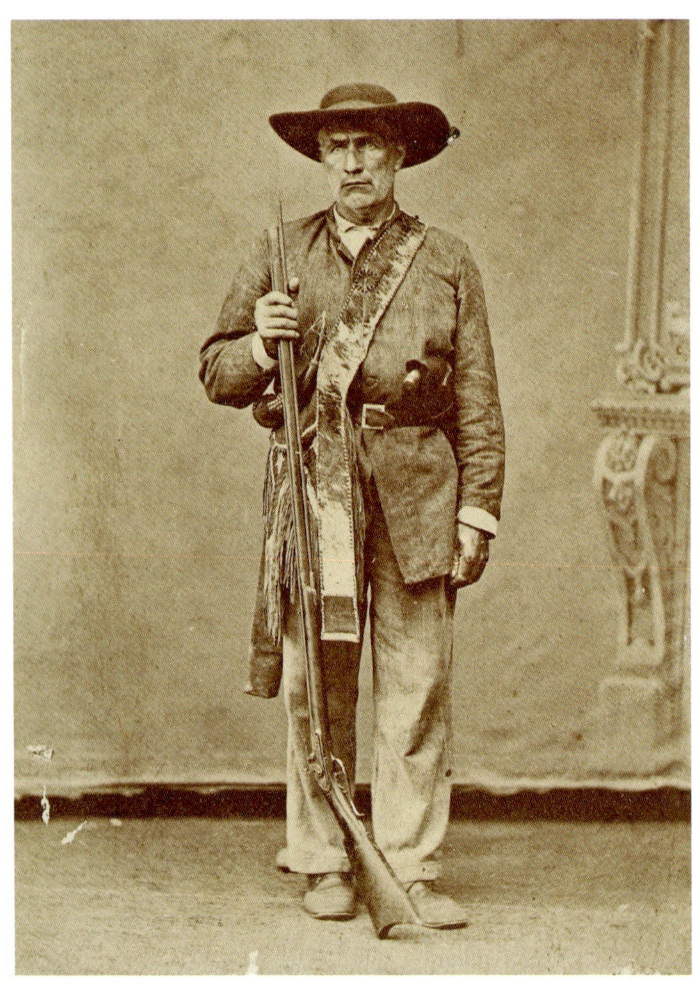

Legendary Texas Ranger William A. A. "Bigfoot" Wallace, Texas. Albumen print by Michael Miley, 1872. *Courtesy of Heritage Auction Gallery / Wiki*

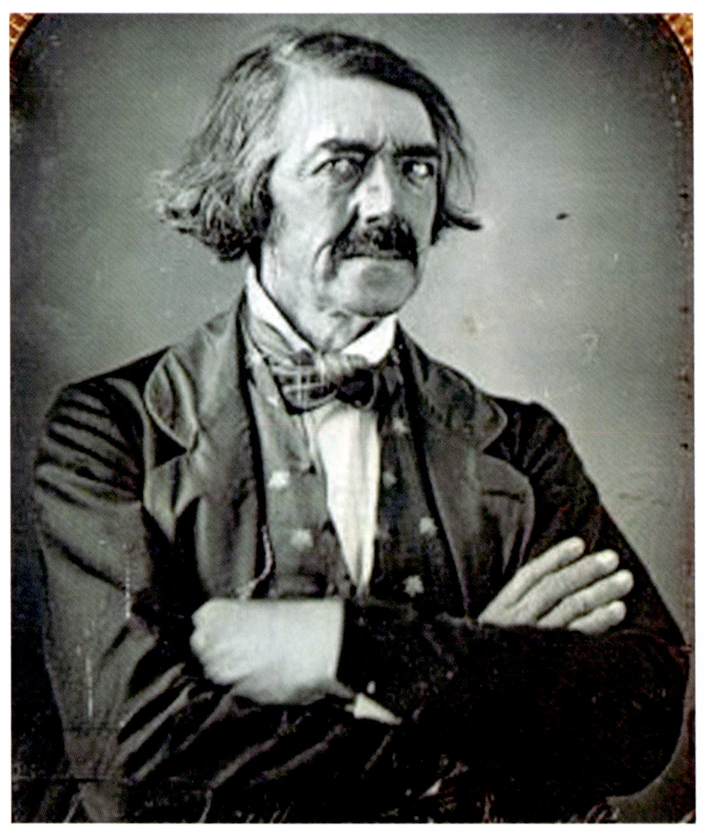

Scalp hunter James Kirker, a.k.a. Don Santiago QuerQuer. Daguerreotype by Thomas Martin Easterly, 1847. *Courtesy of Missouri History Museum Archives, Easterly Daguerreotype Collection / Wiki*

dollar for every Mexican silver peso. Few scalp hunters were more cold-blooded than James "Santiago" Kirker and Captain John Glanton. Their "hair raising" carnage encompassed Mexicans, Indigenous Tarahumara, and even California forty-niners, who were scalped for their sagging poaches of gold nuggets.

"At no time in American history did people show more interest in each other's hair," historian Ralph A. Smith wrote in *The Scalp Hunter in the Borderlands*. "Every ambitious character in the border country eyed the locks of his fellow man."

Santa Elena Canyon was a riparian wonder like no other in the Great Southwest. It was home to beaver, mud turtles, and gar fish that swam back and forth across the border; mountain lions that stalked whitetail deer along river's edge; cliff-climbing black bear migrating between the Chisos Mountains and Sierra del Carmen; and golden eagles and peregrine falcons that soared and plunged after white-wing dove among cliffs, sotol, and mesquite. In 1990, the Chihuahua state government established this canyon as the Área de Protección de Flora y Fauna Cañón de Santa Elena (Protected Area of Flora and Fauna Santa Elena Canyon). Yet, few visitors, canoeists, hikers, or naturalists were aware that Santa Elena Canyon had been home to Indigenous people since 15,000 BCE, when Paleo-Indians hunted, gathered, and fished the Rio Grande. Archaic, Conchos, Jumano, and Chisos peoples, and later the Mescalero Apache, continued the traditions. Theirs was an ancestral homeland, natural sanctuary, and hallowed ground that, during the winter of 1849–50, was sought out for the worst reason on earth.

Paid "by the scalp," Captain John Glanton and his ruthless thugs "finally discovered that an immense [Mescalero] Apache winter camp was stretched along on the American side of the Grand Cañon of the Rio Grande [Santa Elena Canyon]," Colonel Richard Irving Dodge wrote in 1882. "He attacked one end of this camp at daylight one morning, and so scattered were the Indians and so difficult the ground, that his command took over two hundred and fifty scalps of men, women, and children."

The Glanton Gang's heinous depredations caught up with them on the Colorado River five months later at Yuma's Ferry, Arizona Territory, when Quechan chief Caballo en Pelo and his band scalped Glanton and his gang in 1850. Kirker (born in Ulster, Ireland) and his two dozen men, called the Sahuanos, were no less ruthless, scalping 130 peaceful Apache in 1846 at Galeana, Chihuahua, in a single slaughter. The Chihuahua government was bankrupt and couldn't pay Kirker his bounty due, so General Calvo López put a $10,000 bounty on *his* scalp. The American fugitive fled Mexico with his Mexican wife and family, led a wagon train of forty-niners to California, and retired as a scalp hunter in Contra Costa County.

I gazed at the mountain soaring above the river, which turned gold in the afternoon sun. It was right there; the winter sky was so clear, it felt like you could almost reach out and touch it. It was the Sierra del Carmen, an indelible Big Bend landmark, but it was found across the river in the Republic of Mexico. I'd wanted to climb the mountain since I first canoed beneath it on the Rio Grande Wild and Scenic River. So I did my research in the university map collection; packed my food, gear, and camera equipment; and drove twelve hours across two deserts to Big Bend. It was the most remote national park in the contiguous United States. I stopped in the small ranger station and asked the winter host if he had any information about climbing the Sierra del Carmen. He looked at me quizzically and said, "Don't you know that's another country over there?!" I thanked him and walked down to camp and slept within sound of the Rio Grande.

The next morning I caught a ride across the river in a *chalupa* (wooden boat) and walked a mile to the village in the company of smiling children and free-range dogs. Founded in 1897, the village of Boquillas del Carmen was at the end of the road, 160 miles north of Santa Rosa de Músquiz, Coahuila, the nearest town. Two thousand people who once lived in Boquillas traveled the rugged road by foot, burro, and wooden wagon to find work in the Corte Madera Mine. When the silver mine went bust in 1919, the population dwindled to 200 people—hardworking, friendly souls who developed a bond with the desert, river, and sierra. José Falcon was one *fronterizo* who put down roots in the border town and opened a small, colorful restaurant catering to Americans visiting Big Bend.

When I strode into Boquillas, I went right to the restaurant and introduced myself to Sr. Falcon and his family. They sat me down, and I explained that I wanted to climb the Sierra del Carmen. I asked them if they could give me directions to the sierra or the canyon springs. Of course, they assured me. The Falcons served me delicious food and offered a clean room for the night at a bargain price. The next morning their friend named Miguel pointed me in the right direction. "Dios le bendiga" (God bless you), the Falcons wished me. I thanked them profusely and waived goodbye. I wasn't sure what would happen next.

Climbing a remote mountain alone in Mexico can be unnerving. Once you've crossed the border, you're off the grid. American maps turn into medieval charts with blank spaces that seem to insinuate, "Here be whatever demons you hunger for!" In the case of the border, many visitors fear the locals and their customs. In the case of Boquillas and most of Mexico I'd explored—driving from San Xavier del Bac Mission, Arizona, to the Río Usumacinta, Chiapas, to photograph Indigenous peoples on one occasion—locals have gone out of their way to help me. The greater fear was the nature of the Sierra del Carmen's *despoblado*. There was little possibility of being rescued if I made a mistake, so I used caution until I hit my stride and pieced together a route from the arroyo of La Boquilla (the Spout) to the rim of the sierra.

I'd been walking blindly, trudging up a steep, rocky burro trail until I reached an abandoned adobe. I noted it on my Mexican topographical map as Casa Blanca (White House). I continued trekking up to the top of a mesa called Sierra El Terminal. And there it was, a terraced mountain wall that bore a striking resemblance to the stratigraphy of the Grand Canyon. The spectacular band of mountain peaks was linked together by a summit reef of seventy-five-million-year-old, Cretaceous-aged Del Carmen limestone: Cruz de Oro (Cross of Gold), Espinazo del Diablo (Devil's Backbone), and the most conspicuous of them all, El Pico (the Peak).

I kept walking toward El Pico across the creosote-covered plateau, staring at the fault block mountain. It was guarded with 450-foot-high escarpments that would need to be climbed over or detoured around to reach the summit rim. I could see no official trails or trail markers. Orienteering would be essential, on-site route finding. The closer I approached the western headwall, the steeper the mining track became, and the more imposing the mountain appeared. I approached the canyon mouth of Cruz de Oro, but it looked off course, leading to the steep tailings of the old San José Mine. I backtracked, wound around into the next canyon to the north, El Socavón (a gallery where miners work), and camped near a stone cabin. I noted it on my map as Casita Piedra (Little Stone House). The mountain wall towered over me like a tsunami about to break.

At 40 miles long and 8,920 feet high, the Sierra del Carmen forms the northern chain of the Sierra Madre Oriental (Eastern Mother Mountains). It soars out of the Great Chihuahua Desert, reportedly one of the twenty most-important ecosystems on Earth. The Sierra del Carmen and Maderas del Carmen had been inscribed as a UNESCO World Biosphere Reserve. It was also the first official wilderness area designated in Latin America and had long been a wildlife corridor to Big Bend National Park and UNESCO Biosphere Reserve.

The supernal sky islands and desert seas of the 15,625-square-mile Transboundary Megacorridor were home to diverse fauna and flora, including 446 species of birds, 75 species of mammals, and 1,500 species of plants. Among the mammals that form its web of biodiversity are black bear, mountain lion, mule deer, Carmen whitetail deer, elk, antelope, and bighorn sheep, and, at one time, Mexican wolves. In 1988 the governor of Coahuila, economist Eliseo Mendoza Berrueto, tried to kindle the flame of establishing the Sierra del Carmen and Big Bend as the world's largest transborder park along the lines of Waterton/Glacier International Peace Park–UNESCO World Heritage Site. Today, the opportunity stands ready when neighboring countries can join hands across the border, preserving the remarkable region for everyone to visit and treasure.

West of the Pecos, Sierra del Carmen has been called "one of the most remote places on Earth." It has also been called a Lost World. That's how I felt the next morning when I rolled out of my sleeping bag into a *despoblado* where no one else lived or roamed. I was alone to find my way, and to climb until I reached the sky. First, I'd needed to replenish 2 gallons of spring drinking water. It was right where Miguel told me it would be, above the *pozo* (well) in the canyon of El Socavón. I loaded my pack and started for the rim, climbing cross-country 3,000 vertical feet up a hanging canyon. I skirted around the west side of an immense prow of limestone and climbed straight up on the south side of El Pico. "The small high peak at the top of the . . . vertical cliff 2,000 feet or more in height," geologist Ross Maxwell wrote in 1941, was "called Shot Tower" because it was easily identified from a long distance by early Big Bend National Park surveyors.

Slowing to an occasional crawl, I pawed my way up the last thousand feet alongside the pillar of Shot Tower, huffing and puffing, until I finally climbed over the rim and lay on the edge, exhausted from the trailless, river-to-rim Grand Canyon–and-a-half effort.

I staggered to my feet and stood straight up. The sun was starting to set, and the light was starting to turn colors. I had little time. I dropped my pack and ran around the north side of El Pico. From the rim rock on the northern horizon I could see the silver thread of the Rio Grande / Río Bravo del Norte slithering 127 miles east from Presidio, Texas / Ojinaga, Chihuahua, to La Linda, Texas / Acuña, Coahuila. Farther north I spotted the sky island of the Chisos Mountains, Big Bend. The landscape was growing dark to the east, but I could make out the Sierra de San Vincente floating in the Coahuila Desert to the west. I wound back around the east side of El Pico, but the prospect of climbing the last 60 feet or so of the 8,920-foot summit in the darkening sky was not good. The ridgeline of the Sierra del Carmen stretched 40 miles south and faded into the romantic distance of the storied Sierra Madre. I picked my spot and photographed El Pico as Shot Tower turned bronze and the southern rim turned gold and fuchsia.

I had to make a decision: camp on the rim or bail off the sierra and head all the way back down to El Socavón. As the wind started to pick up, I hoisted my pack and plunged down the hanging canyon, bouldering and talus-running along the edge of Shot Tower near the head of El Socavón. I rolled out my sleeping bag on what felt like the bow of a huge ship, kept my shoes tied on, snuggled on the narrow ledge, and stared into the western horizon as the dark sky lit up with stars. I'd made the right call. Like West Texas, I was neither here nor there—summit rim, river gorge, or desert sea—but I was safe and snug for the night. I stared over the legendary western landscape that had carried the hoofbeats of saints, sinners, rangers, and the División del Norte troops of Francisco "Pancho" Villa and the Mexican Revolution. The words of one traveler who'd crossed the frontier to the south stood out: "[I]f you hear of my being stood up against a Mexican stone wall and shot to rags, please know that I think it a pretty good way to depart from this life," American journalist Ambrose Bierce wrote to his niece, Lora Bierce, from Pancho Villa's camp on October 1, 1913. "It beats old age, disease, or falling down the cellar stairs."

It took me most of the next day to descend 7,015 vertical feet out of the sierra to the Rio Grande. Below Casita Piedra, I went down another burro trail I discovered via Cruz de Oro. A friendly miner greeted me and said some Americans and a young girl needed help near Casa Blanca. He didn't say anything else, and little did I know they'd be there waiting when I arrived that afternoon. I looked inside Casa Blanca. I heard noise, but I didn't hear anyone talking. I went inside and the next thing I knew, a woman spun around through a doorway like she had just whirled out of a spaghetti western and pointed what I thought was a Navy Colt .45 revolver at me with two hands. I held up my hands until I realized she didn't have a gun. Had she lost it crossing the desert? I had no idea. I ran out. If there was a girl with her, she'd need food, I thought. "I've got food if you need it!" I yelled. A man and woman yelled back, "We need it. Come in!" I walked inside slowly and saw a scruffy, western-dressed mother, father, and young girl. I tried not to make close eye contact. "Here it is," I said, carefully handing them my remaining food and stealing a glance at what looked like a nine-year-old girl. I wanted to make sure she was okay. "It's all I have. It's your business. I don't need to know anything," I said, gingerly walking away.

I wasn't sure what else I should do for an American family on the lam in Old Mexico. I walked away, glad I was alive. Should I have even gone inside? The girl was the only reason. If they did the right thing, they'd eat, rest until nightfall, wade across the Río Bravo, and turn themselves in. It was 160 miles to Músquiz, and it looked like they'd just walked from there.

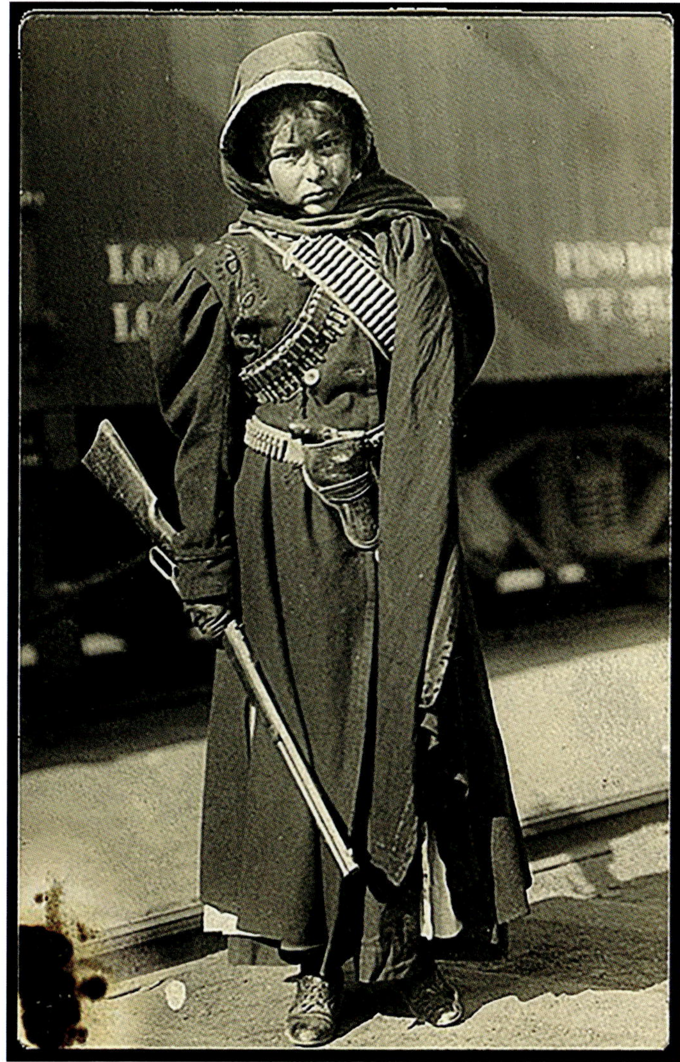

Soldadera of the Mexican Revolution. *Photo by Agustín Victor Casasola, Mexican Association of Press Photographers, circa 1914. Courtesy of Julio Reza Diaz*

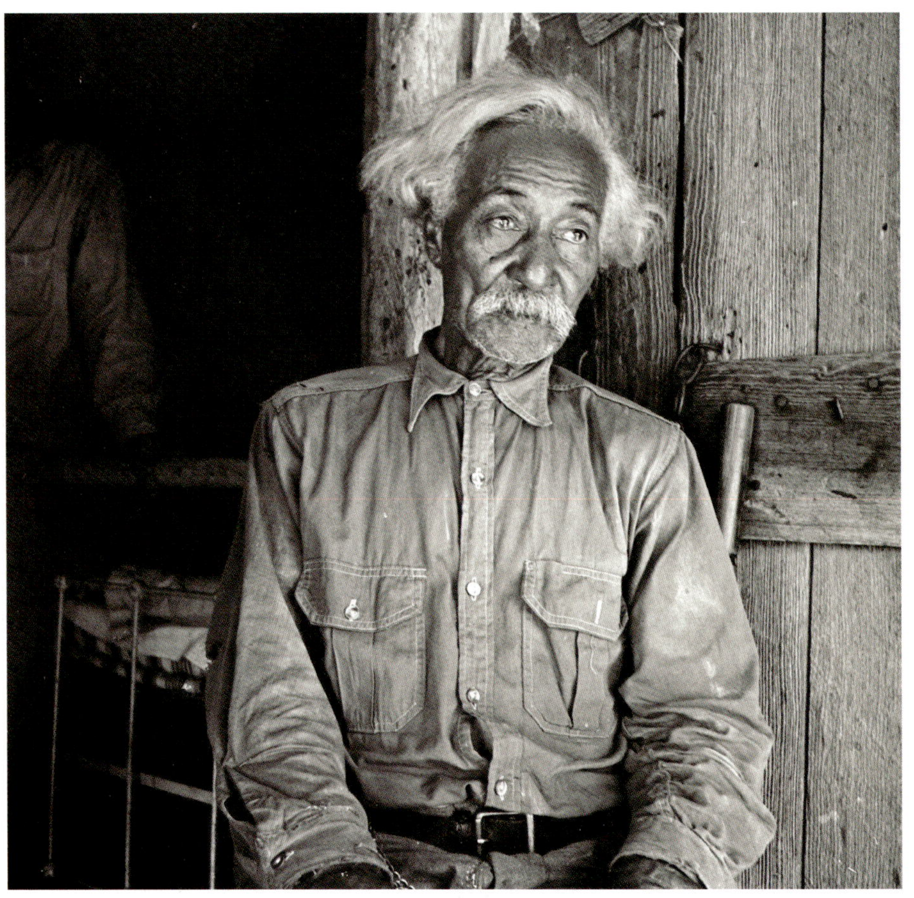

Horse whisperer Robert Lemmons. Nitrate negative print by Dorothea Lange, 1936, Carrizo Springs, Texas. *Courtesy of US Farm Security Administration*

I grew up with the mustangs . . . I worked alone and acted like I was a mustang. I made the mustangs think I was one of them. Maybe I was in those days. After I stayed with a bunch long enough they'd foller me instid of me having to foller them. Show them you're the boss. That's my secret.

—Robert Lemmons, in *The Mustangs*, 1952

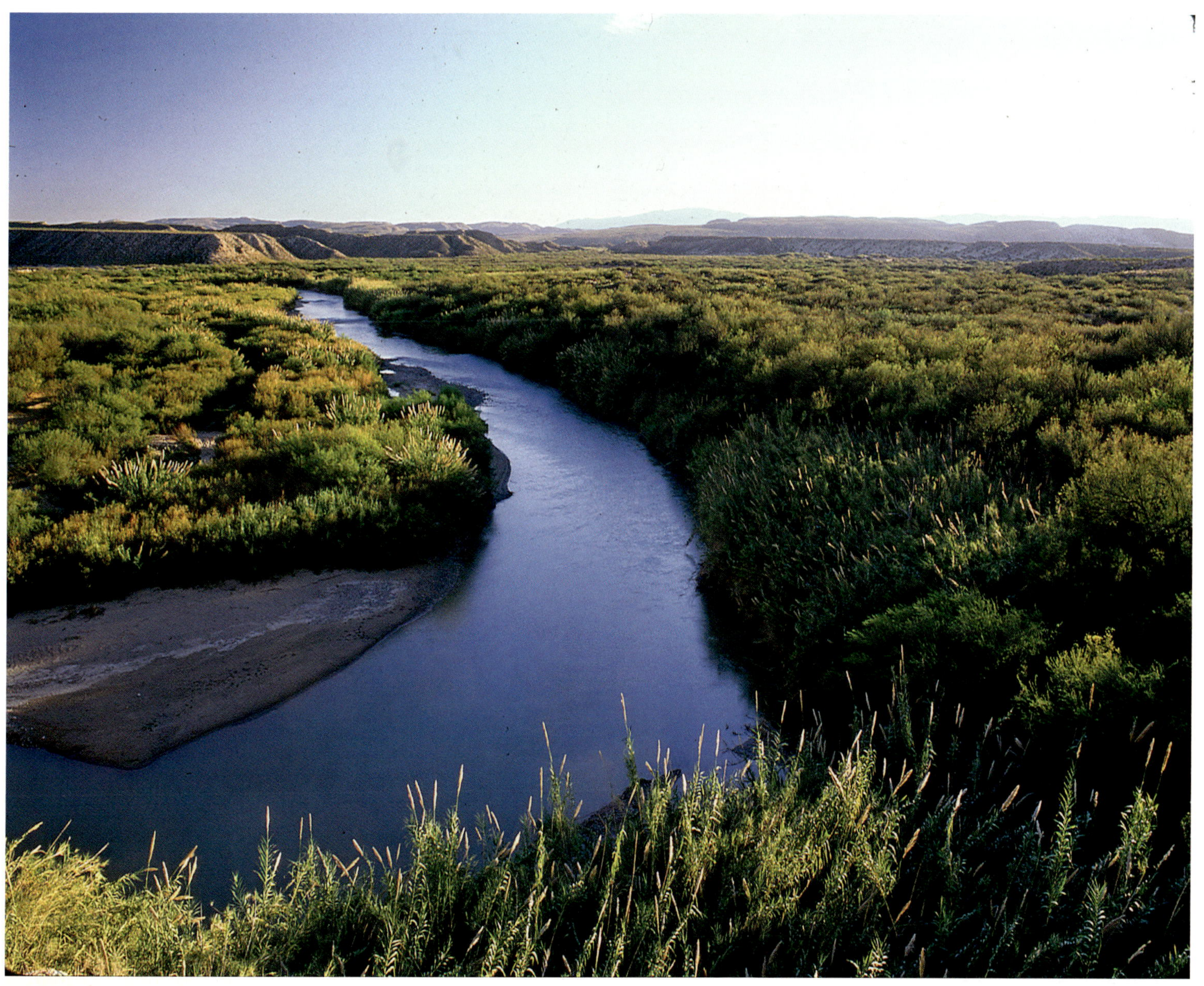

Recharged by the Sierra Madre's Río Conchos, the Río Grande Wild and Scenic River flows through the Chihuahuan Desert of Big Bend to the sea at the Gulf of Mexico.

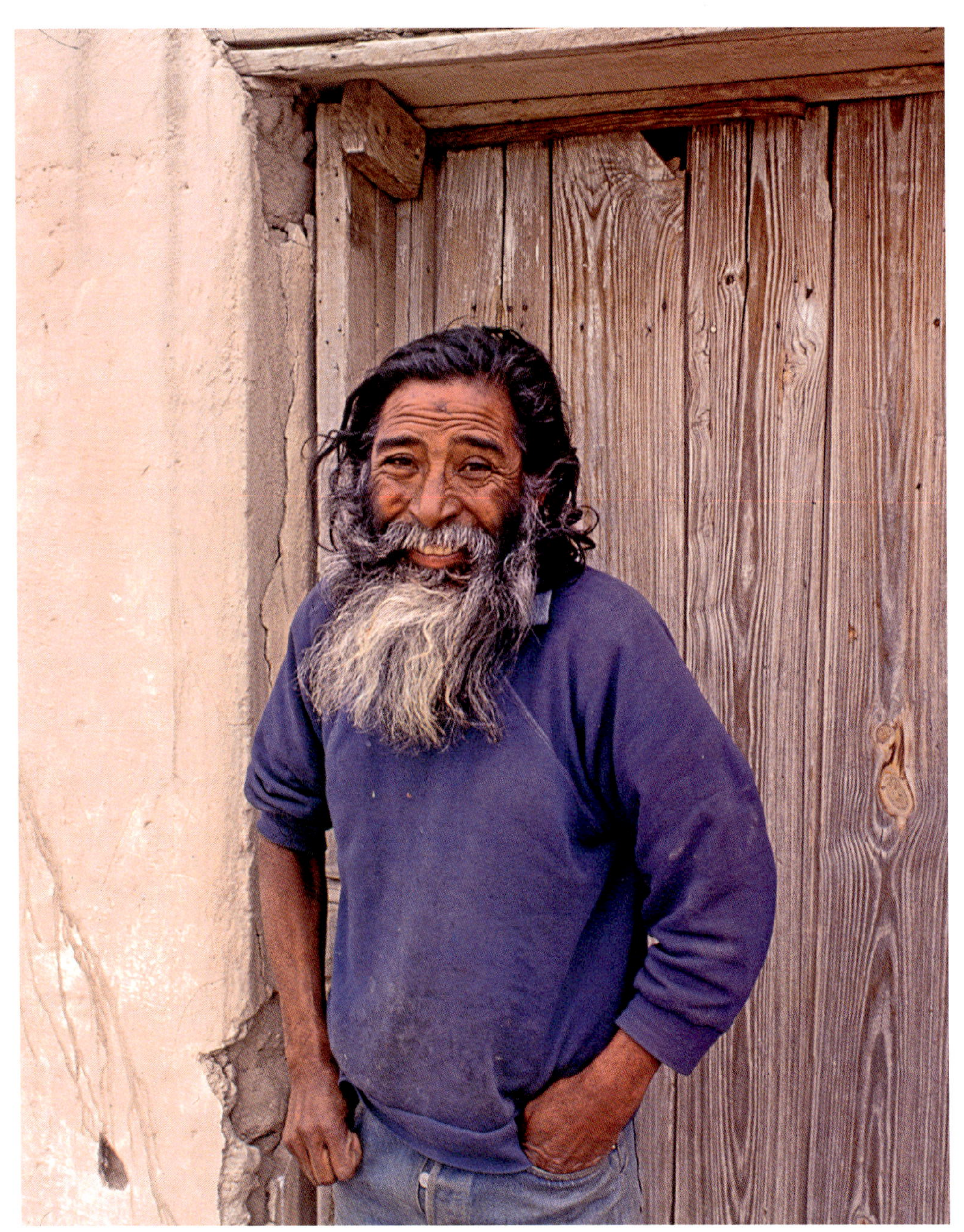

Borderman Juan Valdez stands watch in the Río Bravo del Norte river pueblo of Boquillas del Carmen, Coahuila, Mexico.

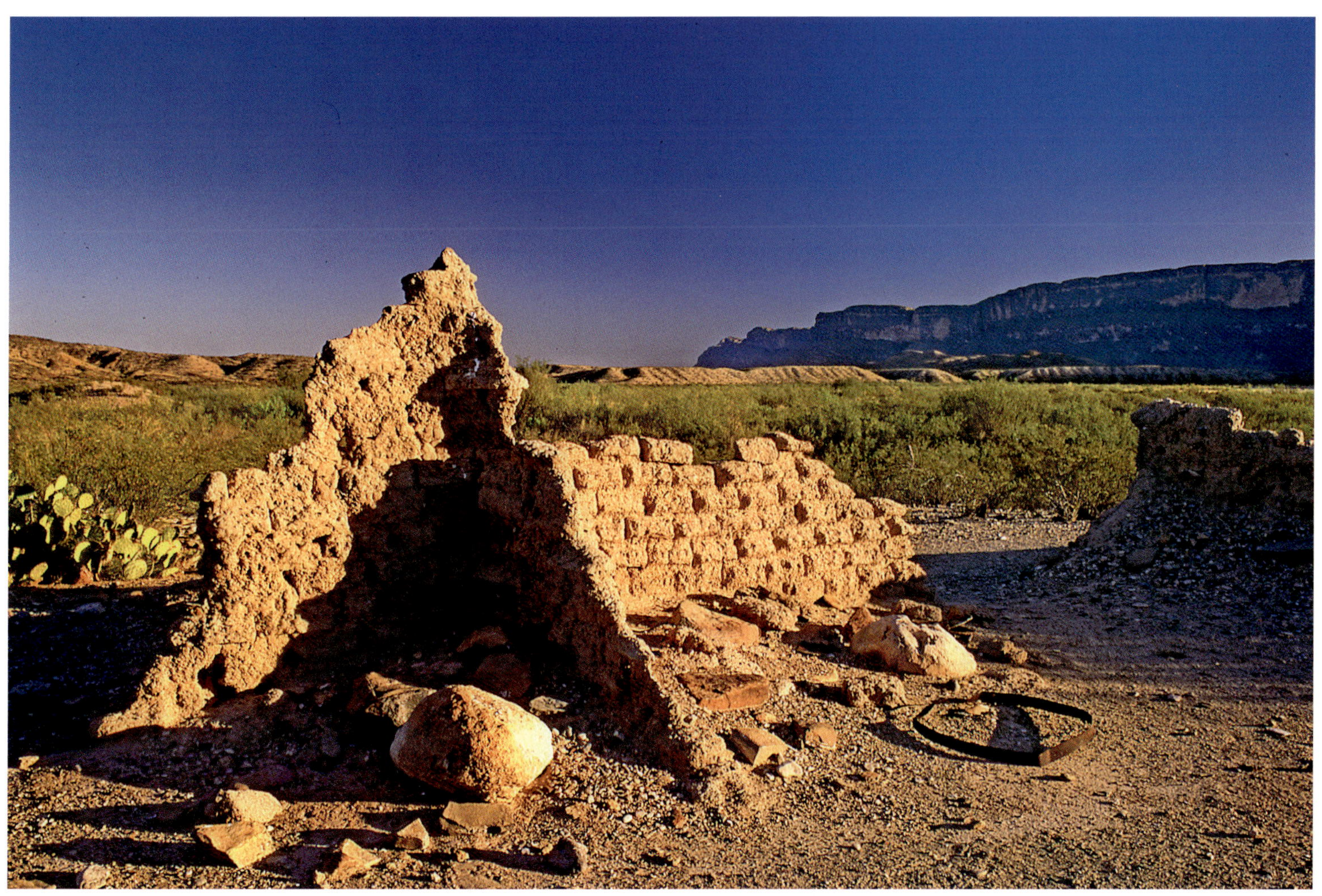

Ruins of Terlingua Abajo ghost town, Chihuahuan Desert, Big Bend National Park, Texas. UNESCO Biosphere Reserve.

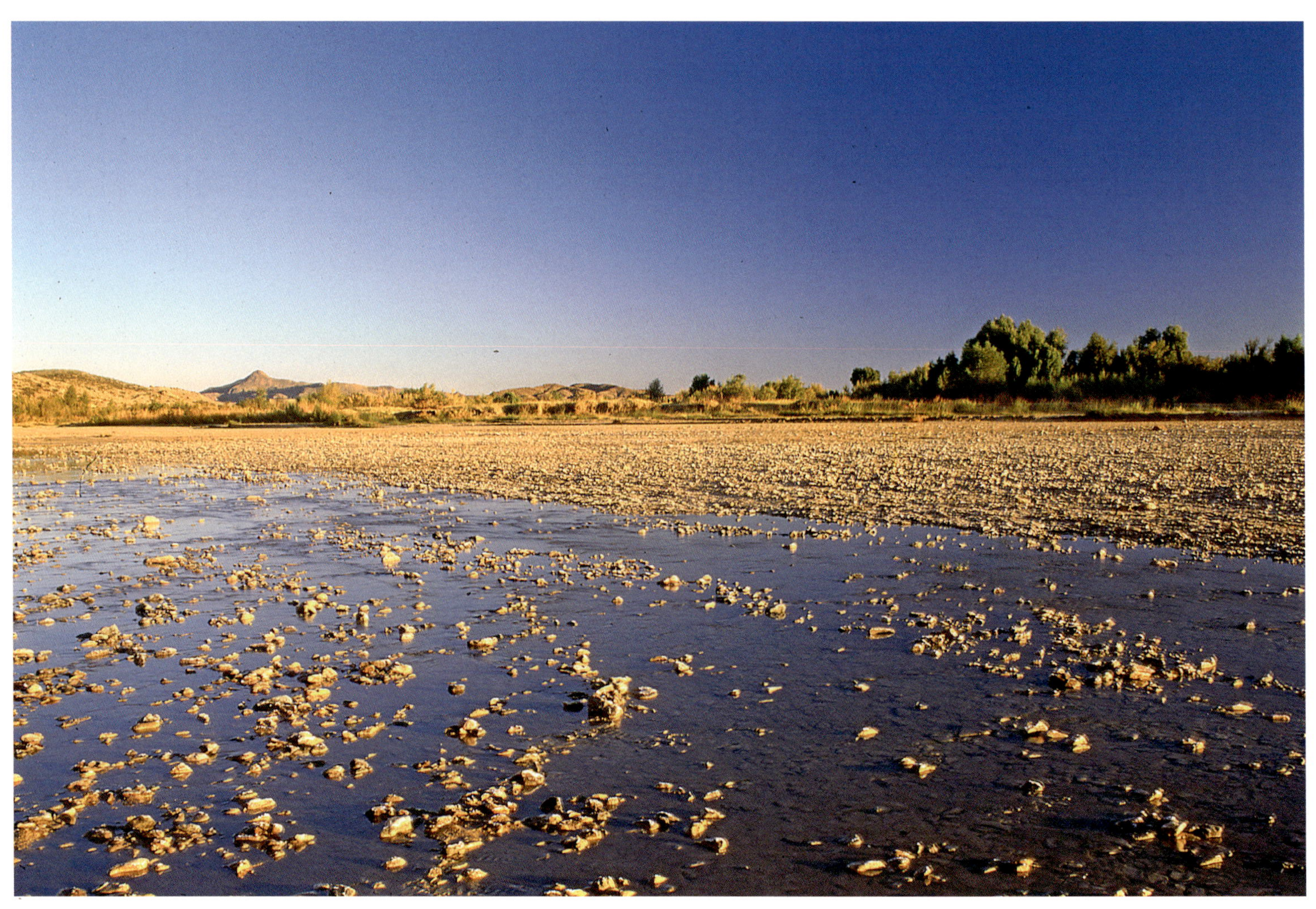

Sheet water flow of Terlingua Creek near Santa Elena Canyon, Big Bend National Park, Texas. UNESCO Biosphere Reserve.

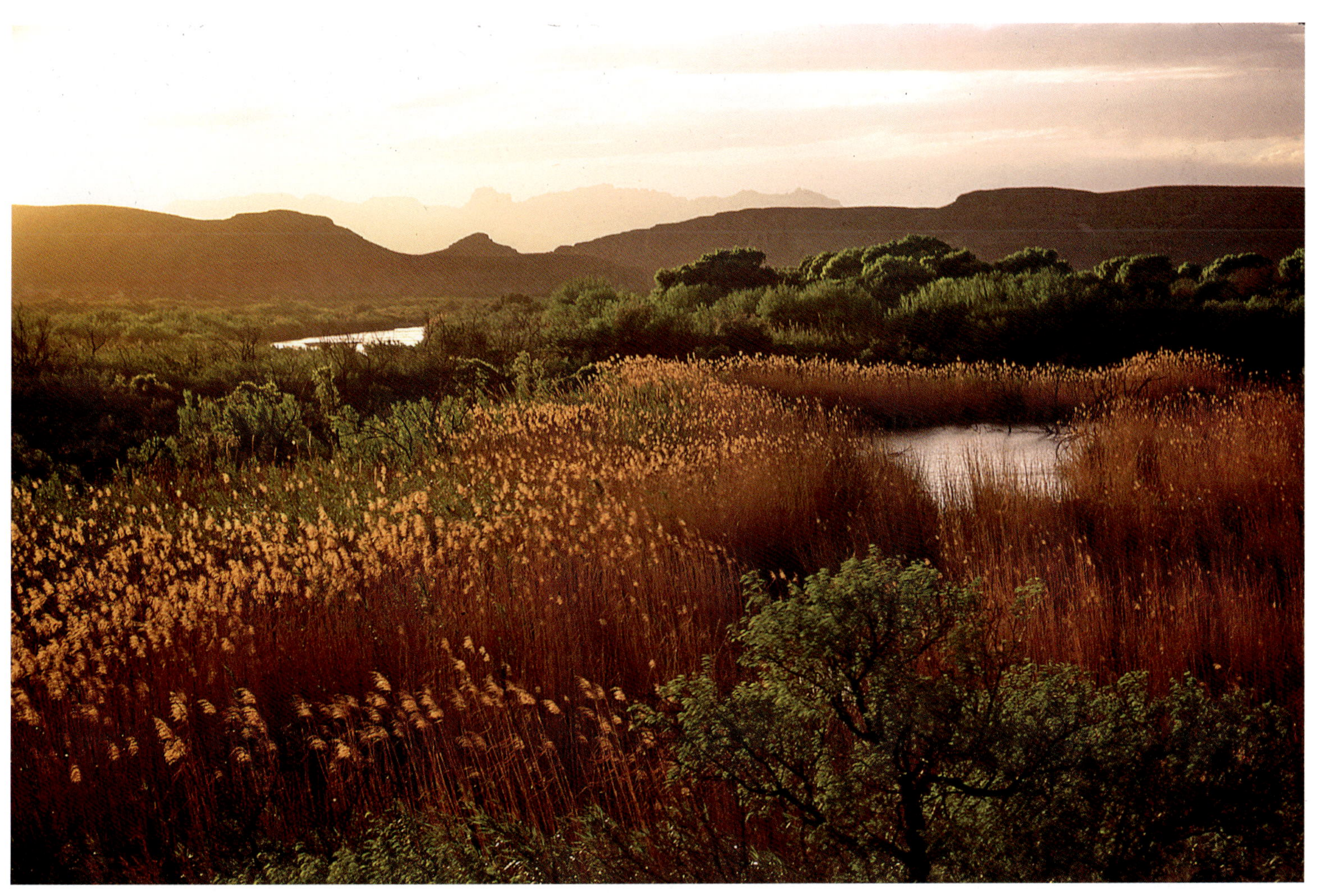

Bosque (wetlands) along the Rio Grande, Big Bend National Park, Texas. UNESCO Biosphere Reserve.

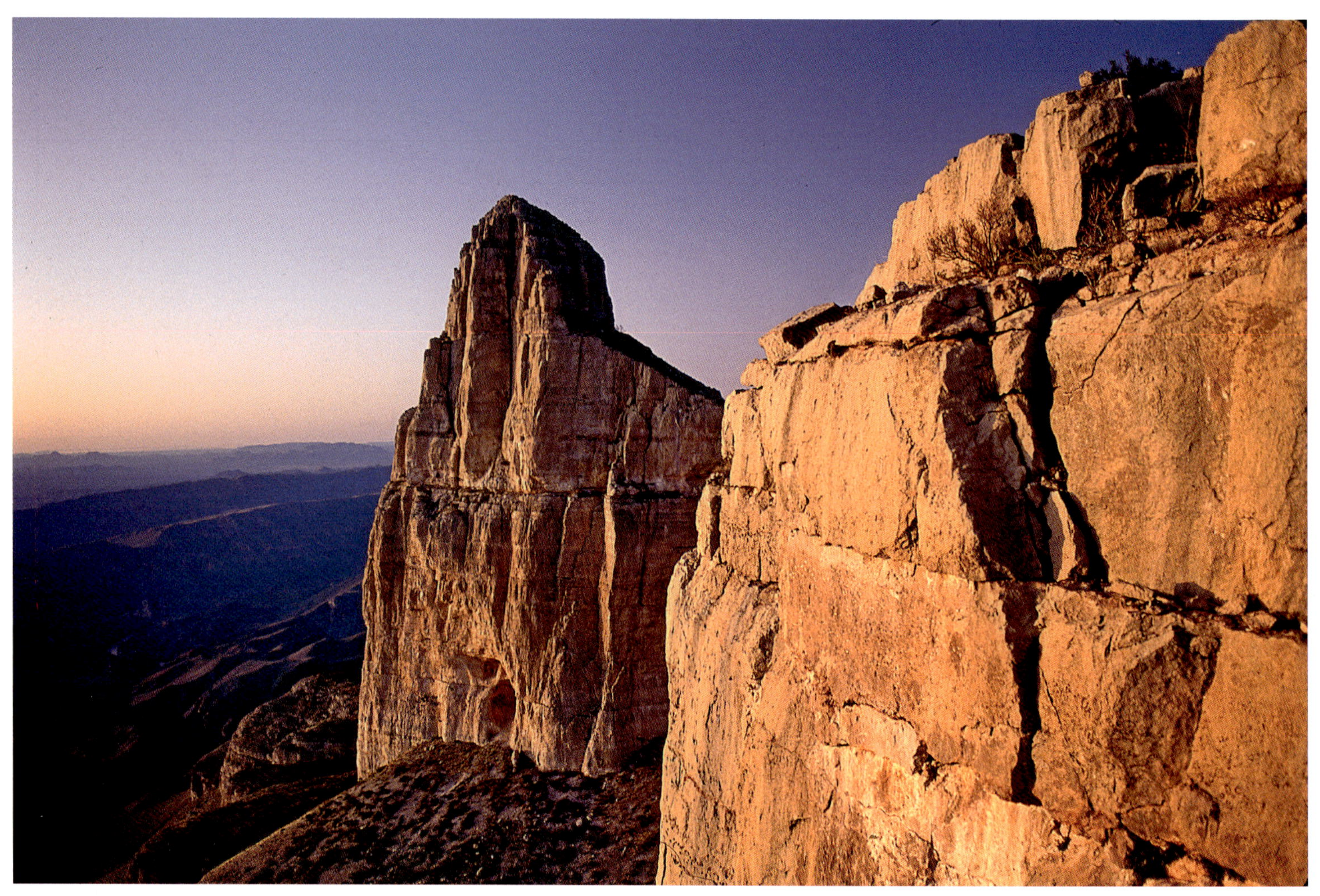

El Pico, as locals called the high point of the northern end of the Sierra del Carmen, was referred to as Shot Tower by Americans who surveyed Big Bend National Park in 1941.

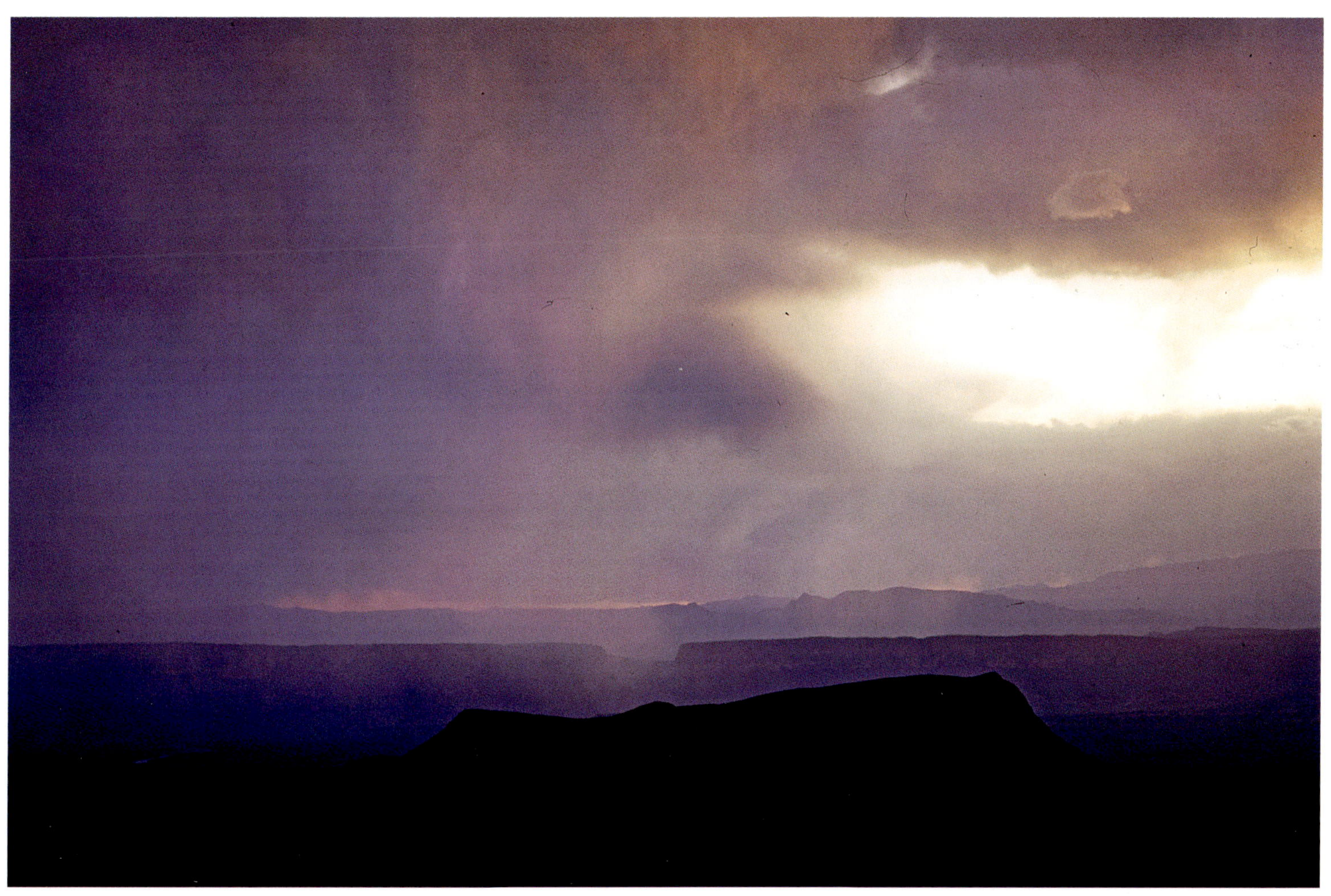

A *despoblado* monsoon extends beyond Texas's Santa Elena Canyon over Coahuila's Sierra de los Hechiceros (Sorcerer's Mountains).

IV. *TIERRAS PERDIDAS* / LOST LANDS

CANYON DE CHELLY, MONUMENT VALLEY, AND THE GRAND CIRCLE

In beauty (happily) I walk.
With beauty before me, I walk.
With beauty behind me, I walk.
With beauty below me, I walk.
With beauty above me, I walk.
With beauty all around me, I walk.
It is finished (again) in beauty.

—*The Night Chant*, Canyon de Chelly, Washington Matthews's recording, 1880

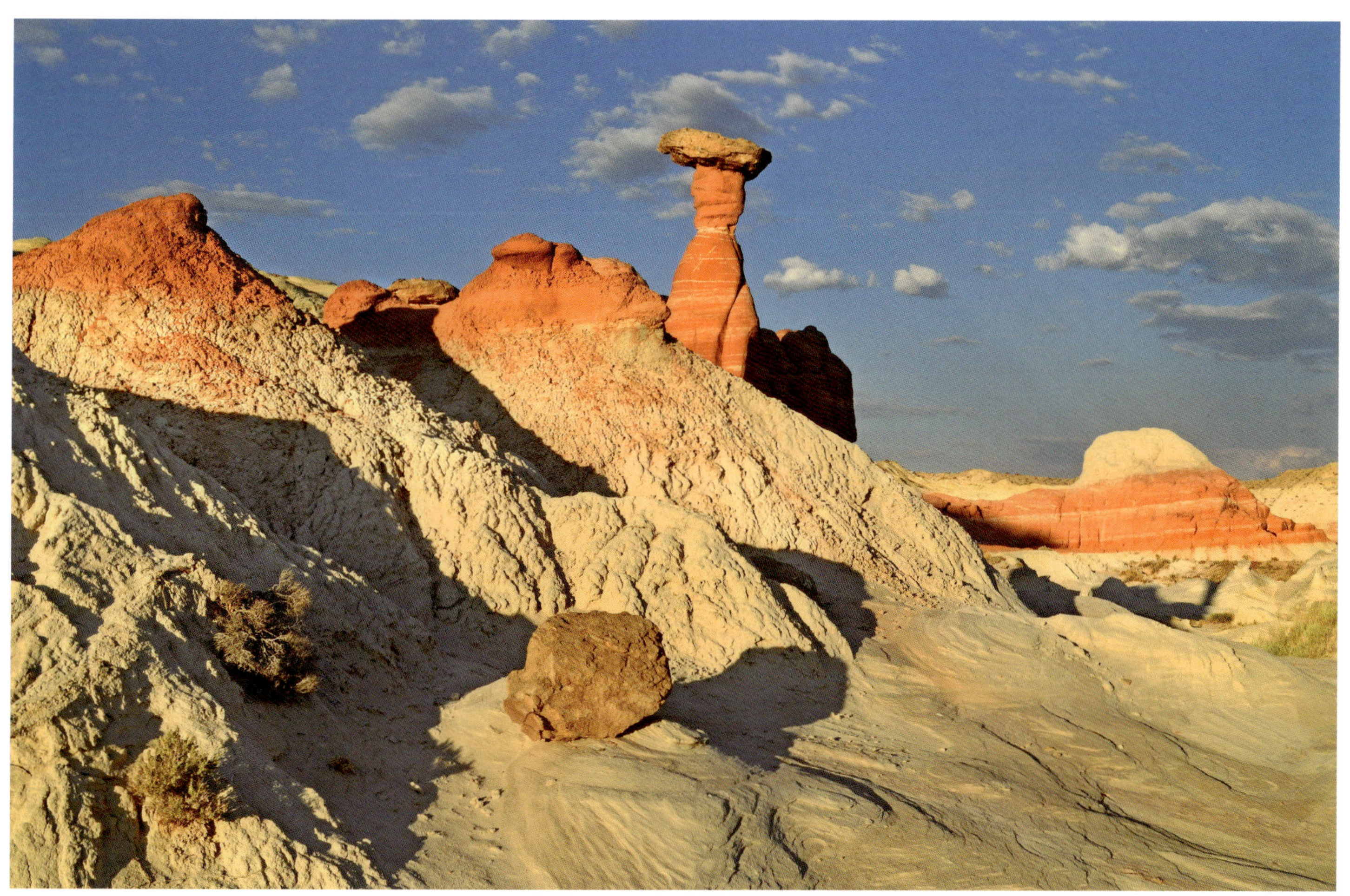

Painted sand hoodoos lure travelers off the Old Spanish National Historic Trail to explore Grand Staircase–Escalante National Monument, Utah.

Many went searching for fortune and gold in the lost lands of Nueva España (New Spain) during the sixteenth century: Francisco Vázquez de Coronado in 1540, Álvar Núñez Cabeza de Vaca in 1542, and Don Juan de Oñate y Salazar in 1598. They crossed the *despoblado* with legions of other conquistadors, padres, explorers, and settlers. They did not come "walking in beauty." They marched, struggled, perished, and massacred strangers during their unrequited search for the Seven Cities of Gold in a country that to them was *tierra perdida* (lost land). But Native peoples knew it intimately and held the spirit of the place as closely as their own heartbeats. It was sacred ground because it provided them with the elements of the earth—air, sky, fire, water—and shelter, game, corn, family, community, and deities they revered.

The Night Chant's reference to "beauty all around me" conceivably also meant stone. Its shapes, colors, and texture were everywhere: arches, badlands, breaks, canyons, cliffs, cracks, hoodoos, mazes, mesas, monuments, natural bridges, needles, petrified sand, sacred mountains, slickrock, spires, and totems. Once American explorers passed through, the landmarks bore such fanciful names as Angels Landing, Bears Ears, Canyon of Death, Dead Horse Point, Devils Garden, Six-Shooter Peak, Temple of the Moon, and other evocative descriptions. By any name, it was an incomparable landscape where Native peoples used adobe mud and stone to build cliff dwellings, granaries, and observatories; hand-carved trails and steps to scale precipitous cliffs; flint-knapped knives and arrowheads; and hand-pecked petroglyphs. Drinking water was collected from rain-fed rock tanks and from sandstone aquifers that held sweet water estimated to be more than 1,000 years old. At shrines and towering stone monuments, homages were paid with eagle-feather prayer sticks and corn pollen. As the long knives of conquistadors began to silence and enslave Native peoples, and their land started slipping away, they prayed to their deities in ceremony and song. There were points of light found throughout the Four Corners of the Great Southwest where the tradition was still observed in the 1880s and beyond.

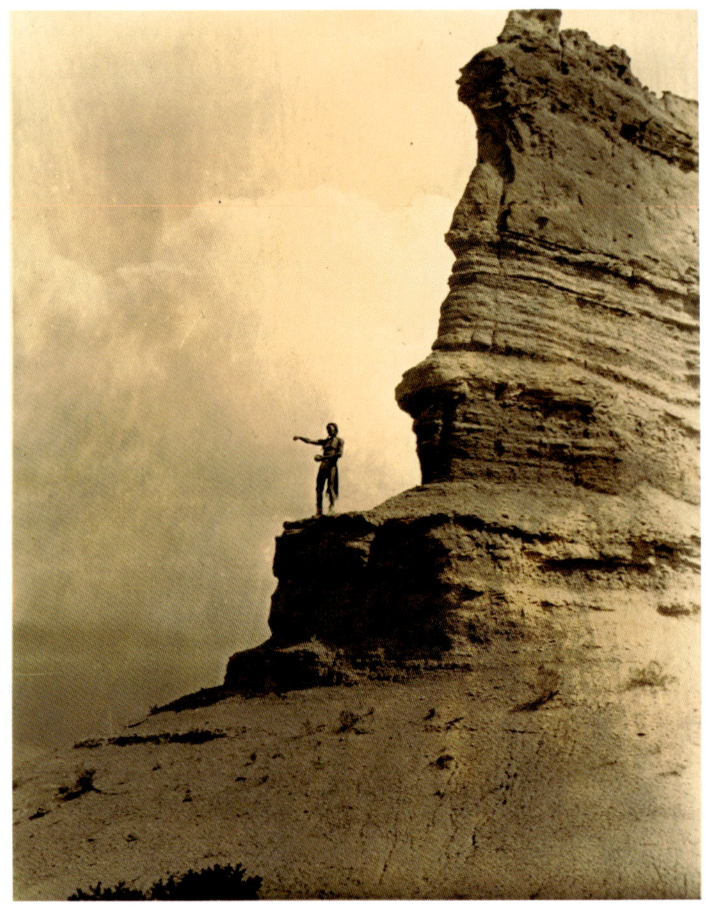

The offering—San Ildefonso, New Mexico. Photomechanical print by Edward S. Curtis, 1927. *Courtesy of Library of Congress*

"When Lololomai, the chief, prays, how does he pray?" musicologist Natalie Curtis Burlin wondered in her 1907 book, *The Indians' Book: An Offering by the American Indians*. "He goes to the edge of the cliff and turns his face to the rising sun, and scatters the sacred corn-meal. Then he prays for all the people . . . And Hopis are not the only people he prays for. He prays for everybody in the whole world, everybody. And not people alone; Lololomai prays for all the animals. And not animals alone; Lololomai prays for all the plants. He prays for everything that has life. That is how Lololomai prays."

CASA BLANCA, CANYON DE CHELLY, AND HOUSE MADE OF DAWN

From the south rim of Canyon de Chelly, I could see the deep terra-cotta chasm that cleaves the 7,622-foot Defiance Plateau into a trident of gorges: Canyon de Chelly, Black Rock Canyon, and Cañon del Muerto (Canyon of Death). Each sinuous arm held cliff dwellings that clung to sandstone walls over 1,000 feet high, from the bed of Chinle Wash to the heights of lookouts that hinted at the canyons' myths, legends, and tragedies: Spider Rock, Massacre Cave, and Mummy Cave. One sacred destination stood out among all others: White House Cliff Dwelling, known to the Navajo as Kininaékai (House of the White Horizontal Streak).

"It was the Indian manner to vanish into the landscape, not to stand out against it," Willa Cather wrote in 1926. "They came and went by the old paths worn into the rock by the feet of their fathers."

I started walking down a cliff high above White House. It lured me into a marvelous canyon whose crystal stream supported lush green cottonwood groves far below. Cottonwood trees provided shade for Indigenous people, horses, cattle, and sheep during summer heat and offered pliable root wood for carving sacred kachina figures that represented *katsina* (spirit beings) and prayer sticks that were known among the Navajo as *k'eet'áán yáłti'* (talking prayer sticks) and among the Hopi as *paahos*. I followed the stony White House Trail that traced the "old paths worn into the rock by the feet of their mothers," the Ásdzání Habitiin (Woman's Trail Up), 600 vertical feet into the canyon rim. I walked across the glistening gravel wash to White House Cliff Dwelling, what Charles Lummis described in *The Swallow's-Nest People* as a phantom: "There is a marvel in the air. The lungs swell to it, in conscious luxury; and in its virgin clarity distance ceases, and the eye is a liar."

In former times, the rugged trail was used for pilgrimages to ceremonies, and as a dependable route to herd horses and sheep in and out of a canyon that was the sacred home of the Haashch'eeh diné (Holy People). Standing at the foot of the magnificent dwelling late that afternoon was unforgettable. Built by Ancestral Puebloans in 1060 CE, the sixty-room "swallow's nest" was inhabited until 1275. Four kivas indicated that the cliff dwellers held ceremonies beneath the 500-foot wall sometime before the Hopi inhabited Koyòngkuktupqa (Turkey Tracks Canyon) from 1300 to the 1600s. That's when the Navajo moved into Tséyi' (In between the Rocks) and lived there from 1700 until the present.

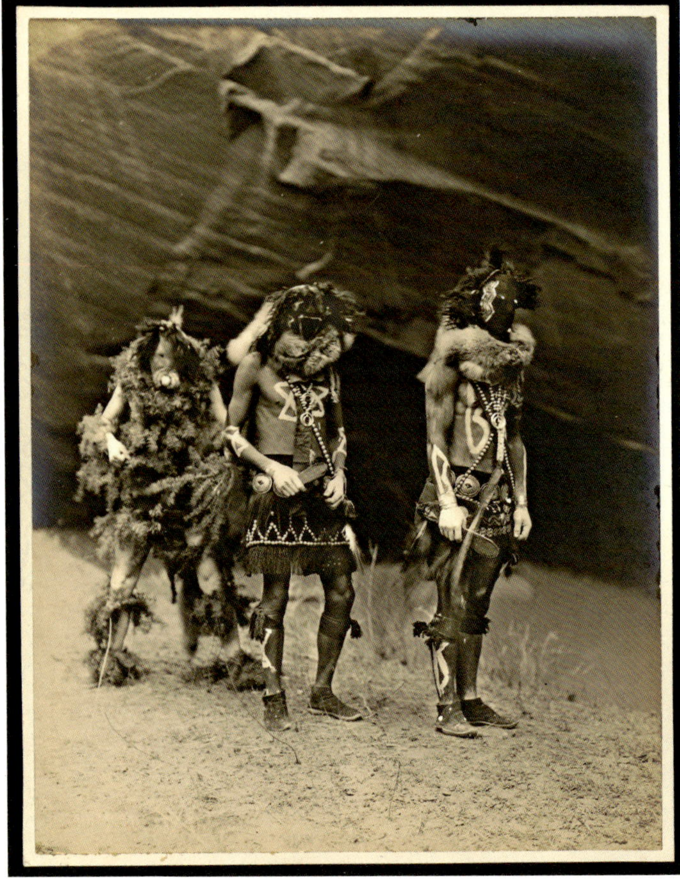

Yebichai war gods. Gelatin silver print by Edward S. Curtis, 1904–1905. *Courtesy of Library of Congress*

Home to the Navajo's Yebichai War Gods, White House Cliff Dwelling had inspired many who'd journeyed long distances to see it over the ages. Editha L. Watson wrote in *Navajo Sacred Places* that "the strange, shadowy figures of the Holy People are still visible to those who believe in them. And it is not difficult to believe, in this cataclysmic country of the Navajo."

On or about December 19, 1880, US Army surgeon and ethnographer Washington Matthews recorded the nine-day Klédze Hatal (Night Chant) ceremony held on the floor of Chinle Wash beneath the White House. They sang "In the House Made of the Dawn." Here, Matthews wrote, "according to the myths, dwelt certain gods who practiced the rites of the Klédze Hatal and taught them to the Navahoes. It is to the gods of this house that these sacrifices are offered. At the White House the patient is supposed to stand in the centre of the world." In part, the Night Chant was heard as a song to the earth, healing, and goodness. How better to reward a journey into the heart of Canyon de Chelly than to imagine the chanting of these beautiful words at the foot of the House Made of the Dawn:

In Tse'gihi
In the house made of the dawn,
In the house made of the evening twilight,
In the house made of the dark cloud,
In the house made of the he-rain,
In the house made of the dark mist,
In the house made of the she-rain,
In the house made of pollen,
In the house made of grasshoppers,
Where the dark mist curtains the doorway,
The path to which is on the rainbow.

The dark wind cut like a flint knife, as the silver pickup barreled toward dawn in the early-morning darkness. The driver's blue eyes glinted in the white hue of the dashboard. Tassels of long gray hair dangled from his sweat-stained cowboy hat. The high-heeled boot kissed the brake pedal, and thick hands caressed the steering wheel into a turn. We rolled to a stop, trailing a red cloud of dust that fell like a phantom over the edge of the rimrock. Through the windshield, two black paws clawed out of the landscape and clutched at the sliver of silver moon. They were Ála Tsoh (Big Hands), or Mitten Buttes. We had come to the Big Hogan to greet whispers of dawn in the sacred valley of Tse Bii Ndzisgaii (Clearing among the Rocks). It became known as Monument Valley.

I slid out of the pickup and walked across the black stones to the edge of the mesa. The world fell away into an abyss, but the delicate brushstrokes of first light blushed the skyline pink. I set up the cold metal tripod, took a seat on the ground, and awaited the first hint of sunlight that would shroud Tse Biyi (Rock Canyon) with long shadows.

Soon, a yellow prism of light blossomed over one of the most famous landscapes on earth. The Navajo revered it, making sacred offerings of corn pollen sprinkled over red-cliff seeps, and ceremonial sand paintings of horned toads and Holy People. Hollywood discovered Monument Valley at the height of the Great Depression, when trading-post owner Harry Goulding camped on director John Ford's doorstep at United Artists with a trove of photographs depicting what would soon epitomize the West around the world.

After Ford's first storm-battered western, movie producers from around the globe queued up to use the Navajos' ancestral ground as their cinematic western canvas. No single location epitomized the American West better than the iconic landscapes in the Navajo ancestral lands revered as Dinétah (Among the People). This 27,000-square-mile area stretches across the Painted Desert between four sacred mountains that are bound by the cardinal directions: on the east by Blanca Peak, or Sisnaajiní (White Shell Mountain); on the south by Mount Taylor, or Tsoodzil (Blue Bead Mountain); on the west by San Francisco Mountains, or Dook'o'oslíid (Abalone Shell Mountain); and on the north by Hesperus Mountain, or Dibé Nitsaa (Big Mountain Sheep). On the border of Utah and Arizona, director Ford re-created the mythic West in *Stagecoach* (1939) and the cavalry trilogy of *Fort Apache* (1948), *She Wore a Yellow Ribbon* (1949), and *Rio Grande* (1950). *The Searchers* followed in 1956; the American Film Institute named it the greatest "'western' as a genre of films set in the American West."

Nearly two decades earlier, western novelist Zane Grey traveled to Cave of the Cliff Dweller (White House Cliff Dwelling), Nonnezoshe (Rainbow Bridge), and Monument Valley for his book of adventures titled *Tales of Lonely Trails*. In it, Grey wrote:

> My first sight of Monument Valley came with a dazzling flash of lightning. It revealed a vast wall, a strange world of colossal shafts and buttes of rock, magnificently sculptored [*sic*], standing isolated and aloof, dark, weird, lonely. . . .

Dawn, with the desert sunrise, changed Monument Valley, bereft it of its night gloom and weird shadow, and showed it in another aspect of beauty. It was hard for me to realize that those monuments were not the works of man.

There was another world of Monument Valley, one in which people lived. Dating to 950 CE, Ancestral Puebloans left their marks in the form of grounded cliff dwellings such as House of Many Hands, so named because delicate white hands had been hand-printed on the graceful sandstone walls overhead. One Paiute elder woman told me these were indications of places where Indigenous people had "crossed over to the spirit world." A hammerstone-pecked form of a shaman bird could be seen flying across one wall. A Kokopeli, or Kókopilau (Humpbacked Flute Player), figure could be seen journeying across another wall. Towering monuments such as Three Sisters, or Haashch'eeh diné (Holy People who turned to stone), and Yéi Becheii Spires, or *k'eet'áánige' ání* (prayer sticks), were revered as deities. Sacred places were everywhere if you knew how to look around Spearhead Mesa, Mystery Valley, Ear of the Wind, and Spider Web Arch. The beauty of Monument Valley was everywhere you turned.

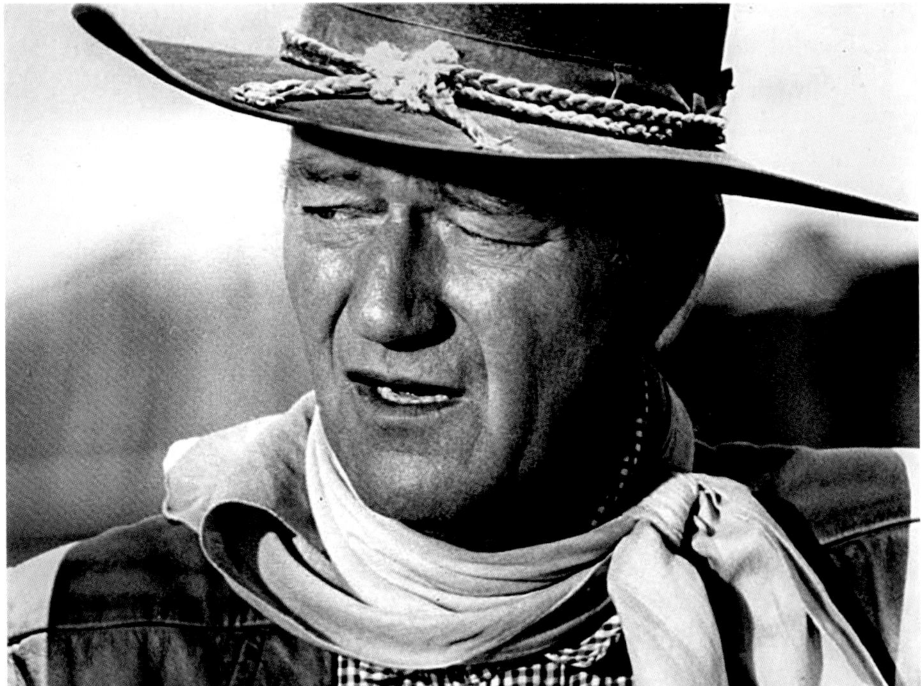

John Wayne on the set of *The Comancheros*, directed by Michael Curtiz, Arizona. Movie still, unknown photographer, 1960. *Courtesy of 20th Century Fox / Wiki*

It was no country for children, they said. Snow-capped, laccolitic peaks lorded over mile-high deserts, deep wilderness chasms, desperate haunts, and landforms that toyed with your imagination. During 1776 and 1777, Franciscan missionaries Francisco Atanasio Domínguez and Silvestre Vélez de Escalante struck out from Santa Fé de Nuevo México to pioneer an impossible route across the frontier to El Presidio Real de San Carlos de Monterrey, California. The missionary explorers endured the toughest country in Nueva España, and they delighted in witnessing the most sublime. Staring winter in the face, and reduced to eating their own horses, Domínguez and Escalante were guided by two Timpanog Utes, Silvestre and twelve-year-old Joaquín, safely back to Santa Fé after making a circuitous 1,700-mile, 159-day journey. The padres completed what was later called a "Grand Circle."

Nearly a hundred years later, another expedition entered the mysterious, unexplored region. On May 25, 1872, topographer Almon H. Thompson led an audacious four-man expedition from Kanab, Utah Territory, across the headwaters of the Paria River, down the beautiful and tortuous Escalante River, and over the 100-mile-long hogback spine of the Waterpocket Fold to the Dirty Devil River. By Thompson's account, they'd journeyed "two hundred and eighty miles, through a country, for the most part, completely unknown." That Major John Wesley Powell's overland expedition succeeded in retrieving their boat, the *Cañonita*, was remarkable. They'd cached the wooden boat in a cave the year before, lost it, and needed it to embark on Powell's Second Colorado River Expedition that August. The canyon country that Frederick S. Dellenbaugh wrote of in his expedition account *A Canyon Voyage* was "this extraordinary locality. No more remote place existed at that time within the United States—no place more difficult of access." It was, Dellenbaugh summarized, "A Wonderland of Crags and Pinnacles, Poverty Rations, Fast and Furious Plunging Waters, Boulders Boom along the Bottom, Chilly Days and Shivering, A Wild Tumultuous Chasm, A Bad Passage by Twilight and a Tornado with a Picture Moonrise, Out of one Canyon into Another." Through it all, the expedition found the boat, "At the Mouth of the Dirty Devil at Last."

In such colossal and treacherous landscapes, children were rarely seen or heard from except in remote and hidden villages and pueblos of Native peoples. But pioneer children were coming with Manifest Destiny: forty-niners, gold seekers, adventurers, homesteaders, and newcomers. They came walking on foot with rifles and axes, on horseback, and by mule-drawn Conestoga wagons, ox-drawn carts, and Mormon push carts, traveling 10 to 15 miles a day for four to five months straight, crossing 2,000 miles of open ground to reach the promised land—if they didn't perish from thirst, hunger, epidemic, childbirth, or battle. Between 1843 and 1869, a half-million pioneers traveled the great western trails of the Santa Fe Trail, Old Spanish Trail, California Trail, Gila Trail, Mormon Trail, and Oregon Trail. Parents and children faced the same odds, weather, hardships, dangers, and terrain that Native peoples did, but they weren't nearly as prepared for the lifestyle and isolation, or adept at surviving hand to mouth in a hostile environment on the far side of eastern civilization. If and when the newcomers finally reached their destination, gold-field, town, or city, most settled in. But some still had a hankering for getting back on the trail through wide-open spaces. Generations later, men, women, and their children created a demand for parks, and in 1916 President Woodrow Wilson signed the National Park Service Organic Act. Explored by Domínguez and Escalante, and later by the Powell Expedition, national parks and monuments were created in the ancestral lands of the Grand Circle, and they became Zion, Bryce, Arches, Canyonlands, Capitol Reef, Grand Staircase–Escalante, and Bears Ears. They were made famous in part by the legacies and travels of Barbencito, or Nabááh Jiłt'áá (Warrior Grabbed Enemy); Everett Ruess, a poet and "Vagabond for Beauty"; Edward Abbey, an environmental essayist who shouted from the slickrock; and Leslie Marmon Silko, a Laguna Pueblo author who brought the Southwest's cultural landscape to life.

I'd always wondered if my son would take to the wilds. I thought—hoped—he might, but I figured he'd need some guidance. Wrong. Camped at the head of Paria Canyon, Utah, my wife, young son, and I walked down the canyon the next morning to look for a series of "windows." Before I could say a word, he climbed into a concave hollow and sat perched in the slickrock sandstone wall, relishing the view across the canyon. Then he jumped down and started looking around to see what he could find. Poking around the streamside cobbles, he found a water-polished stone. He picked it up—it must have weighed 4 pounds—and showed off his prize. "What is it, son?" I asked. "Dad, it's a dinosaur egg," he said, holding up the heavy stone with both arms. Then he lugged it all the way back to camp. He wasn't about to let it get away. It turned out he did take to the wilds. He'd walked in the same rugged country the Old Spanish Trail traversed, between Santa Fé and Nuestra Señora Reina de los Ángeles (Los Angeles) in 1829.

The next day, we drove all the way to Zion National Park, pitched camp, and, the following morning, took the shuttle to Zion Narrows. At 4 feet tall, our son was dwarfed by the raptor's-nest scale of the Temple of Sinawava at the mouth of the North Fork of the Zion Narrows. But he didn't acknowledge the intimidating height. We'd no sooner walked a quarter mile through the neck-craning narrows when he took off running out of sight. Running down the trail after him, we found him climbing up a tall sandstone boulder. He jumped down, picked up a discarded walking stick, and started wading across the North Fork of the Virgin River. It was the same wild stream John Wesley Powell explored on September 12, 1870, when he wrote, "[W]e cross and recross the stream, and wade along the channel where the water is so swift as to almost carry us off our feet . . . we are in danger every moment of being swept down." He kept wading up the narrows, leading us on.

Two days later we drove to Bryce Canyon National Park. Our son wanted to take a short run down the rust-colored cinder trail through the maze of hoodoos of Bryce Canyon. It was named after Mormon pioneer Ebenezer Bryce, who settled in Pine Valley, Utah, in 1868. He also ran cattle in the canyon behind his family's chinked-log cabin. His neighbors called it Bryce Canyon. Bryce reportedly told them it was "a hell of a place to lose a cow." And a son. He discovered it was easier to run down the trail than to climb back up it. It was a lesson well learned, topped with a double-scoop chocolate cone.

It was on to Capitol Reef National Park the next day. We picked peaches from the 1900s-era Gifford Homestead orchards before hiking down a side canyon. It was the haunt of Butch Cassidy, the Sundance Kid, and Etta Place. They rode like bats out of hell through Grand Wash beneath Cassidy Arch, away from a young boy chasing their legend with a plastic pistol across the rimrock canyons toward Robbers Roost. We didn't quite make it to Robbers Roost that day, but here's what early *Atlantic Magazine* writer Rowland E. Robinson reported that Butch told the Wild Bunch about giving up robbin': "If E. F. Harriman paid me what he's paying those guys to stop me from robbing him, I'd stop robbing him."

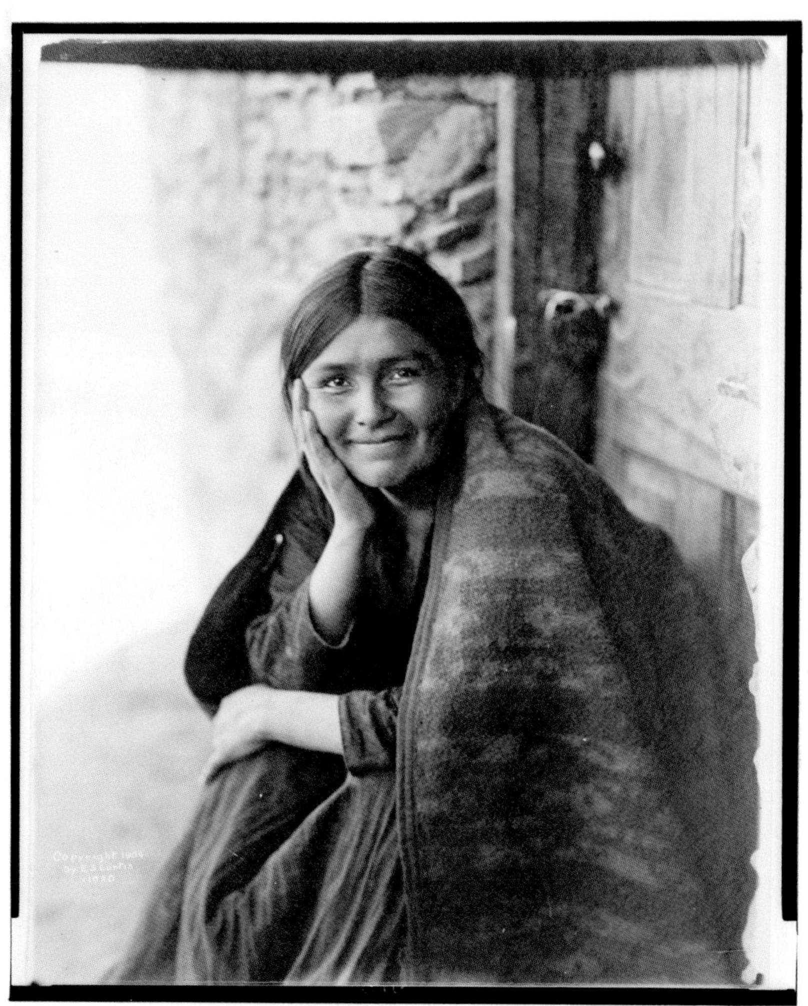

Navajo woman, Arizona. Photographic print by Edward S. Curtis, 1904. *Courtesy of Library of Congress*

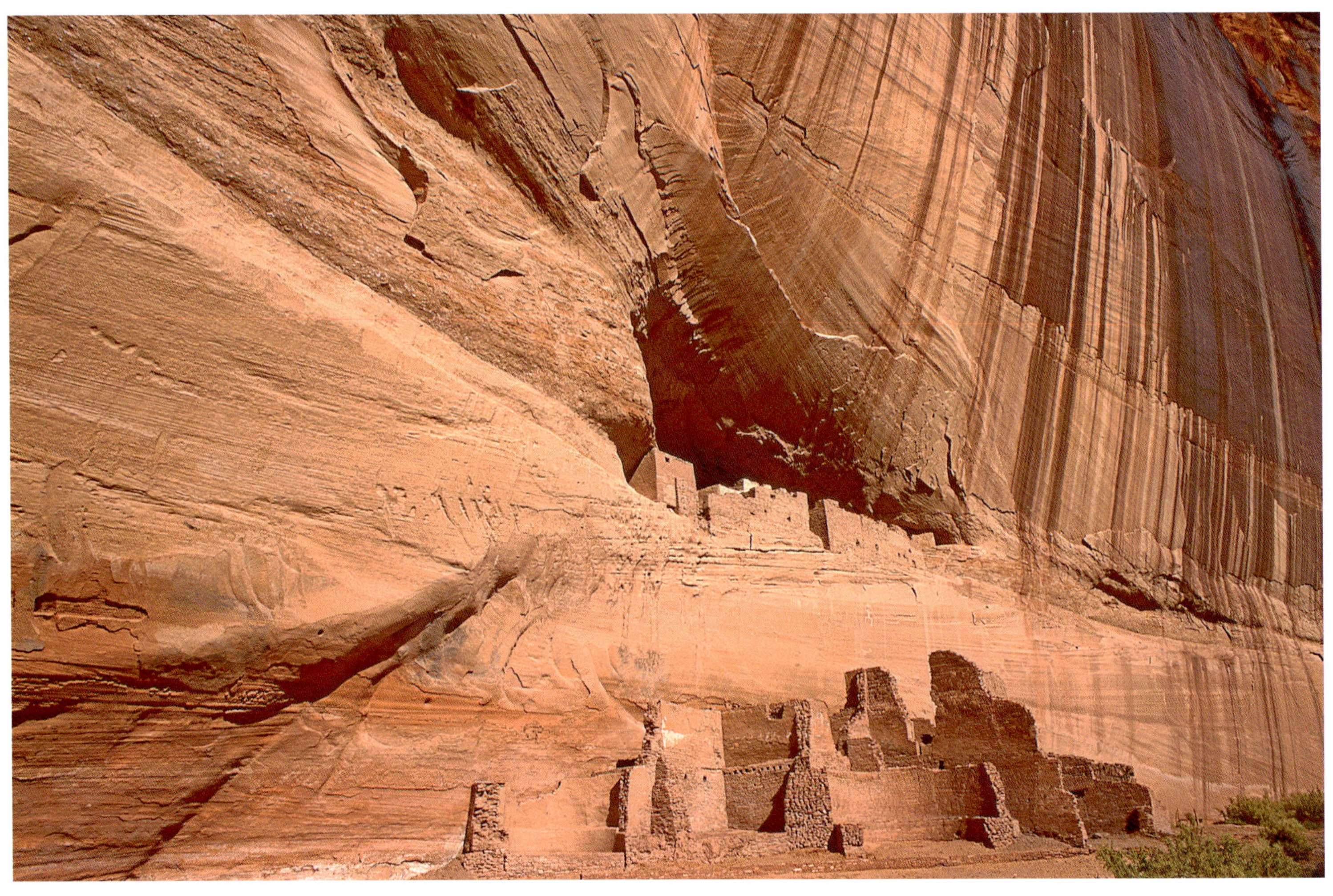

White House Cliff Dwellings, Canyon de Chelly National Monument, Arizona. The nine-day Navajo Klédze Hatal (Night Chant) ceremony was held beneath what was revered as the "House Made of the Dawn," ca. December 19, 1880.

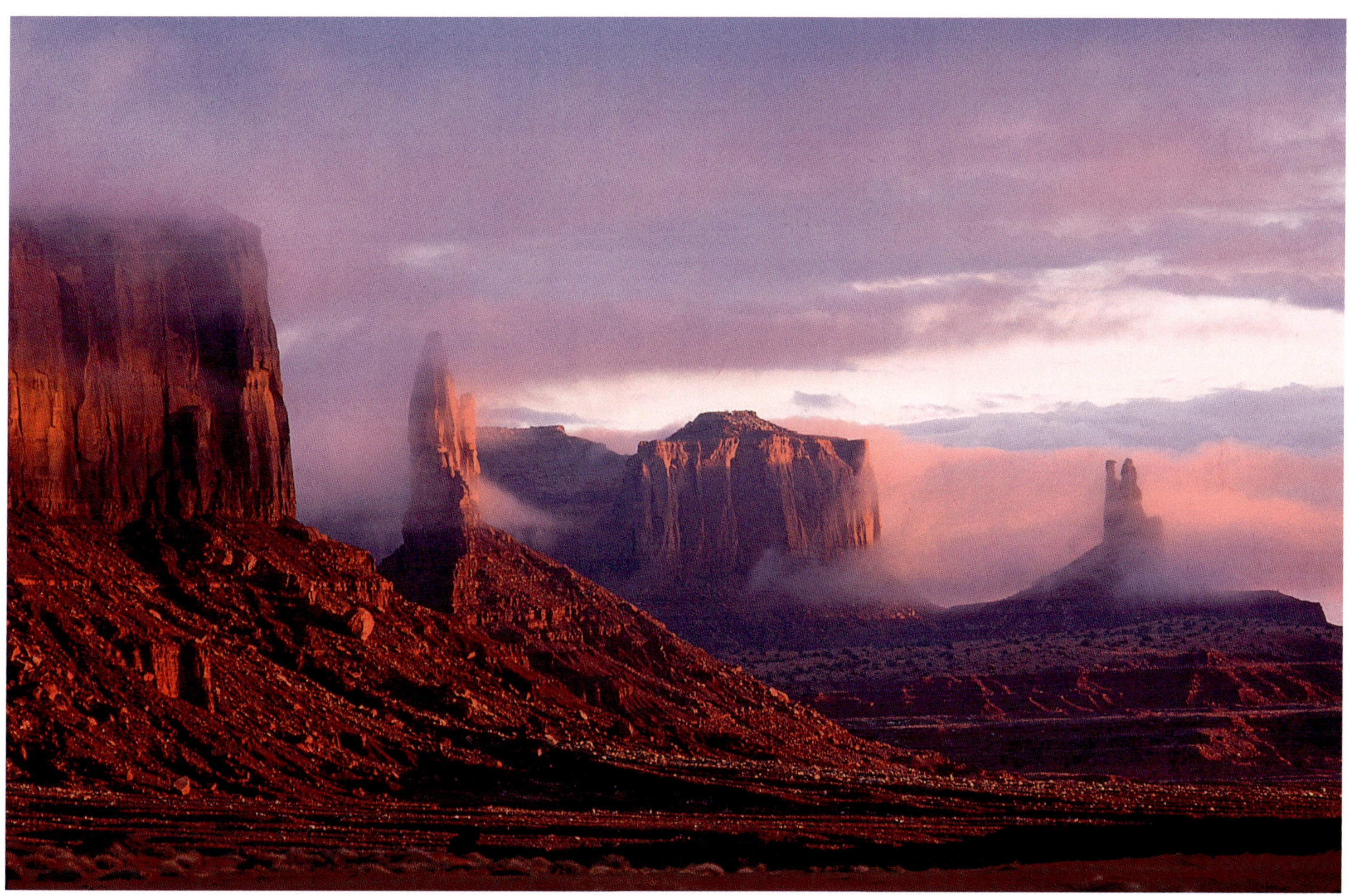

First light washes across the mesas and spires of what Navajo traditionalists call Tsé bii' Ndzisgaii (Clearings among the Rocks), Monument Valley Navajo Tribal Park, Utah-Arizona. Native American Sacred Lands.

So this is where
God put the West.

—John Wayne, 1961

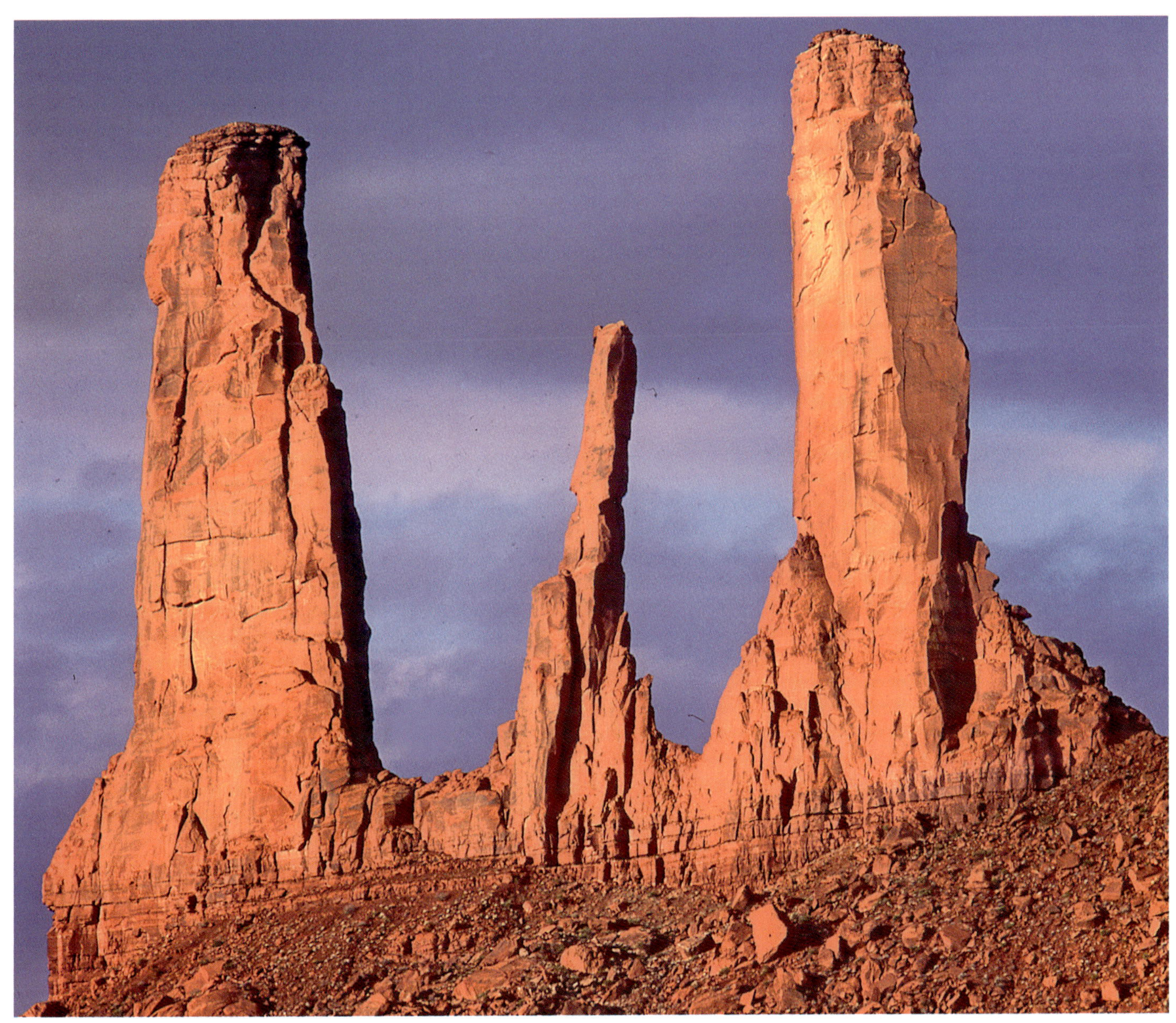

Navajo traditionalists believe the towering spires of Three Sisters represent the Haashch'eeh diné (Holy People Turned to Stone). Monument Valley Navajo Tribal Park, Utah-Arizona.

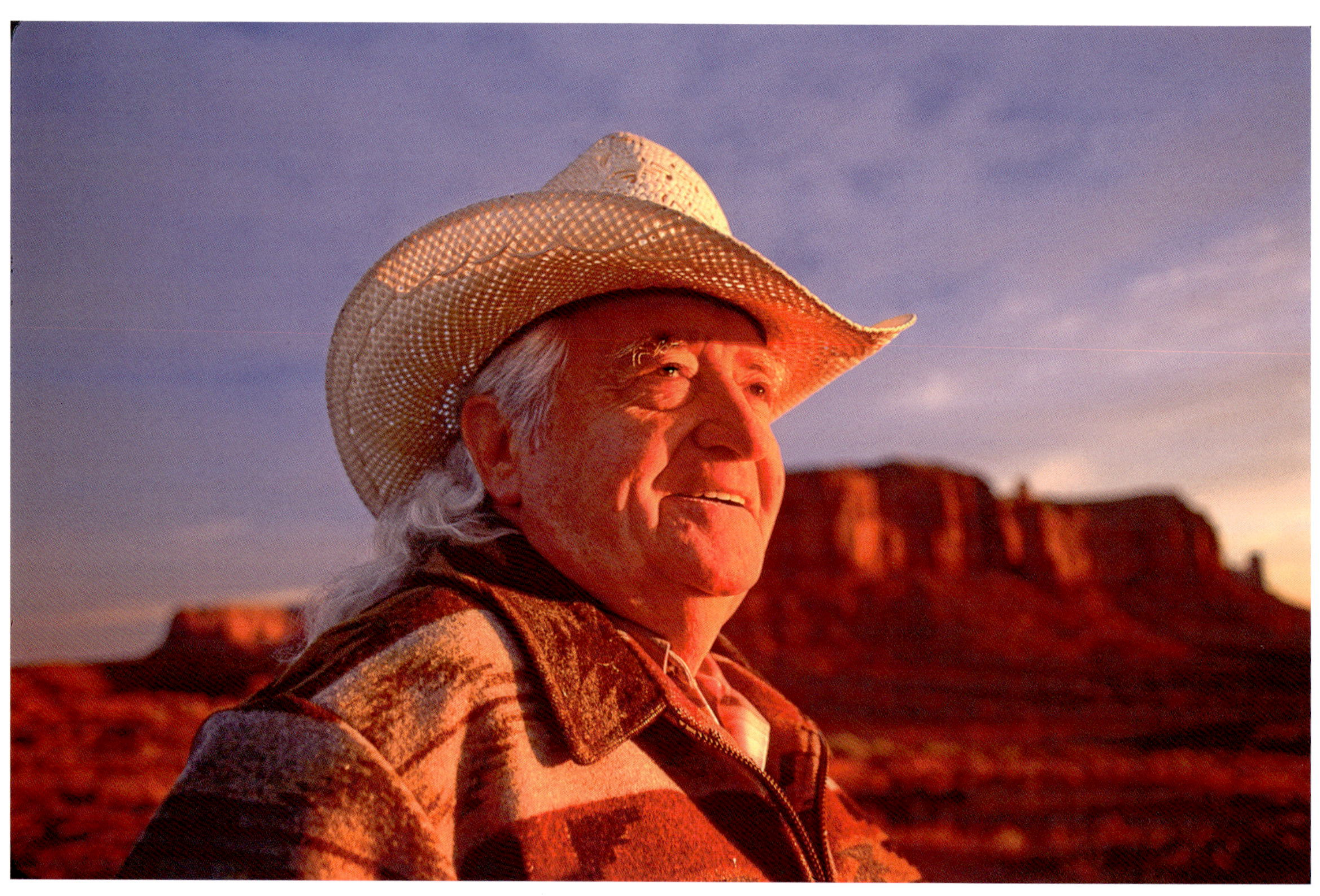

Part Osage-Arizona native, Monument Valley guide and country-western singer Bill Crawley has embraced the spirit of the place for sixty years and has known Suzie Yazzie (*right*) for nearly as long.

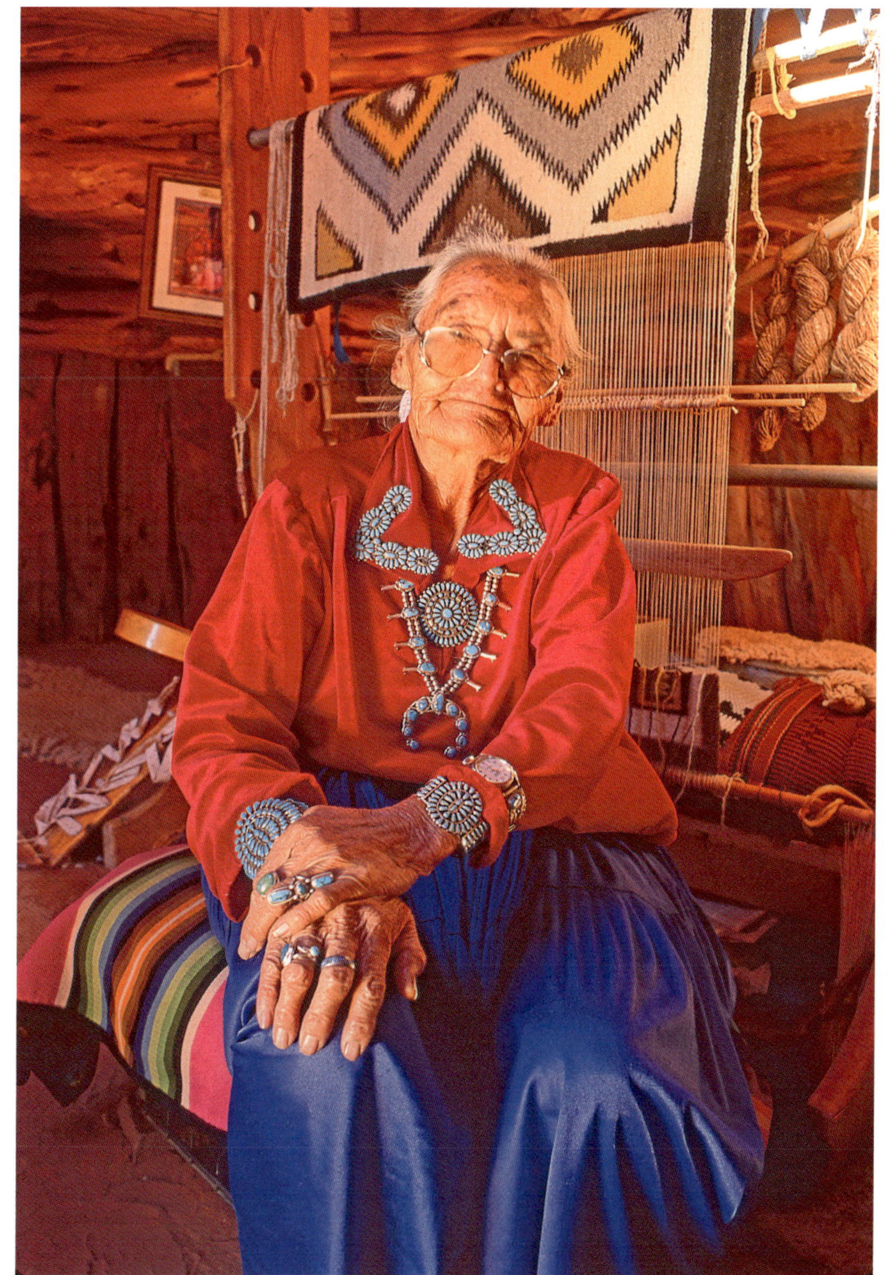

The late ninety-three-year-old Susie T. Yazzie, matriarch, Navajo weaver, and John Ford movie actress, sits next to her loom in a traditional hogan beneath Rain God Mesa, Mystery Valley, Monument Valley, Utah.

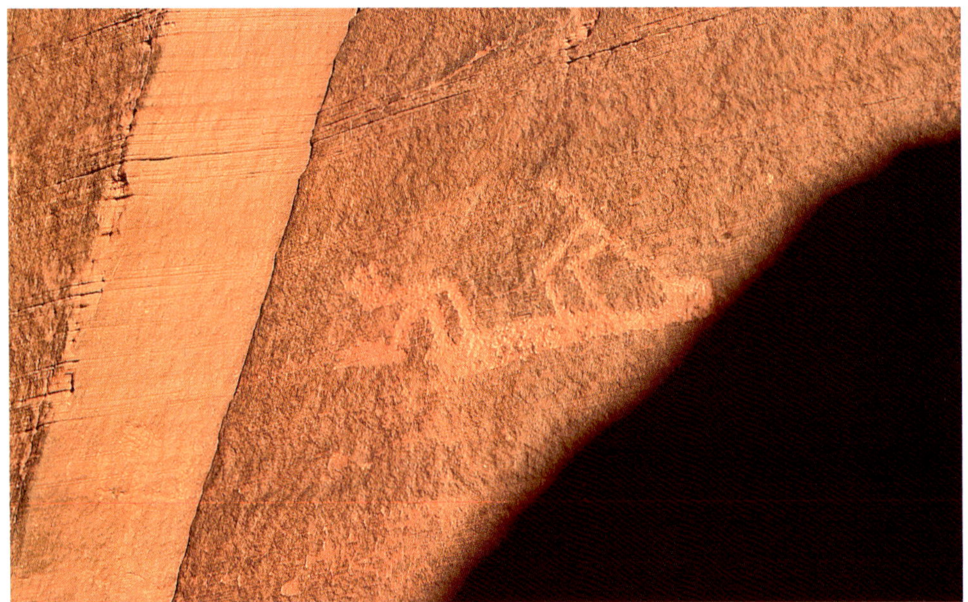

A mythic icon glimpsed throughout the Great Southwest, a Kokopelli petroglyph (humpbacked flute player) was pecked into a towering sandstone panel a millennia ago at an undisclosed location on the Colorado Plateau.

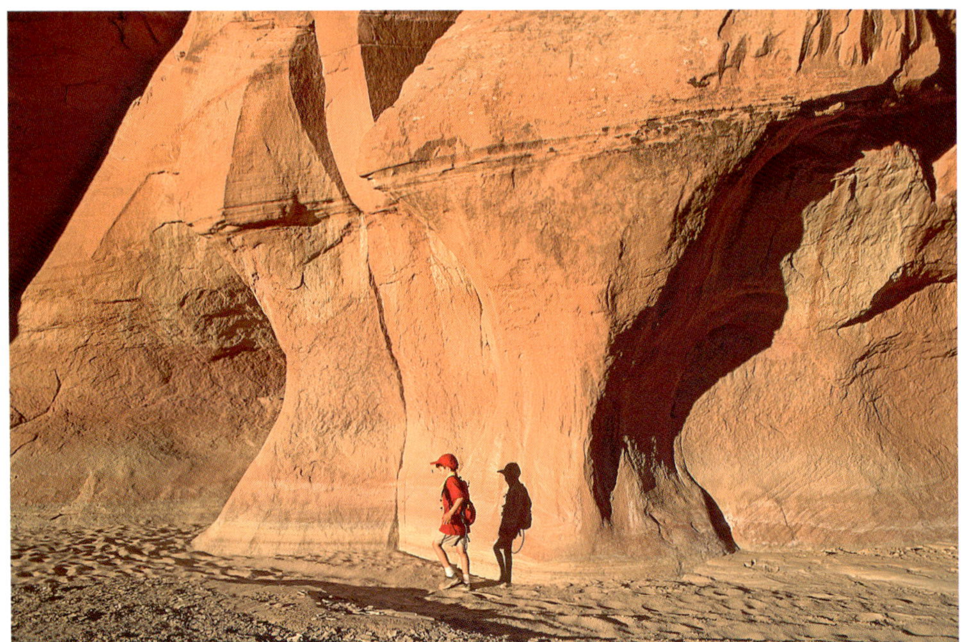

A young boy explores the headwaters of Paria Canyon–Vermilion Cliffs Wilderness, Utah. It was the same rugged country the Old Spanish Trail traversed between Santa Fé de Nuevo México and Nuestra Señora Reina de los Ángeles (Los Angeles) in 1829.

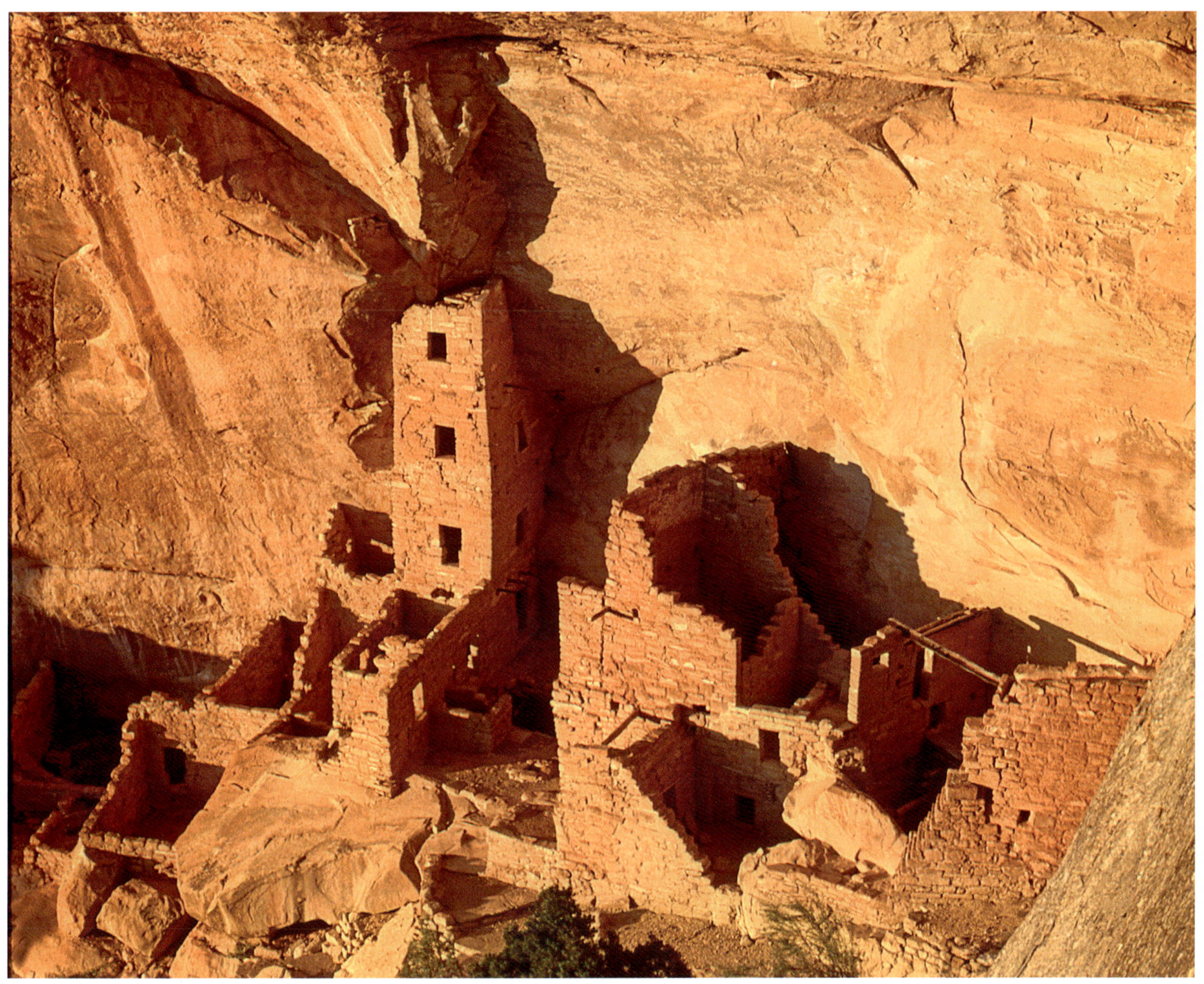

Painted gold in the setting sun of Navajo Canyon, Square Tower House is the tallest cliff dwelling in Mesa Verde National Park, Colorado. Ceremonial kivas encircle the 28-foot-high tower that was home to Ancestral Puebloans between 1204 and 1246 CE. UNESCO World Heritage Site.

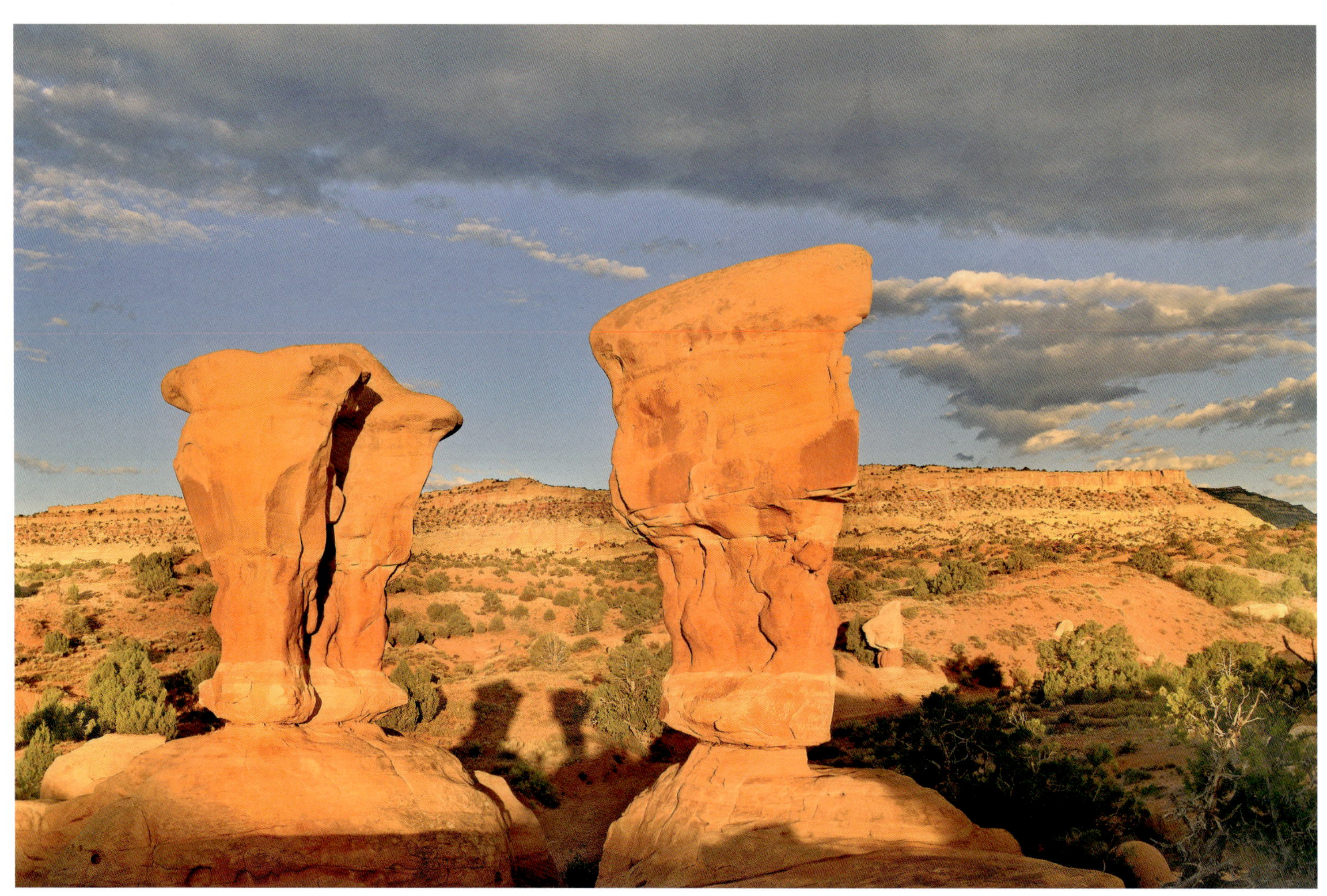

The Goblins' hoodoos, Devils Garden, Grand Staircase–Escalante National Monument, Utah

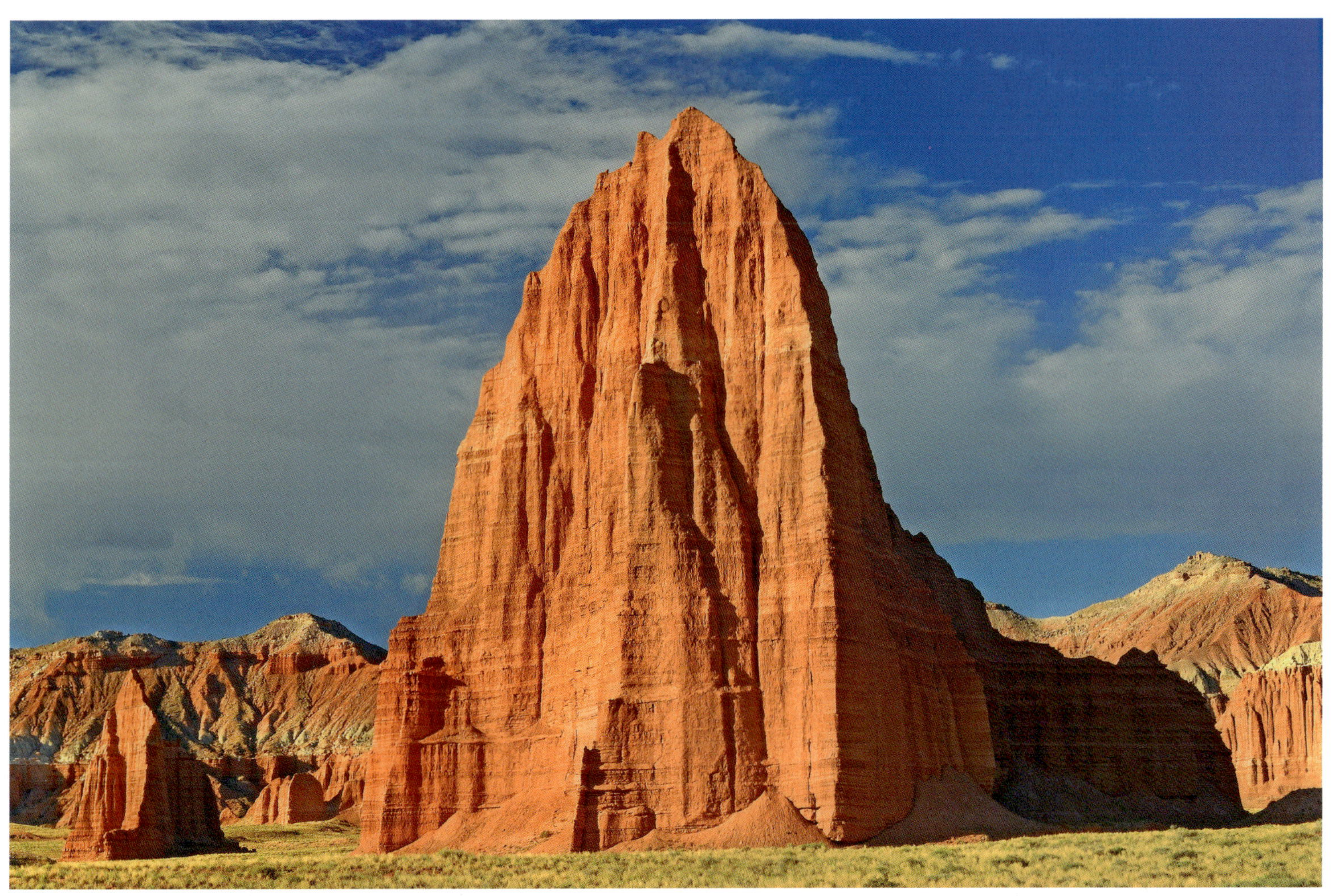

Lost in the Back of Beyond of Capitol Reef National Park, Utah, the 5,665-foot-high Temple of the Moon is one of the most remote desert landmarks in the Great Southwest.

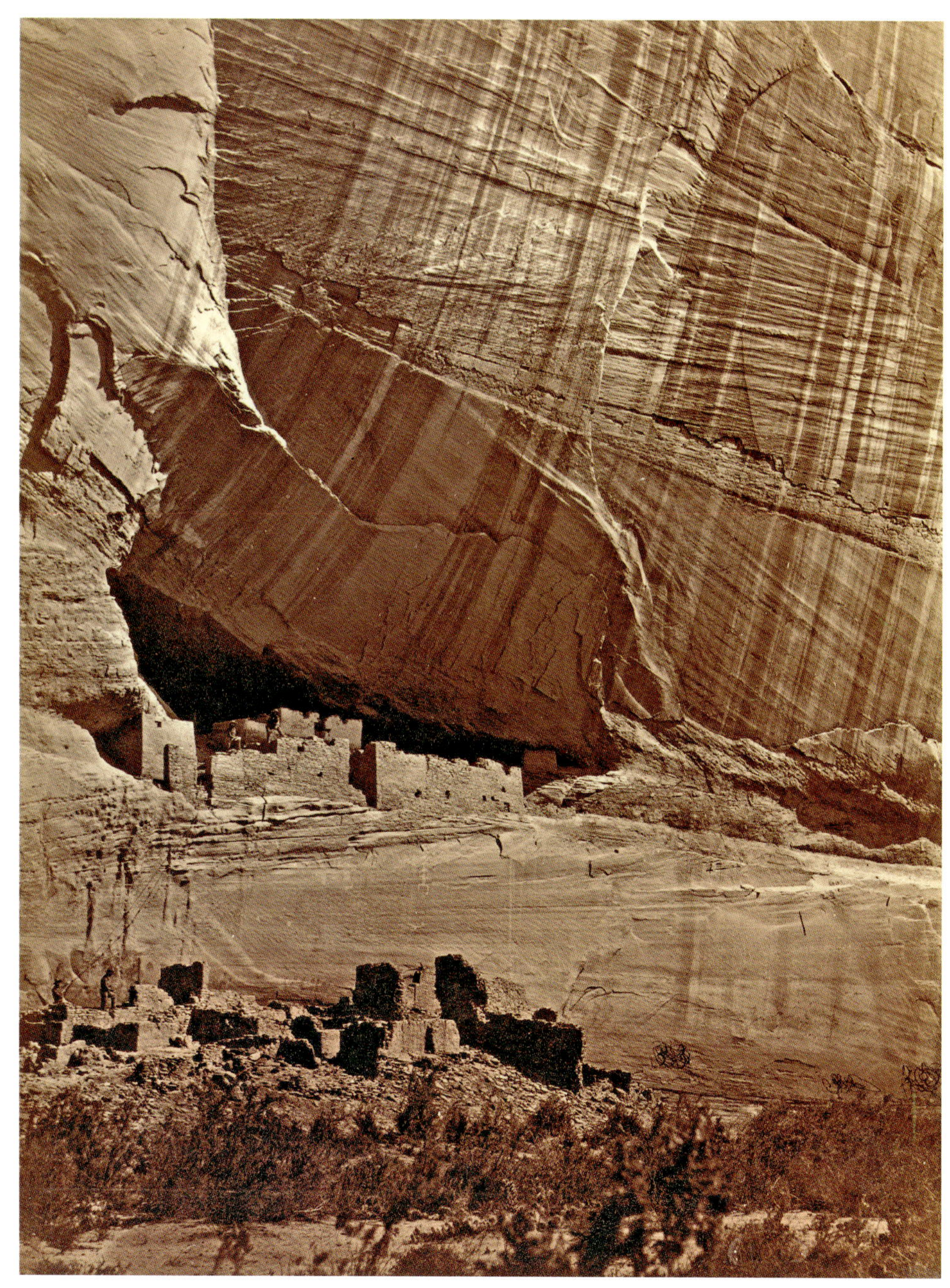

Ancient ruins in a niche 50 feet above the current Canyon de Chelly bed. Albumen print by Timothy H. O'Sullivan, 1873. *Courtesy of Library of Congress*

NOTES

CONTENTS

"With a magnificent Unknown," F. S. Dellenbaugh, "The True Route of Coronado's March," *Journal of the American Geographical Society of New York* 29, no. 4 (1897): 399.

"For many generations," Thomas Banyacya, Hopi traditional elder, "A Letter to the President of the United States of America," in T. C. McLuhan, *Touch the Earth: A Self Portrait of Indian Existence* (New York: Promontory, 1971), 170.

"My heart belongs to no one now," Gertrude Bell, *A Woman in Arabia: The Writings of the Queen of the Desert* (London: Penguin, 1907).

"No man can live this life," Wilfred Thesiger, *Arabian Sands* (London: Longmans, Green, 1959), 1.

INTRODUCTION

"There is a nakedness about the Southwest," Laura Adams Armer, *Southwest* (London and New York: Longmans, Green, 1935), viii.

"An eagle's tail," Clyde P. Ross, *The Lower Gila Region* (Washington, DC: US Government Printing Office, 1923), 192.

Despoblado, Pedro de Casteñada de Nájera, *The Journey of Coronado, 1540–1542*, ed. and trans. George Parker Winship (New York: Allerton Book, 1904), 548.

"Could be heard calling in summer," E. W. Gifford, *Northeastern and Western Yavapai*, University of California Publications in Archaeology and Ethnology 34, no. 4 (Berkeley: University of California Press, June 11, 1936): 308.

Tierra incógnita, uninhabited land, Claudius Ptolemy (Ptolemaeus), *Geographica* (Alexandria, Egypt, ca. 150 CE), https://en.wikipedia.org/wiki/Ptolemy.

El Camino del Diablo (Road of the Devil), D. D. (Capt.) Gaillard, US Corps of Engineers, "The Perils and Wonders of a True Desert," *Cosmopolitan Magazine* 21 (May–October 1896): 603.

Great Malpaís area, Connie L. Stone, *Deceptive Desolation: Prehistory of the Sonoran Desert in West Central Arizona* (Phoenix, AZ: US Bureau of Land Management, 1986), 61.

"Spirit living in the Kofa Mountains," Stone, *Deceptive Desolation*, 121.

"Links of spiritual power," Stone, *Deceptive Desolation*, 121.

"El Grand Desierto," Edwin D. McKee, *A Study of Global Sand Seas*, Geological Survey Professional Paper 1052 (Washington, DC: US Government Printing Office, 1979), 107.

"Hell of a place to lose a cow," Ebenezer Bryce (1875), in Jack Goodman, "A New Look at Old Treasures, *Utah Historical Quarterly* 26, no. 3 (July 1958): 283.

"Climbing this range is arduous work," Kirk Bryan, *The Papago Country, Arizona: A Geographic, Geologic, and Hydrologic Reconnaissance*, US Geological Survey Water-Supply Paper 499 (Washington, DC: US Government Printing Office, 1925), 221.

"Nobody's ever been up there before," Pima elder, Sierra Estrella, "Mountain of the Stars, AZ" file, John Annerino collection, n.d.

America's Outback. Over the years, the terms "America's Outback" and "Back of Beyond" were adopted by Americans from *Terra Australis* (Southern Land). It's a 529,000-square-mile sweep of desert Down Under that characterizes Australia's Outback, and the historic Birdsville Track mail delivery route across the Back of Beyond.

"The Greater Southwest extends," Erik K. Reed, "The Greater Southwest," in *Prehistoric Man in the New World*, ed. Jesse D. Jennings and Edward Norbeck (Chicago: University of Chicago Press, 1964), 175.

"For years I'd pored over the maps," Charles Bowden, *Desierto: Memories of the Future* (New York: W. W. Norton, 1991), 6.

"Not the law, but the land sets the limit," Mary Hunter Austin, *Land of Little Rain* (Boston and New York: Houghton, Mifflin, 1903), 3.

"Least inhabited, last explored region," John Annerino, "Introduction," in *Arizona Wild and Scenic* (San Mateo, CA: BrownTrout, 2012), 2.

"First and last," Mary Hunter Austin, *Lost Borders* (New York and London: Harper and Brothers, 1909), 8.

Austin, *Lost Borders*, 1.

Austin, "Little Rain," in *Land of Little Rain*, 21.

Austin, *Lost Rivers*, 6.

"*Haashch'eeh diné*," Editha L. Watson, *Navajo Sacred Places*, Series 5 (Window Rock, AZ: Navajoland, 1964), 81.

"The scenery was wild and grand," Martha Summerhayes, *Vanished Arizona: Recollections of My Army Life* (Philadelphia: J. B. Lippincott, 1908), 76–77.

"So this is where God put the West," John Wayne (1961), in Bette L. Stanton, *Where God Put the West: Moving Making in the Desert* (Moab, UT: Canyonlands Natural History Association, 1994).

"El Columpio del Diablo," Joaquin H. Jackson with David Marion Wilkinson, *One Ranger: A Memoir* (Austin: University of Texas Press, 2005), 112.

Enchanted Lands: "It is called by the natives Tierra Encantada," Robert Glasgow Dunlop, *Travels in Central America: Being a Journal of Nearly Three Years' Residence in the Country* (London: Longman, Brown, Green, and Longmans, 1847), 57.

"The whole western sky was the colour of golden ashes," Willa Cather, *Death Comes for the Archbishop* (New York: Modern Library, 1927), 92.

"A traveler scarcely knows," Howard Scott Gentry, *The Warihio Indians of Sonora-Chihuahua: An Ethnographic Survey*, Anthropological Papers 65, Smithsonian Institution Bureau of American Ethnology Bulletin 186 (Washington, DC: US Government Printing Office, 1963), 80.

"May your trails be crooked," Edward Abbey, *Desert Solitaire: A Season in the Wilderness* (New York: Ballantine Books, 1968), 12

"Quiet and strange," John Steinbeck and Edward F. Ricketts, *The Log from the Sea of Cortez* (New York:

Viking Penguin, 1941), 104.

"Had to march nearly fourteen hundred miles," B. Traven, *The Treasure of the Sierra Madre* (New York: Alfred A. Knopf, 1935), 202.

"At last I found a trail," Everett Ruess, November 11, 1934, letter to his brother Waldo, in W. L. Rusho, *Everett Ruess: A Vagabond for Beauty* (Salt Lake City, UT: Gibbs Smith, Peregrine Smith Books, 1983), 178, 179, 180.

"A wilderness is hereby recognized as an area," Wilderness Act, Public Law 88-577, 88th Congress, 2nd session, September 3, 1964, codified at U.S. Code 16 (2000), 1131–36.

"Back of Beyond," Ina Doyle, "The Mailmen Back of Beyond," The Tom Kruse Website (Adelaide, Australia: Royal Flying Doctor Service), www.lastmailfrombirdsville.com.au, accessed 2018.

I

"The long, hot days," Sharlot M. Hall, "Sheep-Herding," *Land of Sunshine* 14, no. 5 (May 1901): 363.

"It is not a jolly country," John Ross Browne, "Across the Ninety-Mile Desert," in *Adventures in the Apache Country* (New York: Harper and Brothers, 1869), 27.

"The Hollow of God's Hand," Harold Bell Wright, *The Winning of Barbara Worth* (New York: A. L. Burt, 1911), 94.

"Show a hiker a map," Bill Broyles and Michael P. Berman, *Sunshot: Peril and Wonder in the Gran Desierto* (Tucson: University of Arizona Press, Southwest Center, 2006), 133.

"El Camino del Diablo," Capt. D. D. Gaillard, US Corps of Engineers, "The Perils and Wonders of a True Desert," *Cosmopolitan: A Monthly Illustrated Magazine* 21 (May 1896–October 1896): 603.

"Hant Caai," Richard Stephen Felger and Mary Beck Moser, *People of the Desert and the Sea: Ethnobotany of the Seri Indians* (Tucson: University of Arizona Press, 1985), 39.

"With three other medicine men," Dane Coolidge and Mary Elizabeth Coolidge with Santo Blanco, *The Last of the Seris* (New York: E. P. Dutton, 1939), 93–94.

"Superhuman *xica coosyatoj* Giants," Felger and Moser, *People of the Desert and the Sea*, 10.

"There was no path," Thor Heyerdahl, *The RA Expeditions* (New York: New American Library, 1972), 53.

"Tahéöjc Imozit (Heart of Tiburn)," Felger and Moser, *People of the Desert and the Sea*, 97.

"Father of Denali National Park," Ken Burns, *The National Parks: America's Best Idea* (September 29, 2009), PBS TV / Wiki.

"The Seris assert that mule deer, rabbits, lions, coyotes, jaguars, and rattlesnakes," Charles Sheldon, "A Journey to Seriland, Sonora, 1921–1922," in *The Wilderness of the Southwest*, ed. Neil B. Carmony and David E. Brown (Salt Lake City: University of Utah Press, 1993), 172.

"The world's aquarium, " Tim Ecott, "Sea of Cortez: The World's Aquarium," *The Telegraph* (UK), July 18, 2015, www.telegraph.co.uk/travel/destinations/central-america/mexico/articles/Sea-of-Cortez-the-worlds-aquarium, accessed 2018.

"I finally reached the north peak," John W. Robinson, *Camping and Climbing in Baja* (Glendale, CA: La Siesta, 1983), 77.

"Via an old Indian trail in San Pedro Canyon," Robinson, *Camping and Climbing in Baja*, 77.

"On every side the peak dropped away," Norman Clyde, "The Conquest of Lower California's Highest Peak," *Touring Topics* 24, no. 9 (September 1932): 14–15.

"Selecting the best mules, we ascended this very high peak," Father Eusebio Francisco Kino, *Kino's Historical Memoir of Pimería Alta, 1683–1711* (Cleveland, OH: Arthur H. Clark, 1919), 205.

"Lava, ash, and sand," Ronald L. Ives, *Land of Lava, Ash, and Sand: The Pinacate Region of Northwestern Mexico* (Tucson: Arizona Historical Society, 1989), iii.

"Empty Quarter of the Sonoran Desert," Charles Bowden, "The Importance of Being Nothing, Pinacate—Empty Quarter of the Sonoran Desert," *National Parks Magazine* 63, no. 9 (September/October 1989): 26.

"If at any time I get an invitation," Ronald L. Lives, in Bill Broyles, "Loyal Loner: The Life of Ronald L. Ives, Southwest Geographer," *Journal of the Southwest* 61, no. 2 (Summer 2019): 269.

"This region is the bleakest, flattest, hottest," Edward Abbey and editors, *Cactus Country* (New York: Time-Life Books, 1972), 159.

II

"Pretty soon he would be hundreds and hundreds of miles away," Mark Twain, *Roughing It* (New York: Harper and Brothers, 1913), 1–2.

Photo quote, "On these gypsum sands is the playground of the mirage, and here it plays its greatest pranks with distance, perspective, and color," Miguel A. Otero, "Playground of the Mirage," in *Report of the Governor of New Mexico to the Secretary of the Interior* (Washington, DC: US Government Printing Office, 1903), 122. Cited in Territorial Archives of New Mexico, microfilm roll 149, frame 411, State Records Center and Archives.

Arthur Chapman, *Out Where the West Begins: And Other Western Verses* (New York: Houghton Mifflin, 1917).

"On the way Geronimo looked out," Angie Debo, *Geronimo: The Man, His Time, His Place* (Norman: University of Oklahoma Press, 1976), 262, 293.

"Land of Standing-Up Rocks," Chiricahua National Monument, Arizona, www.nps.gov/chir/learn/nature/index.htm.

"Around the camp fires of Mexico," A. Starker Leopold, *Wildlife of Mexico: The Game Birds and Mammals*, illustrated by Charles W. Schwartz (Berkeley: University of California Press, 1959), 465–66, 469, https://archive.org/details/wildlifeofmexic00leop.

"Like No Place Else on Earth," White Sands National Park, New Mexico, www.nps.gov/whsa/index.htm.

"In the desert of dead men," Cleve Hallenbeck and Juanita H. Williams, "The White Sands of La Jornada del Muerte," in *Legends of the Spanish Southwest* (Glendale, CA: Arthur H. Clark, 1938), 61, 68.

"These mountains represent the four directions of the universe," Wendell Chino, "The Sacred Mountains," *Mescalero Apache Religion and Lifestyle, 1890–1990*, April 22, 2013 (online), http://mescalerolife.blogspot.

com/2013/04/the-sacred-mountains-original.html.

"The bones seem to cut sharply," Georgia O'Keeffe, "About Myself," in *Georgia O'Keeffe: Exhibition of Oils and Pastels*, January 22–March 17, 1939 (New York: Yale University Library, 1939), 3, https://brbl-dl.library.yale.edu/vufind/Record/4212776, accessed 2018.

"It had a splendid silent terror," D. H. Lawrence, "New Mexico," in *Selected Essays* (London: Penguin Books, 1960), 180.

"Everywhere there is the evidence of Chaco," Mary Hunter Austin, *Land of Journey Ending* (New York and London: Century Company, 1924), 107.

"I had to adopt the Indian's method," Zane Grey, *Tales of Lonely Trails* (New York and London: Harper and Brothers, 1922), 6.

"I grew up with mustangs," Robert Lemmons, quoted in J. Frank Dobie, *The Mustangs* (Boston: Little, Brown, 1952): 235–36.

III

"Down in the gorge," Zane Grey, *The Lone Star Ranger* (New York, Harper & Brothers, 1914), 134, 212, 219.

"They spent their lives crossing frontiers," Carlos Fuentes, *Gringo Viejo* (México: Fondo de Cultura Económica, 1985), 5.

"Here they brought a man to me," Álvar Núñez Cabeza de Vaca, in *La relación y comentarios de governador Álvar Núñez Cabeza de Vaca* (1542), quoted in Jesse E. Thompson, MD, "Cabeza de Vaca: The First Texas Surgeon," *Baylor University Medical Center Proceedings* 8, no. 8 (1995): 4 (excerpt translated by Sally Thompson McPherson).

"And so I say that this is what befell me," Sor María de Jesús de Ágreda, May 15, 1631, in Frederick Webb Hodge, George P. Hammond, and Agapito Rey, eds. and trans., *Fray Alonso de Benavides' Revised Memorial of 1634 with Numerous Supplementary Documents Elaborately Annotated* (Albuquerque: University of New Mexico Press, 1945), 148.

"At no time in American history," Ralph A. Smith, "The Scalp Hunter in the Borderlands, 1835–1850," *Arizona and the West: A Quarterly Journal of History* 6, no. 1 (Spring 1964): 19.

"Paid by the scalp," Colonel Richard Irving Dodge, *Our Wild Indians: Thirty-three Years' Personal Experience among the Red Men of the Great West; A Popular Account of Their Social Life, Religion, Habits, Traits, Customs, Exploits, etc. with Thrilling Adventures and Experiences on the Great Plains and in the Mountains of Our Wide Frontier* (Hartford, CT: A. D. Worthington, 1888), 245.

"He attacked one end of this camp," Dodge, *Our Wild Indians*, 245.

"One of the most remote places on Earth," Mexico Less Traveled, http://mexicolesstraveled.com/sierradelcarmen.htm, accessed August 20, 2020.

"The small high peak," Dr. Ross A. Maxwell, regional geologist, "The Big Bend of Texas," *Regional III Quarterly* 3, no. 1 (January 1941): 1, http://npshistory.com/newsletters/region_iii_quarterly/vol3-1d.htm.

"If you hear of my being stood up against a Mexican stone wall," Ambrose Bierce, *The Letters of Ambrose Bierce* (San Francisco: Book Club of California, 1922), 196–97.

IV

"In beauty (happily) I walk," Washington Matthews, *The Night Chant: A Navaho Ceremony* (New York: Knickerbocker, 1902), 145.

"When Lololomai, the chief, prays," Natalie Curtis Burlin, *The Indians' Book: An Offering by the American Indians* (New York and London: Harper and Brothers, 1907), 494.

"He goes to the edge of the cliff," Burlin, *The Indians' Book*, 494.

"It was the Indian manner to vanish into the landscape," Cather, *Death Comes for the Archbishop*, 235.

"Old paths worn into the rock," Laurance D. Linford, *Navajo Places: History, Legend, Landscape* (Salt Lake City: University of Utah Press, 2000), 47.

"There is a marvel in the air," Charles F. Lummis, "The Swallow's-Nest People," *Out West: A Magazine of the Old Pacific and the New* 26, no. 6 (June 1907): 503.

"The strange shadowy figures of the Holy People," Watson, *Navajo Sacred Places*, 5.

"According to the myths," Matthews, *The Night Chant*, 90.

"In the house made of the dawn," Matthews, *The Night Chant*, 143.

"Western as a genre of films," *The Searchers*, release date May 26, 1956, AFI's 10 TOP 10, American Film Institute, 2016, Los Angeles, http://afi.com/10top10.

"My first sight of Monument Valley," Zane Grey, *Tales of Lonely Trails*, 4–5.

"Holy People who turned to stone," Watson, *Navajo Sacred Places*, 81.

"Two hundred and eighty miles," A. H. Thompson, "Report on a Trip to the Mouth of the Dirty Devil River," in J. W. Powell, *Exploration of the Colorado River of the West and Its Tributaries: Explored in 1869, 1870, 1871, and 1872* (Washington, DC: US Government Printing Office, 1875), 145.

"This extraordinary locality," Frederick Samuel Dellenbaugh, *A Canyon Voyage: The Narrative of the Second Powell Expedition down the Green-Colorado River from Wyoming, and the Explorations on Land, in the Years 1871 and 1872* (New York and London: Knickerbocker, 1908), 115–16.

"A Wonderland of Crags and Pinnacles," Dellenbaugh, *A Canyon Voyage*, 115.

"We cross and recross the stream," Powell, *Exploration of the Colorado River of the West and Its Tributaries*, 109–10.

"If E. F. Harriman paid me," Butch Cassidy, in Rowland E. Robinson, "An Ancestral Gun," *Sportsman Tourist: A Weekly Journal of Rod and Gun* 52 (March 5, 1900), 342.

The Hopi *katsina* (spirit being) Kókopilau has also been recognized as a deity of fertility, messenger from sacred springs, and a flute-playing ancient trader. The unmistakable symbol has been found on broken pottery shards in the Great House mounds of Chaco Canyon; the ruins of Aztec, New Mexico; and south along Chaco Meridian to Paquimé, Casas Grande, Chihuahua. In 1921 archeologists unearthed clay vessels at Paquimé of effigies that bore "on their backs distinct humps which suggest the humpbacked erotic figure of Kokopelli." Some scholars profess that Kokopelli may have derived from Nahualt (Aztec) long-distance traveling merchants, *pochteca* (*pochtecatl*), who journeyed from Mesoamerica's Valley of Mexico to Paquimé and "crossed the vast deserts and mountains of the north in search of raw materials, especially turquoise."

Author's note: Not long after I first returned from Canyon de Chelly, I discovered I was not the only photographer to make a pilgrimage to this hallowed shrine. I knew little about them and started digging. In 1904, Edward S. Curtis photographed "Yebichai War Gods" Tonenili, Tobadzischini, and Nayenezgani in a gelatin silver print, who appeared to be in Canyon de Chelly. Many other pioneer western photographers explored Canyon de Chelly and Cañon del Muerto in search of cliff dwellings, led by Navajo guides George and Charlie. White House was the most sought-after ruin because Lieutenant James H. Simpson of the Corps of Topographical Engineers first drew attention to Casa Blanca (White House) in Canyon de Chelly in 1849. Among the photographers who followed Simpson's lead were Timothy H. O'Sullivan, who described his albumen silver print in 1873 as the "Ancient Ruins in the Cañon de Chelle, Arizona"; William Henry Jackson, who described his albumen silver print in 1877 as a "Ruined Cave Town on the Rio de Chelly, Arizona"; John K. Hillers, who described his albumen silver print ca. in 1879 as the "Ruins of Cliff Dwellings, Canon de Chelley"; and Ben Wittick, who described his albumen silver print on October 17, 1882, as the "Ruins of Ancient Cliff Town, Aztec Ruins [*sic*], Canyon de Chelly, White House Cave, Arizona."

BIBLIOGRAPHY

Abbey, Edward. *Desert Solitaire: A Season in the Wilderness*. New York: Ballantine Books, 1968.

Abbey, Edward, and editors. *Cactus Country*. The American Wilderness. New York: Time-Life Books, 1972.

Abbey, Edward, and Philip Hyde. *Slickrock: Endangered Canyons of the Southwest*. New York: Sierra Club Books and Charles Scribner's Sons, 1971.

Abbott, E. C. ("Teddy Blue"), Helena Huntington Smith, and Ross Santee. *We Pointed Them North: Recollections of a Cow Puncher*. New York: Farrar and Rinehart, 1939.

Ágreda, Sor María de Jesús de. *Mística ciudad de Dios y biografía de su autora V*. Barcelona: Heredos de Juan Gil Editores, 1914.

Annerino, John. "Exposiciones remotas: La historia detrás de la fotografía" ("Remote exposures: The story behind the photographs"). *México Desconocido* ("Unknown Mexico") 398 (April 2016).

———. *In the Chasms of Water, Stone, and Light: Passages through the Grand Canyon*. Atglen, PA: Schiffer, 2019.

———. *Indian Country: Sacred Ground, Native Peoples*. New York: W. W. Norton, 2007.

——— "Introduction." In *Arizona Wild and Scenic Calendar*. San Mateo, CA: BrownTrout, 2012.

———. *Roughstock: The Toughest Events in Rodeo*. New York and London: Four Walls, Eight Windows, 2000.

———. Sierra Estrella. Mountain of the Stars, AZ, file, John Annerino Collection, n.d., accessed 2020.

———. *The Virgin of Guadalupe: Art and Legend*. Layton, UT: Gibbs Smith, 2012.

———. "10.01.05, 6:10 PM, Monument Valley: Between Myth and Mystery: A Cowboy Guide and a Navajo Elder Weave the Threads of Monument Valley." In *Special Issue: Once upon a Day in Arizona: 50 Writers and Photographers, Every Corner of the State*. Edited by Peter Aleshire. *Arizona Highways Magazine* 82, no. 10 (October 2006).

Armer, Laura Adams. *Southwest*. London and New York: Longmans, Green, 1935.

"Atención Gringo. For Gold & Glory, Come South of the Border . . ." Chihuahua, Mexico, Francisco "Pancho" Villa recruitment poster, January 1915.

Austin, Mary Hunter. *The Land of Journey's Ending*. New York and London: Century, 1924.

———. *Land of Little Rain*. Boston and New York: Houghton, Mifflin, 1903.

———. *Lost Borders*. New York and London: Harper and Brothers, 1909.

Banyacya, Thomas, Hopi traditional elder. "A Letter to the President of the United States of America." In *Touch the Earth: A Self Portrait of Indian Existence*. By T. C. McLuhan. New York: Promontory, 1971.

Bell, Gertrude. *A Woman in Arabia: The Writings of the Queen of the Desert*. London: Penguin, 1907.

Bickford, F. T. "Prehistoric Cave-Dwellings." *Century Illustrated Monthly Magazine* 40, no. 6 (October 1890).

Bierce, Ambrose. *The Letters of Ambrose Bierce*. Edited by Bertha Clarke Pope. Memoir by George Sterling. San Francisco: Book Club of California, 1922.

Bloom, Lansing B. "A Campaign against the Moqui Pueblos [Arizona] under Governor Félix Martínez, 1716."

Annotated by Ralph E. Twitchell. *New Mexico Historical Review* 6, no. 2 (April 1931).

Bolton, Herbert Eugene. *Spanish Exploration in the Southwest: 1542–1706.* New York: Charles Scribner's Sons, 1916.

Bourke, John G. "Popular Medicine, Customs, and Superstitions of the Rio Grande." *Journal of American Folklore* 7, no. 25 (1894): 119–146.

Bowden, Charles. *Desierto: Memories of the Future.* New York: W. W. Norton, 1991.

———. "The Importance of Being Nothing, Pinacate—Empty Quarter of the Sonoran Desert." *National Parks Magazine* 63, no. 9 (September/October 1989).

Brandes, Ray, and Ralph A. Smith, with Don Bufkin. "The Scalp Business on the Border, 1837–1850: Accounts of the 'Hair-Raising' Exploits of Two of History's Bloodiest Barbers, Kirker and Glanton." *Smoke Signal* 6: *Tucson Westerners* (Fall 1962).

Brown, David E., and Carlos A. López González. *Borderland Jaguars / Tigres de la Frontera*. Salt Lake City: University of Utah Press, 2001.

Browne, J. Ross. "Across the Ninety-Mile Desert." In *Adventures in the Apache Country: A Tour through Arizona and Sonora. with Notes on the Silver Regions of Nevada*. New York: Harper and Brothers, 1869.

Broyles, Bill. "Loyal Loner: The Life of Ronald L. Ives, Southwest Geographer." *Journal of the Southwest* 61, no. 2 (Summer 2019): 223–435.

Broyles, Bill, and Michael P. Berman. *Sunshot: Peril and Wonder in the Gran Desierto*. Tucson: University of Arizona Press, Southwest Center, 2006.

Broyles, Bill, Luke Evans, Richard S. Felger, et al. "Our Grand Desert: A Gazetteer for Northwestern Sonora, Southwestern Arizona, and Northeastern Baja California." *Dry Borders: Journal of the Southwest* 39, nos. 3–4 (Autumn/Winter, 1997.

Bryan, Kirk. *The Papago Country, Arizona: A Geographic, Geologic, and Hydrologic Reconnaissance, with a Guide to Desert Watering Places.* US Geological Survey Water-Supply Paper 499. Washington, DC: US Government Printing Office, 1925.

Bryce, Ebenezer (1875). In "A New Look at Old Treasures," by Jack Goodman. *Utah Historical Quarterly* 26, no. 3 (July 1958).

Burdick, Arthur J. *The Mystic Mid-Region: The Deserts of the Southwest*. New York: G. P. Putnam's Sons, 1904.

Burlin, Natalie Curtis, comp. and ed. *The Indians' Book: An Offering by the American Indians of Indian Lore, Musical and Narrative, to Form a Record of the Songs and Legends of Their Race*. Illustrations from photographs and from original drawings by Indians. New York and London: Harper and Brothers, 1907.

Burns, Ken. *The National Parks: America's Best Idea*. PBS TV / Wiki, September 29, 2009.

Burrus, Ernest J. *Wenceslaus Linck's Diary of His 1766 Expedition to Northern Baja*. Los Angeles: Dawson's Book Shop, 1966.

Cabeza de Vaca, Álvar Núñez. *La relación de Álvar Núñez Cabeza de Vaca*. Zamora, Spain: Augustin de Paz y Juan Picardo, 1542.

Cabeza de Vaca, Álvar Núñez (1542). Excerpt from *La relación de Álvar Núñez Cabeza de Vaca*. Cited in "Cabeza de Vaca: The First Texas Surgeon," by Jesse E. Thompson, MD. *Baylor University Medical Center Proceedings* 8, no. 8 (1995). Excerpt translated by Sally Thompson McPherson.

Carmony, Neil B., and David E. Brown, eds. *Tales of Tiburon: An Anthology of Adventures in Seriland*. Phoenix, AZ: Southwestern Natural History Association, 1983.

Cather, Willa. *Death Comes for the Archbishop*. New York: Modern Library, 1927.

Chapman, Arthur. *Out Where the West Begins: And Other Western Verses*. New York: Houghton Mifflin, 1917.

Charles, Mrs. Tom "Bula." *Tales of the Tularosa*. Alamogordo, NM: Mrs. Tom Charles, 1953.

Chatwin, Bruce. *The Songlines*. New York: Penguin Books, 1987.

Childs, Thomas. "History from an Old-Timer: Letters, Comments of Desert Readers." *Desert Magazine* 12, no. 12 (October 1949).

Childs, Thomas, as written to Henry F. Dobyns. "Sketch of the Sand Indians." *The Kiva* 19, nos. 2–4 (Spring 1954).

Chino, Wendell. "The Sacred Mountains." *Mescalero Apache Religion and Lifestyle, 1890–1990*. http://mescalerolife.blogspot.com, April 22, 2013.

Clyde, Norman. "The Conquest of Lower California's Highest Peak." *Touring Topics, Magazine of the Auto Club Southern California* 24, no. 9 (September 1932).

Coolidge, Dane, and Mary Elizabeth Coolidge, with Santo Blanco. *The Last of the Seris*. New York: E. P. Dutton, 1939.

Crampton, C. Gregory. *Standing Up Country: The Canyon Lands of Utah and Arizona*. Salt Lake City: University of Utah Press in association with the Amon Carter Museum of Western Art, 1964.

Cremony, John C. *Life among the Apaches*. San Francisco and New York: A. Roman, 1868.

Cudahy, John. *Mañanaland: Adventuring with Camera and Rifle through California in Mexico*. New York: Duffield, 1928.

Curtis, Edward S. *The North American Indian: Being a Series of Volumes Picturing and Describing the Indians of United States and Alaska*. 20 vols. Cambridge, MA: Harvard University Press, 1907–1930.

Daniels, George G. *The Spanish West*. The Old West. Alexandria, VA: Time-Life Books, 1976.

Debo, Angie. *Geronimo: The Man, His Time, His Place*. Norman: University of Oklahoma Press, 1976.

DeGrazia, Ted, with William Neil Smith. *The Seri Indians: A Primitive People of Tiburón Island in the Gulf of California*. Flagstaff, AZ: Northland, 1970.

Dellenbaugh, Frederick Samuel. *A Canyon Voyage: The Narrative of the Second Powell Expedition down the Green-Colorado River from Wyoming, and the Explorations on Land, in the Years 1871 and 1872*. New York and London: Knickerbocker, 1908.

———. "True Route of Coronado's March." *Journal of the American Geographical Society of New York* 29, no. 4 (1897).

Dobie, J. Frank. *The Mustangs*. Boston: Little, Brown, 1952.

———. *Guide to Life and Literature of the Southwest, with a Few Observations*. Austin: University of Texas Press, 1943.

Dodge, Colonel Richard Irving. *Our Wild Indians: Thirty-Three Years' Personal Experience among the Red Men of the Great West; A Popular Account of Their Social

Life, Religion, Habits, Traits, Customs, Exploits, etc. with Thrilling Adventures and Experiences on the Great Plains and in the Mountains of Our Wide Frontier. Hartford, CT: A. D. Worthington, 1888.

Domenech, Abbe Emanuel. *Seven Years Residence in the Great Deserts of North America*. 2 vols. London: Longman, Green, Longman, and Roberts, 1860.

Doyle, Ian. "The Mailmen Back of Beyond." *Last Mail from Birdsville . . . The Story of Tom Kruse*. The Tom Kruse Website, Royal Flying Doctor Service. www.lastmailfrombirdsville.com.au, retrieved 2018.

Dunlap, Robert Glasgow. *Travels in Central America: Being a Journal of Nearly Three Years' Residence in the Country*. London: Longman, Brown, Green, and Longmans, 1847.

Dutton, Clarence E. *Report on the Geology of the High Plateaus of Utah, with Atlas*. US Geographical and Geological Survey of the Rocky Mountain Region, J. W. Powell in charge. Washington, DC: US Government Printing Office, 1880.

Ecott, Tim. "Sea of Cortez: The World's Aquarium." *The Telegraph* (UK), July 18, 2015. www.telegraph.co.uk, retrieved 2018.

Emery, William H. *Notes of a Military Reconnaissance, from Fort Leavenworth, in Missouri, to San Diego, in California, including Part of the Arkansas, Del Norte, and Gila Rivers*. 39th Congress, 1st Session. Ex. Doc. No. 41. Washington, DC: Wendell and Van Benthuysen, 1848.

———. *Report on the United States and Mexico Boundary Survey*. Vol. 1. 34th Congress, 1st Session, House of Representatives. Ex. Doc. No. 135. Washington, DC: Cornelius Wendell, 1857.

Felger, Richard Stephen, and Mary Beck Moser. *People of the Desert and the Sea: Ethnobotany of the Seri Indians*. Tucson: University of Arizona Press, 1985.

Fergusson, Erna. *Dancing Gods: Indian Ceremonials of New Mexico and Arizona*. New York: Alfred A. Knopf, 1931.

Fewkes, Jesse Walter. *Antiquities of the Mesa Verde National Park, Cliff Palace*. Washington, DC: US Government Printing Office, 1911.

Fuentes, Carlos. *Gringo Viejo, México: Fondo de cultura económica* / *The Old Gringo: A Novel*. New York: Farrar, Straus, and Giroux, 1985.

Gaillard, Capt. D. D., US Corps of Engineers. "The Perils and Wonders of a True Desert." *Cosmopolitan: A Monthly Illustrated Magazine* 21 (May 1896–October 1896): 603.

Gannett, Henry. *A Gazetteer of Utah*. Geological Survey Bulletin 166. Washington, DC: US Government Printing Office, 1900.

Geronimo (or Goyaklah, "one who yawns"). *Geronimo: His Own Story: The Autobiography of Great Patriot Warrior, as Told to S. M. Barrett*. Edited by Frederick Turner. New York: Meridian, 1970. Originally published as *Geronimo's Story of His Life* (New York: Duffield, 1906).

Gifford, E. W. *Northeastern and Western Yavapai*. University of California Publications in Archaeology and Ethnology 34, no. 4. Berkeley: University of California Press, June 11, 1936.

Goodman, Jack. "A New Look at Old Treasures." *Utah Historical Quarterly* 26, no. 3 (July 1958).

Grant, Ulysses S. "Chiricahua Indian Reservation, Executive Mansion, December 14, 1872." Executive Orders Relating to Indian Reservations: from May 14, 1855 to July 1, 1912. Washington, DC: US Government Printing Office, 1912.

Gregory, Herbert E. *Geology and Geography of the Zion Park Region Utah and Arizona: A Comprehensive Report on a Scenic and Historic Region of the Southwest*. Geological Survey Professional Paper 220. Washington, DC: US Government Printing Office, 1950.

Gregory, Herbert E., and J. C. Anderson. "Geographic and Geologic Sketch of the Capitol Reef Region of Utah." *Bulletin of the Geological Society of America* 50 (December 1939): 1827–50.

Gregory, Herbert E., and Robert C. Moore. *The Kaiparowits Region: A Geographic and Geologic Reconnaissance of Utah and Arizona*. US Department of the Interior Professional Paper 164. Washington, DC: US Government Printing Office, 1931.

Grey, Zane. *The Lone Star Ranger*. New York, Harper & Brothers, 1914.

———. *Tales of Lonely Trails*. New York and London: Harper and Brothers, 1922.

Griffen, William B. *Notes on the Seri Indian Culture, Sonora, Mexico*. School of Inter-America Studies, Latin American Monographs 10. Gainesville: University of Florida Press, 1959.

Grindell, Edward P., and Jack Hoffman. "The Lost Explorers: The Mystery of a Vanished Expedition." *Wide World Magazine: An Illustrated Monthly of True Narrative, Adventure, Travel, Customs, and Sport* 19, no. 112 (April 1907).

Haley, J. Evetts, and Harold Bugbee. *Charles Goodnight: Cowman and Plainsman*. Boston and New York: Houghton, Mifflin, 1936.

———. *Jeff Milton: A Good Man with a Gun*. Norman: University of Oklahoma Press, 1948.

Hall, Sharlot M. "Sheep-Herding." *Land of Sunshine* 14, no. 5 (May 1901), cover.

Hallenbeck, Cleve. *Álvar Núñez Cabeza de Vaca: The Journey and Route of the First European to Cross the Continent of North America, 1530–1536*. Glendale, CA: Arthur H. Clark, 1940.

Hallenbeck, Cleve, and Juanita H. Williams. "The White Sands of La Jornada del Muerte." In *Legends of the Spanish Southwest*. Glendale, CA: Arthur H. Clark, 1938.

Hardman, Peggy. "Lemmons, Bob." In *Handbook of Texas Online*. www.tshaonline.org/handbook/online/articles/fle72, accessed 2018.

Hayden, Julian D. "Seri Indians on Tiburon Island," *Arizona Highways Magazine* 18, no. 1 (January 1942).

———. *The Sierra Pinacate*. Essays by Charles Bowden and Bernard L. Fontana. Tucson: University of Arizona Press, Southwest Center, 1998.

Heyerdahl, Thor. *The RA Expeditions*. Translated by Patricia Crampton. New York: New American Library, 1972.

Hieb, Louis A. "'The Flavor of Adventure Now Rare': H. C. Rizer's Account of James Stevenson's 1882 Bureau of Ethnology Expedition to Canyon de Chelly." *Journal of Arizona History* 46, no. 3 (2005): 205–48. www.jstor.org/stable/41696914.

Hodge, Frederick Webb, George P. Hammond, and Agapito Rey, eds and trans. *Fray Alonso de Benavides' Revised Memorial of 1634 with Numerous Supplementary Documents Elaborately Annotated*. Albuquerque: University of New Mexico Press, 1945.

Horgan, Paul. *Great River: The Rio Grande in North American History*. 2 vols. New York: Rinehart, 1954.

Hornaday, William T. *Camp-Fires on Desert and Lava*. New York: Charles Scribner's Sons, 1909.

Howell, Georgina. *Gertrude Bell: Queen of the Desert*. New York: Farrar, Straus, and Giroux, 2007.

Ives, Ronald L. "Excursionando en los Pinacates." *La Montaña*, April 1934: 11–12.

———. "The Legend of the "White Queen" of the Seri." *Western Folklore* 1, no 3 (July 1962).

Ives, Ronald L., Don Bufkin, James W. Byrkit, and Karen J. Dahood. *Land of Lava, Ash, and Sand: The Pinacate Region of Northwestern Mexico*. Tucson: Arizona Historical Society, 1989.

Jackson, H. Joaquin, and David Marion Wilkinson. *One Ranger: A Memoir*. Austin: University of Texas Press, 2005.

Jaeger, Edmund C. *The North American Deserts*. Stanford, CA: Stanford University Press, 1957.

James, George Wharton. *The Wonders of the Colorado Desert (Southern California): Its Rivers and Its Mountains, Its Canyons and Its Springs, Its Life and Its History, Pictured and Described*. Boston: Little, Brown, 1906.

Janvier, Thomas Allibone. "'Legend of La Llorona' by Gilberto Cano." In *Legends of the City of Mexico*. New York and London: Harper and Brothers, 1910.

Johnson, Boma. "Earth Figures of the Lower Colorado and Gila River Deserts: A Function Analysis." *Arizona Archaeologist* 20 (December 1986).

Kendell, George Wilkins. *Narrative of the Texan Santa Fé Expedition: Comprising a Description of a Tour through Texas, and across the Great Southwestern Prairies, the Camanche and Caygüa Hunting-Grounds, with an Account of the Sufferings from Want of Food, Losses from Hostile Indians, and Finale Capture of the Texans, and Their March, as Prisoners, to the City of Mexico*. Vol. 2. New York: Harper and Brothers, 1847.

Kidder, Alfred V. "The Pottery of the Casas Grandes District, Chihuahua." In *Holmes Anniversary Volume: Anthropological Essays Presented to William Henry Holmes in Honor of His Seventieth Birthday, December 1, 1916*. Edited by Allison V. Amour, 253–68. Washington, DC: J. W. Bryan, 1916.

King, Clarence, geologist in charge. *United States Geological Exploration of the Fortieth Parallel / U.S. Army Corps. of Engineers*. Photographed by T. H. O'Sullivan. Washington, DC: US Government Printing Office, 1872.

Kino, Father Eusebio Francisco. *Kino's Historical Memoir of Pimería Alta: A Contemporary Account of the Beginnings of California, Sonora, and Arizona, 1683–1711*. Edited and translated by Herbert Eugene Bolton. Cleveland, OH: Arthur H. Clark, 1919.

Klah, Hasteen. *Navajo Creation Myth: The Story of Emergence*. Recorded by Mary C. Wheelwright. Navajo Religion Series 1. Santa Fe, NM: Museum of Ceremonial Art, 1942.

Klauber, Laurence M. *Rattlesnakes: Their Habits, Life Histories, and Influence on Mankind*. Berkeley: University of California Press, 1984.

Kluckhorn, Clyde M. *Navaho Witchcraft*. Papers of the Peabody Museum of American Archaeology and Ethnology 22, no. 2. Cambridge, MA: Harvard University, 1944.

Knipmeyer, James H. *Butch Cassidy Was Here: Historic Inscriptions of the Colorado Plateau*. Salt Lake City: University of Utah Press, 2002.

Lacy, Hugh. "Say I Kept My Dream!" *Desert Magazine* 1 (September 1938).

Laird, Carobeth, and George Laird. *The Chemehuevis*. Banning, CA: Malki Museum Press, 1976.

"Land of Standing-Up Rocks." Chiricahua National Monument, Arizona. www.nps.gov/chir/learn/nature/index.htm.

Lawrence, D. H. "New Mexico." In *Selected Essays*. London: Penguin Books, 1960.

"Legend of Pavla Blanca." www.nps.gov/whsa/planyourvisit/upload/pavla_blanca_final_4_17_11.pdf, retrieved 2018.

Leopold, A. Starker. *Wildlife of Mexico: The Game Birds and Mammals*. Illustrated by Charles W. Schwartz. Berkeley: University of California Press, 1959.

"Like No Place Else on Earth." White Sands National Park, New Mexico. www.nps.gov/whsa/index.htm.

Linford, Laurance D. *Navajo Places: History, Legend, Landscape*. Salt Lake City: University of Utah Press, 2000.

Lowell, E. S. "A Comparison of Mexican and Seri Indian Versions of the Legend of Lola Cassanova." *The Kiva* 35, no. 4 (Summer 1970).

Lumholtz, Carl. *New Trails in Mexico: An Account of One Year's Exploration in Northwestern Sonora, Mexico, and South-western Arizona, 1909–1910*. New York: Charles Scribner's Sons, 1912.

Lummis, Charles F. "The Swallow's-Nest People." *Out West: A Magazine of the Old Pacific and the New* 26, no. 6 (June 1907).

Macomb, J. N. *Report of the Exploring Expedition from Sante Fé, New Mexico, to the Junction of the Grand and Green Rivers of the Great Colorado of the West, in 1859, under the Command of Capt. J. N. Macomb; with a Geological Report by Prof. J. S. Newberry*. Washington, DC: US Government Printing Office, 1876.

Mangum, Neil C. *In the Land of Frozen Fires: A History of Occupation in El Malpais Country*. Southwest Regional Office Division of History, Professional Papers 32. Santa Fe, NM: Southwest Cultural Resources Center, 1990.

Manje, Captain Juan Mateo. *Luz de Tierra Incógnita, Unknown Arizona and Sonora, 1693–1701, from the Francisco Fernández del Castillo Version of Luz de Tierra Incógnita*. Edited and translated by Harry J. Karns. Tucson, AZ: Arizona Silhouettes, 1954.

Matthews, Washington. *The Night Chant: A Navaho Ceremony*. New York: Knickerbocker, 1902.

Matthews, Washington, and John K. Hillers. *Navaho Legends, with Introduction, Notes, Illustrations, Texts, Interlinear Translations, and Melodies*. Boston, New York, and London: Houghton, Mifflin, 1897.

Maxwell, Ross A., regional geologist. "The Big Bend of

Texas." *Regional III Quarterly* 3, no. 1 (January, 1941). http://npshistory.com/newsletters/region_iii_quarterly/vol3-1d.htm.

McGee, W. J. "The Wildest Tribe in North America, Seriland and the Seri." *Land of Sunshine* 14, no. 5 (May 1901).

McKee, Edwin D. *A Study of Global Sand Seas*. Geological Survey Professional Paper 1052, prepared in cooperation with the National Aeronautics and Space Administration. Washington, DC: US Government Printing Office, 1979.

McPherson, Robert S. *Sacred Land, Sacred View: Navajo Perceptions of the Four Corner Region*. Salt Lake City, UT: Brigham Young University, 1992.

Meinig, D. W., chief editorial consultant. "The Southwest" (map). Supplement to *National Geographic Magazine* 162, no. 5 (November 1982).

Meinig, D. W. *Southwest: Three Peoples in Geographical Change, 1500–1970*. New York, Toronto, and London: Oxford University Press, 1971.

Momaday, N. Scott. *House Made of Dawn*. New York: Harper and Row, 1968.

Moore, James L., Nancy J. Akins, Robert Dello-Russo, and Stephen S. Post. *A Research Design for the Archaeological Investigation of 14 Sites at Spaceport America, Sierra County, New Mexico*. Archaeological Notes 430. Santa Fe: Museum of New Mexico, Office of Archaeological Studies, 2010.

Morris, Roy, Jr. *Ambrose Bierce: Alone in Bad Company*. New York: Oxford University Press, 1999.

Nájera, Pedro de Casteñada de, Francisco Vásquez de Coronado, Antonio de Mendoza, and Juan Camilo Jaramillo. *The Journey of Coronado, 1540–1542, from the City of Mexico to the Grand Cañon of the Colorado and the Buffalo Plains of Texas, Kansas and Nebraska*. New York: Allerton Book, 1904.

Niza, Fray Marcos de. *The Journey of Fray Marcos de Niza*. Edited and translated by Cleve Hallenbeck. Dallas: Southern Methodist University Press, 1987.

North, Arthur W. *Camp and Camino in Lower California*. New York: Baker and Taylor, 1910.

O'Bryon, Eleanor Dart. *Coming Home from Devil Mountain*. Tucson, AZ: Harbinger House, 1989.

O'Keeffe, Georgia. "About Myself." *Georgia O'Keeffe: Exhibition of Oils and Pastels*, January 22–March 17, 1939, An American Place, 509 Madison Avenue, New York City. Beinecke Rare Book and Manuscript Library, Yale University Library. https://brbl-dl.library.yale.edu/vufind/Record/4212776, accessed 2018.

Oñate y Salazar, Don Juan de, colonizer of New Mexico (1595–1628). *Record of the Marches by the Army, New Spain to New Mexico, 1596–99*. Edited and translated by George P. Hammond and Agapito Rey. American Journeys Collection, document AJ-102, Madison: Wisconsin Historical Society Digital Library and Archives, 2003.

Ortiz, Alfonso, ed. *Handbook of North American Indians*. Vol. 10, *Southwest*. Washington, DC: Smithsonian Institution, 1983.

Palmer, William R. "Utah Indians Past and Present: An Etymological and Historical Study of Tribes and Tribal Names from Original Sources by Wm. R. Palmer, Cedar City, Utah." *Utah Historical Quarterly* 1, no. 1 (April 1928).

Pattie, James Ohio. *The Personal Narrative of James Ohio Pattie, of Kentucky: During an Expedition from St. Louis, through the Vast Regions between That Place and the Pacific Ocean, and Thence Back through the City of Mexico to Vera Cruz; During Journeyings of Six Years, in Which He and His Father, Who Accompanied Him, Suffered Unheard of Hardships and Dangers*. Edited by Timothy Flint. Cincinnati, OH: John H. Wood, 1831.

Perkins, Clifford Alan, and W. D. Smithers. *Border Patrol: With the US Immigration Service on the Mexican Boundary, 1910–1954*. El Paso: Texas Western Press, 1978.

Porter, Eliot, and Daniel Beard. *The Place No One Knew: Glen Canyon on the Colorado*. San Francisco: Sierra Club Books, 1963.

Powell, J. W. *Exploration of the Colorado River of the West and Its Tributaries. Explored in 1869, 1870, 1871, and 1872*. Washington, DC: US Government Printing Office, 1875.

———. *Report on the Arid Lands of the United States, with a More Detailed Account of the Lands of Utah*. Washington, DC: US Government Printing Office, 1879.

Priestly, J. B. *Midnight on the Desert: A Chapter of Autobiography*. London and Toronto: William Heineman, 1917.

Ptolemy (Ptolemaeus), Claudius. *Geographica*. Alexandria, Egypt, ca. 150 CE. https://en.wikipedia.org/wiki/Ptolemy.

Ragsdale, John W., Jr. "Values in Transition: The Chiricahua Apache from 1886–1914." *American Indian Law Review* 35, no. 1 (2010).

Reed, Erik K. "The Greater Southwest." In *Prehistoric Man in the New World*. Edited by Jesse D. Jennings and Edward Norbeck, 175–91. Chicago: University of Chicago Press, 1964.

Reed, John. *Insurgent Mexico*. New York and London: D. Appleton, 1914.

Reichard, Gladys A. *Navajo Religion: A Study in Symbolism*. Bollingen Series 18. Princeton, NJ: Princeton University Press, 1963.

Reisner, Marc. *Cadillac Desert: The American West and Its Disappearing Water*. New York: Penguin Books, 1987.

Robinson, John W. *Camping and Climbing in Baja*. 5th ed. Glendale, CA: La Siesta, 1983.

Robinson, Rowland E. "An Ancestral Gun." *Sportsman Tourist: A Weekly Journal of Rod and Gun* 52 (March 5, 1900): 342.

Rojas, Manuel. *Joaquín Murrieta, "el Patrio": El "Far West" del México Cercenado*. Mexicali, México: Gobierno del Estado de Baja California, 1986.

Roosevelt, Theodore. "Across the Navajo Desert." In *A Book-Lover's Holidays in the Open*. New York: Charles Scribner's Sons, 1916.

Ross, Clyde P. *The Lower Gila Region, Arizona: A Geographic, Geologic, and Hydrologic Reconnaissance with a Guide to Desert Watering Places*. Water-Supply Paper 498. Washington, DC: US Government Printing Office, 1923.

Ruess, Everett. "1127 A.D. in Arizona." *Desert Magazine* 2, no. 9 (July 1939).

Ruess, Everett, Hugh Lacy, Randall Henderson, and W. L.

Rusho. *On Desert Trails with Everett Ruess*. Salt Lake City, UT: Gibbs Smith, 2000.

Ruess, Stella Knight. "Son!" *Desert Magazine* 1, no. 11 (September 1938).

Rush, W. L. *Everett Ruess: A Vagabond for Beauty*. Salt Lake City, UT: Gibbs Smith, 1983.

Salas, Elizabeth. *Soldaderas in the Mexican Military: Myth and History*. Austin: University of Texas Press, 1990.

Schwed, Mark. "Cousteau's 5-Year Grand Finale: A Farewell Voyage of Rediscovery." *Los Angeles Times*, August 15, 1986. http://articles.latimes.com, accessed 2018.

The Searchers. Release date May 26, 1956. AFI's 10 TOP 10, American Film Institute, 2016, Los Angeles. http://afi.com/10top10/.

Sheldon, Charles. "A Journey to Seriland, Sonora, 1921–1922." In *The Wilderness of the Southwest: Charles Sheldon's Quest for Desert Bighorn Sheep and Adventures with the Havasupai and Seri Indians*. Edited by Neil B. Carmony and David E. Brown. Salt Lake City: University of Utah Press, 1993.

———. *The Wilderness of Desert Bighorns & Seri Indians: A Historical Classic of the Southwest: the Southwestern Journals of Charles Sheldon*. Edited by Neil B. Carmony and David E. Brown. Phoenix, AZ: Arizona Desert Bighorn Sheep Society, 1979.

Silko, Leslie Marmon. *The Turquoise Ledge: A Memoir*. New York: Penguin Books, 2010.

Smith, Fred J., Jr., Lyman C. Huff, E. Neal Hinrichs, and Robert G. Luedke. *Geology of the Capitol Reef Area, Wayne and Garfield Counties, Utah*. Geological Survey Professional Paper 363. Washington, DC: US Government Printing Office, 1963.

Smith, Ralph A. *Borderlander: The Life of James Kirker. 1793–1852*. Norman: University of Oklahoma Press, 2000.

———. "The Scalp Hunter in the Borderlands, 1835–1850." *Arizona and the West: A Quarterly Journal of History* 6, no. 1 (Spring 1964).

Smithers, Wilfred Dudley. *Chronicles of the Big Bend: A Photographic Memoir of Life on the Border*. Austin, TX: Madrona, 1976.

———. "Nature's Pharmacy and the Curandero." *West Texas Historical and Scientific Society Publications* 18 (September 1, 1961): 15–39.

Stanton, Bette L. *Where God Put the West: Movie Making in the Desert*. Moab, UT: Canyonlands Natural History Association, 1994.

Steinbeck, John, and Edward F. Ricketts. *The Log from the Sea of Cortez*. New York: Viking Penguin, 1941.

Stone, Connie L. *Deceptive Desolation: Prehistory of the Sonoran Desert in West Central Arizona*. Cultural Resource Series 1. Phoenix: US Bureau of Land Management, Arizona State Office, 1986.

Summerhayes, Martha. *Vanished Arizona: Recollections of My Army Life*. Philadelphia: J. B. Lippincott, 1908.

Thesiger, Wilfred. *Arabian Sands*. London: Longmans, Green, 1959.

———. *A Vanished World*. New York and London: W. W. Norton, 2002.

Thompson, Jesse E., MD. "Cabeza de Vaca: The First Texas Surgeon." Excerpts from *La relación de Álvar Núñez Cabeza de Vaca* translated from the original Spanish by Sally Thompson McPherson. *Baylor University Medical Center Proceedings* 8, no. 8 (1995). www.baylorhealth.edu, accessed 2018.

———. "Sagittectomy—First Recorded Surgical Procedure in the American Southwest, 1535—the Journey and Ministrations of Álvar Núñez Cabeza de Vaca." *New England Journal of Medicine* 289 (December 27, 1973).

Toor, Frances. "*La Llorona* (The Weeper)." From Tehuantepec, Oaxaca Collection, recorded by Concha Michel. In *A Treasury of Mexican Folkways: The Customs, Myths, Folklore, Traditions, Beliefs, Fiestas, Dances, and Songs of the Mexican People*. New York: Crown, 1947.

Traven, B. *The Treasure of the Sierra Madre*. New York: Alfred A. Knopf, 1935. First published in Germany in 1927 as *Der Schatz der Sierra Madre*.

Twain, Mark. *Roughing It*. New York: Harper and Brothers, 1913.

Tyler, Ronnie C. *The Big Bend: A History of the Last Texas Frontier*. Washington DC: US Department of the Interior, 1975.

Underhill, Ruth, Donald M. Bahr, Baptisto Lopez, Jose Pancho, and David Lopez. *Rainhouse and Ocean: Speeches for the Papago Year*. American Tribal Religions 4. Flagstaff: Museum of Northern Arizona Press, 1979.

Van Valkenburgh, Richard F. *Diné Bikéyah (the Navaho's Country)*. Edited by Lucy Wilcox Adams and John McPhee. Window Rock, AZ: US Department of the Interior, Office of Indian Affairs, Navajo Service, 1941.

Van Valkenburgh, Richard F., and Scotty Begay. "Sacred Places and Shrines of the Navajo, Part I: The Sacred Mountains." *Museum Notes* (Museum of Northern Arizona) 11, no. 3 (September 1938).

Van Valkenburgh, Richard F., and Clyde Kluckhorn, eds. *Navajo Indians III: Navajo Sacred Places*. New York: Garland, 1974.

Van Valkenburgh, Richard F., and Frank O. Walker. "Old Place Names in Navajo Country," *Master Key* 19, no. 3 (1945).

Waters, Frank. *Eternal Desert*. Phoenix: Arizona Highways Books, 1990.

Watson, Editha L. *Navajo Sacred Places*. Navajoland Publications 5. Window Rock, AZ: Navajo Tribal Museum, 1964.

Wheeler, George M., director of Geographical Surveys West of the 100th Meridian (US). *Wheeler's Photographic Survey of the American West, 1871–1873*. Photographs by Timothy H. O'Sullivan and William Bell. New York: Dover, 1983.

White, Stewart Edward. *Arizona Nights*. New York: McClure, 1907.

Wilcove, David S. *No Way Home: The Decline of the World's Great Animal Migrations*. Washington, DC: Island, 2007.

Wilderness Act, Public Law 88-577, 88th Congress, 2nd session, September 3, 1964, codified at US Code 16, 2000, 1131–36.

Woodhead, Henry, ed. *The Spirit World*. Alexandria, VA: Time-Life Books, 1993.

Wright, Harold Bell. *The Winning of Barbara Worth*. New York: A. L. Burt, 1911.

ABOUT THE AUTHOR

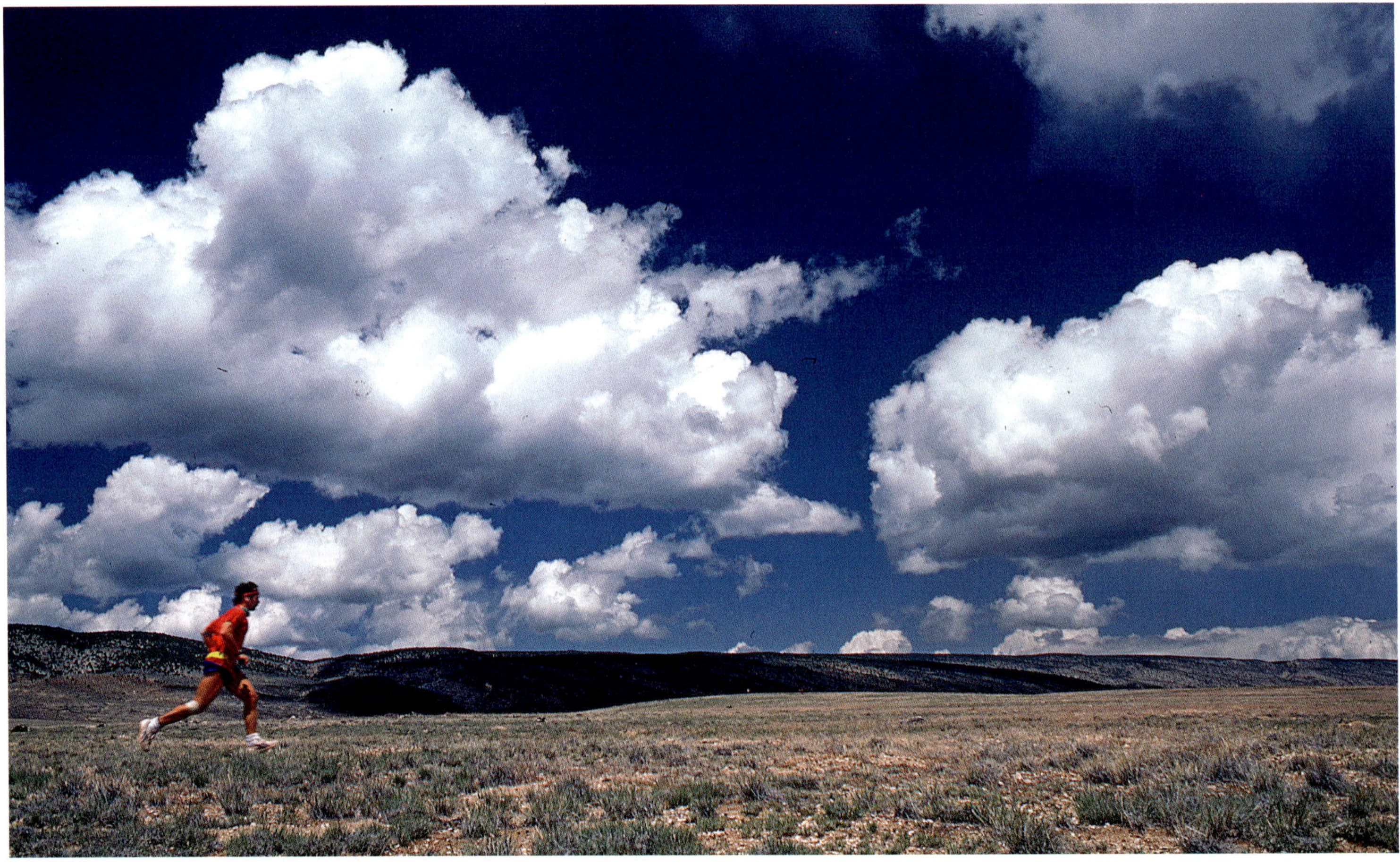

John Annerino is a photographer and author of photography books, photographic essays, and calendars of the American West and Old Mexico. His work has appeared in *Time*, *LIFE*, the *New York Times*, *Scientific American*, *Travel & Leisure*, *Browntrout*, and *National Geographic Adventure*, among other publications. His map "The Grand Canyon Explored" is on display at the Grand Canyon National Geographic Visitor Center. John has dedicated his life to photographing, researching, and writing about endangered landscapes, native peoples, western cowboys, and Spanish traditions. In his quest to explore the Grand Canyon's and Great Southwest's mythic landscapes and secret places by foot, raft, rope, camera, and pen, John has climbed hallowed peaks, rafted wild and scenic rivers, traversed deep chasms and painted deserts, and traced ancient Indian, missionary, and pioneer trails.

The author runs on the Domínguez-Escalante National Historic Trail near Vermilion Cliffs National Monument near the end of his fleet-footed, monthlong journey from Mexico to the Utah-Arizona border.

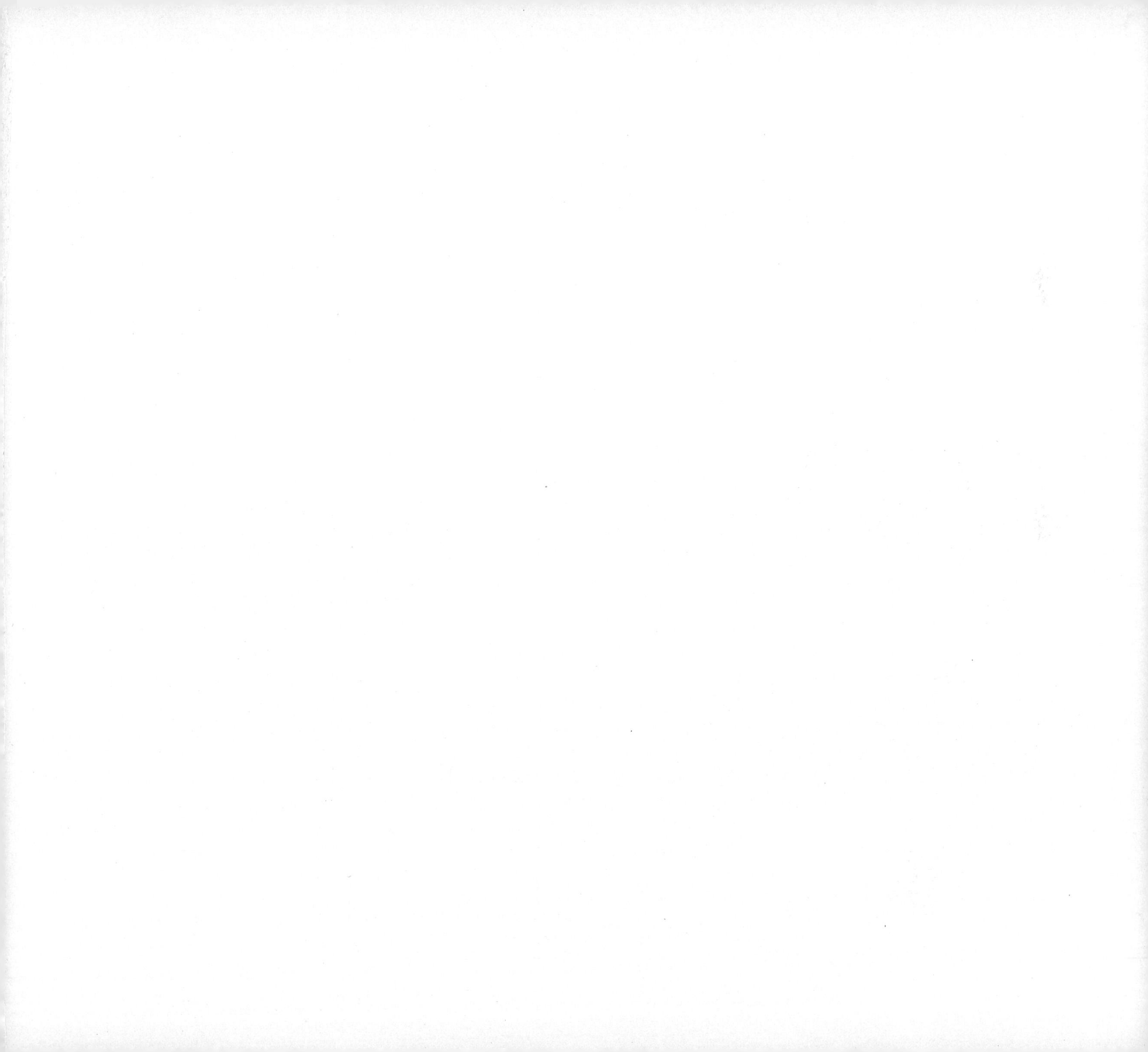